ANCIENT
GREECE
AND
ROME

AN ENCYCLOPEDIA
FOR STUDENTS

ANCIENT GREECE AND ROME

AN ENCYCLOPEDIA FOR STUDENTS

Carroll Moulton, *Editor in Chief*

VOLUME I

CHARLES SCRIBNER'S SONS
Macmillan Library Reference USA
Simon & Schuster Macmillan
New York

SIMON & SCHUSTER AND PRENTICE HALL INTERNATIONAL
London   Mexico City   New Delhi   Singapore   Sydney   Toronto

Developed for Charles Scribner's Sons by Visual Education Corporation, Princeton, N.J.

For Scribners

PUBLISHER: Karen Day
EDITORS: Timothy J. DeWerff
          Stephen Wagley
COVER DESIGN: George Berrian

For Visual Education

PROJECT DIRECTOR: Jewel G. Moulthrop
WRITERS: Jean Brainard, John Haley, Charles Patterson, Adrienne Ruggiero, Rebecca Stefoff
EDITORS: Kevin Downing, Jeanine D. Evans, Charles Roebuck
EDITORIAL ASSISTANT: Jacqueline Morais
COPY EDITOR: Maureen Ryan Pancza
INDEXER: Sallie Steele
PHOTO RESEARCH: Martin A. Levick
PRODUCTION SUPERVISOR: Christine Osborne
PRODUCTION ASSISTANT: Liz Ryan-Sax
INTERIOR DESIGN: Maxson Crandall
ELECTRONIC PREPARATION: Cynthia C. Feldner, Fiona Torphy
ELECTRONIC PRODUCTION: Elise Dodeles, Lisa Evans-Skopas, Deirdre Sheean, Isabelle Verret

Library of Congress Cataloging-in-Publication Data

Ancient Greece and Rome : an encyclopedia for students / Carroll Moulton, editor in chief.
   p. cm.
  Includes bibliographical references and index.
  Summary: Presents a history of Ancient Greece and Rome as well as information about the literature and daily life of these early civilizations.
   ISBN 0-684-80507-3 (4 vol. set : alk. paper). — ISBN 0-684-80503-0 (vol. 1 : alk. paper). — ISBN 0-684-80504-9 (vol. 2 : alk. paper) — ISBN 0-684-80505-7 (vol. 3 : alk. paper) — ISBN 0-684-80506-5 (vol. 4 : alk. paper)
   1. Civilization, Classical—Encyclopedias—Juvenile literature. [1. Civilization, Classical—Encyclopedias.]   I. Moulton, Carroll.
DE5.A57 1998
938—dc21
        98-13728
        CIP
        AC

TABLE OF CONTENTS

MAPS

COLOR PLATES

VOLUME I

A

Achaea

Achilles

Acropolis

Adonis

Aedile

Aegean Sea

Aeneid

Aeschylus

Aetolia

Africa

Afterlife

Agamemnon

Agora

Agriculture, Greek

Agriculture, Roman

Alcibiades

Alexander the Great

Alexandria

Alphabets and Writing

Alps

Amazons

Ammianus Marcellinus

Amphitheater, Roman

Animals

Antigone

Antioch

Antonius, Marcus

Aphrodite

Apollo

Appian Way

Apuleius

Aqueducts

Arabia

Archaeology of Ancient Sites

Arches

Archimedes

Architecture, Greek

Architecture, Roman

Aristophanes

Aristotle

Armies, Greek

Armies, Roman

Art, Greek

Art, Roman

Artemis

TABLE OF CONTENTS

VOLUME II

VOLUME III

VOLUME IV

Table of Contents

PREFACE

Why study the classics? A generation ago, before the culture wars and the dawn of being digital, some common answers to this question stressed that Greek and Latin train students in analytical thinking, expose them to some of the "great books" of Western literature, and develop such practical skills as vocabulary building. The theory was that this kind of liberal education was readily transferable—in that students could apply it in a wide range of professions and careers. Although the specific skills I have singled out continue to be among the by-products of a classical education, no one to my knowledge has offered a very persuasive rationale for the study of ancient Greece and Rome in modern America, at least not at the university level or in the original, so-called "dead" languages. This failure to develop such a defense of the classics at the end of the 20th century is related, no doubt, to a broader set of trends in American education: strident (but occasionally productive) turf wars over the traditional curriculum, the ascendancy of a cost-effective mentality about the classroom, and a general impatience with all but the most practical and immediate results of teaching and learning. The overall sense of beleaguerment or retreat felt by many scholars and teachers was captured by the title of a collection of essays on higher education published in 1997: *What's Happened to the Humanities?*

As the following informal case study suggests, teachers, scholars, and publishers across the board must do a better job of presenting the relevance of classical Greece and Rome. Around the time of the Bicentennial in 1976, a brief flurry of effort among classicists focused on the influence of ancient Greece and Rome on 18th-century colonial culture in general, and on many of the Founding Fathers in particular. Just a few weeks ago, however, when I checked the latest editions of American literature and history textbooks at the secondary level, I found virtually no mention of the profound impact of the classical heritage on Thomas Jefferson, John and Abigail Adams, James

Madison, and their contemporaries. The name of the Senate, the constitutional concepts of the separation of powers and of checks and balances, the unit rule in our electoral system, the assimilation of George Washington to the legend of Cincinnatus, and the layout and much of the architecture of Washington, D.C.: all were derived from ancient Roman models by those who fought the American Revolution and nurtured the new nation. So, too, were their lessons in practical persuasion, which came from the rhetoric of Cicero, Livy, and Tacitus. But most of our school textbooks, as well as many college-level surveys and specialized studies of the period, are silent about these connections.

The information about the classical world contained in *Ancient Greece and Rome* can offer no more than a glimpse of the vitality and continuing relevance of the classical tradition. What it *can* facilitate is a renewed exploration of the Mediterranean cultures that left such a critical, enduring impact on Europe and the Americas. The spirit of this reexploring, it is to be hoped, will be as inclusive as teachers and students can make it. It will blend practical utility with aesthetic appreciation, cultural literacy with pluralist awareness. As the Harvard political theorist Seyla Benhabib remarks in an essay published in *Field Work* (1996): "The globalization and pluralization of the canon will not destroy those values of the life of the mind that the ancient Greeks first discovered in their encounter with the power of *logos*, of reason and speech: curiosity, courage, the power to question and to resist, to challenge the given, and the urge to go 'beyond the appearances.'"

In this regard, one more mini-lesson may be helpful. Homer's *Iliad* and *Odyssey* have been translated into English—which is now, of course, a global language—more often than any other texts in history, including the Bible. Homer's orally composed poems are universally acknowledged as the fountainhead of Western literature. Yet the insights that a familiarity with Homer may yield range across a wide spectrum, embracing (for example) the West African *Epic of Son-Jara,* the recent

documentation of South Asian epics, the Caribbean world of Derek Walcott's *Omeros,* the pervasive sense of ritual in the jewel-like collages of Romare Bearden, and the celluloid vistas of *Star Wars.* A study of ancient mythology may help us to unravel the process of myth-making in our own time, and an acquaintance with oral tradition and performance in ancient cultures may suggest new insights into some of the structures and challenges of digitally generated texts. Yes, a knowledge of Greek and Latin word roots will still be useful for budding doctors and lawyers, and the study of these two ancient languages still serves as an excellent training for learning many modern ones in a shrinking world. But the most exciting possibilities for the practical applications of classical studies lie at a deeper level. They will be the result of a dynamic interplay between past and present within the mind of every individual student.

The information in *Ancient Greece and Rome* is substantially (but not exclusively) a distillation of two previous works, both published by Scribners: *Ancient Writers: Greece and Rome* (1982), edited by T. James Luce, and *Civilizations of the Ancient Mediterranean: Greece and Rome* (1988), edited by Michael Grant and Rachel Kitzinger. These volumes, intended for a college-level audience, consist of essays written by experts in Greek and Roman literature, history, art and archaeology, philosophy, religion, and material culture. The task of reshaping this material for a younger audience has been undertaken by the editorial staff of Visual Education Corp. in Princeton, N.J. I would like to acknowledge the contributions of the Editorial Board and the Board of Teaching Consultants, as well as the welcome support and encouragement of Karen Day, Publisher of Scribner Reference Books.

Lastly, a special word of affectionate thanks to my former Princeton University colleague and fellow Editorial Board member, T. James Luce. Nearly 20 years ago, Jim Luce invited me to contribute the essays on Greek comedy for *Ancient Writers: Greece and Rome.* His patient advice, sound scholarship, and unflagging support in behalf of these new volumes have been invaluable.

Carroll Moulton
Southampton, New York
February 5, 1998

ca. 2000–ca. 1400 B.C. *Minoan civilization flourishes in Crete*

ca. 1400–ca. 1200 B.C. *Mycenaean civilization flourishes on mainland Greece*

ca. 1200 B.C. *Dorians migrate to southern Greece; Greek Dark Age begins (to ca. 750 B.C.)*

1183 B.C. *Fall of Troy*

776 B.C. *First Olympic Games*

753 B.C. *Legendary founding of Rome by Romulus and Remus; monarchy begins in Rome (to 510 B.C.)*

ca. 750 B.C. *Archaic period begins in Greece (to 500 B.C.); Greeks found colonies in other regions of the Mediterranean region*

Homer *(700s B.C.)*

Hesiod *(ca. 700 B.C.)*

736 B.C. *Messenian revolt against Sparta (to 716 B.C.)*

Solon *(ca. 630–ca. 560 B.C.)*

Thales of Miletus *(ca. 625–547 B.C.)*

ca. 620 B.C. *Draco formulates his law code in Athens*

Sappho *(born ca. 612 B.C.)*

ca. 592 B.C. *Solon alters Athenian law code and reforms political system*

Pythagoras *(born ca. 580 B.C.)*

ca. 560 B.C. *Pisistratid dynasty of tyrants begins in Athens (to 510 B.C.)*

Croesus *(reigned ca. 560–546 B.C.)*

Aeschylus *(525–456 B.C.)*

550 B.C. *Persian Empire is founded*

Themistocles *(ca. 524–459 B.C.)*

Pindar *(ca. 518–ca. 438 B.C.)*

510 B.C. *Tarquin the Proud, the last king of Rome, is exiled*

509 B.C. *Roman Republic is founded (to 31 B.C.)*

508/507 B.C. *Cleisthenes reforms government of Athens*

ca. 500 B.C. *Classical period in Greece begins (to 323 B.C.)*

Heraclitus *(ca. 500s B.C.)*

499 B.C. *Ionian Revolt by Greek cities in Asia Minor against the Persian Empire (to 493 B.C.); Persian Wars begin (to 479 B.C.)*

Sophocles *(ca. 496–406 B.C.)*

Pericles *(ca. 495–429 B.C.)*

490 B.C. *Battle of Marathon*

Phidias *(ca. 490–ca. 430 B.C.)*

480 B.C. *Battle of Thermopylae and Battle of Salamis; Persian king Xerxes withdraws from Greece*

Xerxes *(reigned 486–465 B.C.)*

Herodotus *(ca. 484–ca. 420 B.C.)*

Leonidas *(died 480 B.C.)*

Euripides *(ca. 480–406 B.C.)*

479 B.C. *Greeks defeat Persians at Battle of Plataea*

478 B.C. *Delian League, alliance of Greek cities led by Athens, is founded*

Pausanias *(died 470 B.C.)*

Socrates *(469–399 B.C.)*

460 B.C. *Pericles dominates Athenian politics (to 429 B.C.)*

Democritus *(460–370 B.C.)*

Hippocrates *(ca. 460–ca. 380 B.C.)*

Thucydides *(ca. 459–399 B.C.)*

450 B.C. *The Twelve Tables, first written Roman law code, is established*

Alcibiades *(ca. 450–404 B.C.)*

449 B.C. *Peace is established between Persian Empire and Delian League*

447 B.C. *Construction of Parthenon begins on Athenian Acropolis (finished 438 B.C.)*

Aristophanes *(ca. 445–385 B.C.)*

431 B.C. *Peloponnesian War begins (to 404 B.C.)*

Isocrates *(ca. 435–338 B.C.)*

Xenophon *(ca. 428–ca. 355 B.C.)*

Plato *(428–348 B.C.)*

421 B.C. *Peace of Nicias temporarily halts Peloponnesian War*

415 B.C. *Athens sends expedition against Sicily (to 413 B.C.)*

405 B.C. *Sparta defeats Athens at Aegospotami in last sea battle of the Peloponnesian War*

404 B.C. *The "Thirty Tyrants" rule Athens (to 403 B.C.)*

399 B.C. *Socrates is sentenced to death for "corrupting the young"*

Aristotle *(384–322 B.C.)*

Demosthenes *(ca. 384–322 B.C.)*

Philip II *(382–336 B.C.)*

387 B.C. *Gauls invade Rome*

Praxiteles *(300s B.C.)*

Theophrastus *(ca. 371–287 B.C.)*

358 B.C. *Philip II becomes king of Macedonia*

Alexander the Great *(356–323 B.C.)*

Menander *(ca. 342–ca. 291 B.C.)*

338 B.C. *Philip defeats Athenians and Thebans at Battle of Chaeronea*

Epicurus *(341–270 B.C.)*

336 B.C. *Philip is assassinated; Alexander the Great becomes king of Macedonia*

334 B.C.   *Alexander invades Asia*

331 B.C.   *Alexander founds the city of Alexandria in Egypt and defeats King Darius of Persia at Battle of Gaugamela*

330 B.C.   *Darius assassinated; Alexander expands Macedonian empire*

323 B.C.   *Alexander dies; Hellenistic period begins (to 31 B.C.)*

312 B.C.   *Construction of Appian Way begins (finishes 244 B.C.)*

305 B.C.   *Ptolemaic dynasty of rulers of Egypt begins (to 30 B.C.)*

Callimachus *(ca. 305–ca. 240 B.C.)*

Euclid *(active ca. 300 B.C.)*

Theocritus *(ca. 300–ca. 260 B.C.)*

ca. 295 B.C.   *Library of Alexandria is founded*

Archimedes *(ca. 287–212 B.C.)*

Eratosthenes *(ca. 285–ca. 195 B.C.)*

280 B.C.   *Pyrrhic War between Rome and Pyrrhus, king of Epirus, begins (to 275 B.C.)*

264 B.C.   *First Punic War between Rome and Carthage begins (to 241 B.C.)*

Plautus *(254–184 B.C.)*

Hannibal *(ca. 246–182 B.C.)*

227 B.C.   *Sicily becomes the first Roman province*

Scipio Africanus *(236–183 B.C.)*

Cato the Elder *(234–149 B.C.)*

218 B.C.   *Hannibal marches the Carthaginian army across the Alps to Italy; Second Punic War begins (to 201 B.C.)*

Polybius *(ca. 205–125 B.C.)*

Terence *(ca. 185–159 B.C.)*

149 B.C.   *Third Punic War begins (to 146 B.C.)*

Tiberius Gracchus *(163–133 B.C.)*

Marius *(ca. 157–86 B.C.)*

146 B.C.   *Rome destroys Carthage and Corinth*

Gaius Gracchus *(154–121 B.C.)*

Sulla *(ca. 138–78 B.C.)*

133 B.C.   *Last king of Pergamum wills his kingdom to Rome; Tiberius Gracchus attempts reform of Roman government and is assassinated*

Crassus *(112–53 B.C.)*

Pompey *(106–48 B.C.)*

Cicero *(106–43 B.C.)*

Julius Caesar *(100–44 B.C.)*

123 B.C.   *Gaius Gracchus extends the reforms of his brother*

Cato the Younger *(95–46 B.C.)*

Lucretius *(ca. 94–ca. 50 B.C.)*

Sallust *(86–35 B.C.)*

121 B.C.   *Gaius Gracchus is assassinated*

Brutus *(85–42 B.C.)*

Catullus *(84–54 B.C.)*

82 B.C.   *Sulla is named dictator (to 79 B.C.)*

Mark Antony *(ca. 82–30 B.C.)*

73 B.C. *Spartacus leads slave revolt (to 71 B.C.)*	Vitruvius Pollio *(first century B.C.)*
	Herod the Great *(ca. 73–4 B.C.)*
63 B.C. *Catiline leads conspiracy against Rome, is exposed by Cicero*	Vergil *(70–19 B.C.)*
	Cleopatra *(69–30 B.C.)*
	Horace *(65–8 B.C.)*
60 B.C. *First Triumvirate is formed by Pompey, Julius Caesar, and Crassus*	Strabo *(ca. 64 B.C.–after A.D. 21)*
	Augustus, Caesar Octavianus *(63 B.C.–A.D. 14)*
58 B.C. *Caesar's conquests of Gauls (to 50 B.C.)*	Livy *(ca. 59 B.C.–ca. A.D. 17)*
53 B.C. *Crassus is defeated and killed by Parthians*	Tibullus *(ca. 54 B.C.–A.D. 18)*
	Propertius *(ca. 50 B.C.–ca. A.D. 16)*
49 B.C. *Caesar enters Italy with his army, beginning a civil war with Pompey and his followers (to 45 B.C.)*	
44 B.C. *Caesar becomes dictator for life; senators led by Brutus and Cassius assassinate Caesar*	
43 B.C. *Second Triumvirate is formed by Mark Antony, Octavian (later Augustus), and Marcus Lepidus*	Ovid *(43 B.C.–A.D. 18)*
42 B.C. *Antony and Octavian defeat Brutus and Cassius*	Tiberius *(42 B.C.–A.D. 37)*
31 B.C. *Octavian defeats Antony and Cleopatra; Roman Republic ends and Roman Empire begins*	Claudius *(10 B.C.–A.D. 54)*
	Seneca the Younger *(ca. 4 B.C.–A.D. 65)*
	Vespasian *(A.D. 9–79)*
27 B.C. *Octavian receives title of Augustus; Augustus becomes first Roman emperor (to A.D. 14)*	Caligula *(A.D. 12–41)*
	Pliny the Elder *(ca. A.D. 23–79)*
	Persius *(A.D. 34–62)*
	Nero *(A.D. 37–68)*
A.D. 6 *Judaea becomes Roman province*	Josephus *(ca. A.D. 37–100)*
	Lucan *(A.D. 39–65)*
A.D. 14 *Tiberius becomes emperor (to A.D. 37)*	Titus *(A.D. 39–81)*
	Quintilian *(ca. A.D. 40–ca. 96)*
	Martial *(ca. A.D. 40–ca. 104)*
A.D. 37 *Caligula becomes emperor (to A.D. 41)*	Plutarch *(ca. A.D. 40–ca. 120)*
	Statius *(ca. A.D. 45–ca. 96)*
A.D. 41 *Caligula is assassinated; Claudius becomes emperor (to A.D. 54)*	Epictetus *(ca. A.D. 50–ca. 120)*
	Domitian *(A.D. 51–96)*
A.D. 43 *Claudius invades Britain and makes it a Roman province (to A.D. 47)*	Tacitus *(ca. A.D. 55–ca. 120)*
	Trajan *(A.D. 57–117)*
	Juvenal *(ca. A.D. 60–130)*
A.D. 54 *Nero becomes emperor (to A.D. 68)*	Pliny the Younger *(ca. A.D. 61–ca. 112)*

A.D. 66	Jewish Revolt begins (to A.D. 70)	Petronius Arbiter (dies A.D. 66)
A.D. 68	Nero commits suicide	
A.D. 69	Vespasian becomes emperor (to A.D. 79)	Suetonius (ca. A.D. 69–after 122)
		Longinus (first century A.D.)
A.D. 79	Titus becomes emperor (to A.D. 81)	Hadrian (A.D. 76–138)
A.D. 79	Mt. Vesuvius erupts and destroys the cities of Pompeii and Herculaneum	
A.D. 80	Colosseum opens for public entertainments	
A.D. 81	Domitian becomes emperor (to A.D. 96)	
A.D. 98	Trajan becomes emperor (to A.D. 117)	
A.D. 101	Trajan wages war against Dacia (to A.D. 106)	Ptolemy (ca. A.D. 100–ca. 170)
A.D. 117	Hadrian becomes emperor following the death of Trajan (to A.D. 138)	Lucian (born ca. A.D. 120)
		Apuleius (born ca. A.D. 120)
		Marcus Aurelius (A.D. 121–180)
A.D. 122	Construction of Hadrian's Wall begins	Galen (A.D. 129–ca. 200)
A.D. 161	Marcus Aurelius becomes emperor (to A.D. 180)	Septimius Severus (ca. A.D. 145–211)
		Tertullian (ca. A.D. 160–ca. 240)
A.D. 193	Septimius Severus becomes emperor (to A.D. 211)	
A.D. 200s	Germans raid Roman Empire	Plotinus (A.D. 205–269/270)
A.D. 212	Emperor Caracalla grants citizenship to all free persons of the Roman Empire	Diocletian (ca. A.D. 240–313)
		Constantine I (A.D. 272–337)
A.D. 284	Diocletian becomes emperor (to A.D. 305)	
A.D. 303	Persecution of Christians begins (to A.D. 311)	
A.D. 312	Constantine I becomes emperor (to A.D. 337)	
A.D. 313	Constantine issues edict granting tolerance to Christianity	
A.D. 330	Constantinople is founded	Ammianus Marcellinus (ca. A.D. 330–ca. 395)

ACHAEA

* **Peloponnese** peninsula forming the southern part of the mainland of Greece

* **epic** long poem about legendary or historical heroes, written in a grand style

* **city-state** independent state consisting of a city and its surrounding territory

See map in Greece, History of (vol. 2).

Achaea was a narrow region of ancient Greece that included southeastern Thessaly and the north coast of the Peloponnese*. The poet HOMER used the name *Achaeans* in his epic* poem the *Iliad* to refer to the Greeks who fought in the Trojan War.

In the 700s B.C., Achaea established colonies in southern Italy that supplied grain and other foods to Greece. The Achaeans prospered, and by the 400s B.C., the growing towns of the region had joined to form a military confederation known as the Achaean League. The league reached the height of its power in the 200s B.C. At that time, it included both Achaean and non-Achaean city-states* and controlled most of the Peloponnese and parts of central Greece. The Achaean League created an early form of representative government in which member city-states, rather than individual citizens, voted on issues.

Conflict with the city-state of SPARTA led the Achaean League into an alliance with MACEDONIA in 224 B.C. This alliance lasted until the league joined Rome against Macedonia in 198 B.C. Later, Achaea became part of the Roman province of Macedonia. Then in 27 B.C., Rome created a new province called Achaea that included all of central Greece, the Peloponnese, and the CYCLADES islands in the Aegean Sea. The region remained part of the Roman Empire until the A.D. 400s, when Greece became part of the Byzantine Empire. (*See also* **Cities, Greek; Colonies, Roman; Federalism.**)

ACHILLES

* **underworld** kingdom of the dead; also called Hades

See color plate 12, vol. 4.

Achilles, the great warrior of Greek mythology, was the hero of the war between the Greeks and the Trojans. The Greeks revered him for his strength and courage in battle. The story of Achilles' daring exploits at TROY provides much of the action in Homer's *Iliad*.

Achilles was the son of King Peleus and the sea nymph Thetis. Predictions had been made that Achilles would die in battle at Troy, but Thetis tried to change his fate. To protect her son, she dipped him in the River Styx of the underworld*. Only one spot—the heel by which she held Achilles—remained unprotected. The modern expression "Achilles' heel" thus refers to a person's area of vulnerability or weakness.

When the Trojan War began, Thetis tried to hide Achilles. She disguised him as a young girl and sent him to another kingdom. But her plan failed. Knowing of Achilles' great skills as a warrior, the Greeks sent one of their leaders, ODYSSEUS, to search for him. Odysseus pretended to be a merchant and showed pieces of jewelry and other ornaments to the women at court. Among the ornaments, he had placed some weapons. When Achilles admired the weapons, Odysseus identified him immediately and convinced him to join the Greek forces.

In the midst of the Trojan War, Achilles—known for his temper—had a bitter argument with AGAMEMNON, the leader of the Greek forces. Feeling dishonored, Achilles absolutely refused to continue fighting. But this headstrong warrior also displayed great loyalty. When his good friend Patroclus died fighting the Trojan prince Hector, Achilles rushed back into battle to seek revenge. Achilles killed Hector and then tied the body to his chariot and dragged it back to the Greek camp. As predicted,

1

Achilles met his own death in battle at Troy—wounded in the heel by an arrow shot from the bow of the Trojan prince Paris. (*See also* ***Iliad;*** **Myths, Greek.**)

ACROPOLIS

* **city-state** independent state consisting of a city and its surrounding territory

* **classical** in Greek history, refers to the period of great political and cultural achievement from about 500 B.C. to 323 B.C.

An acropolis is a high, fortified site that was an important feature of many city-states* in ancient Greece. The word *acropolis* means upper part of a city. Originally, it served as a hilltop fortress—a place of refuge in time of war.

The Athenians built the most famous acropolis in Greece, which is referred to as the Acropolis. Its public buildings, temples, porches, and gates—all in white stone or marble—remain one of the supreme accomplishments of classical* Greek art. Rising near the center of Athens, the Acropolis is a steep rocky hill with a flat oval-shaped top about 500 feet wide and 1,150 feet long.

Ancient peoples built settlements and fortifications on the Acropolis of Athens, perhaps as early as 6000 B.C. During the time of the Mycenaeans, between 1600 and 1100 B.C., a massive wall was constructed around the site, which included a small fortified city and palace. Natural springs on the slopes of the hill supplied water for the inhabitants. The first temples on the Acropolis were built in the 500s B.C., during the reign of King Pisistratus. These included temples to ATHENA, the goddess who protected the city.

In 480 B.C., Persian invaders swept into Athens and destroyed the Acropolis. The Athenian general PERICLES rebuilt the Acropolis during the mid-400s B.C. with funds borrowed from allies of Athens. To work on the new Acropolis, Pericles hired the leading architects and artists of the day. In later years, other structures were added to the Acropolis and its slopes.

Athenians entered the Acropolis from the west end. There they climbed the stairs of the Propylaea, a massive gateway that also served as

This model depicts how the Acropolis of Athens looked during the classical period. The largest structure is the Parthenon (A), and the smaller temple with columns at the left is the Erechtheum (B). The stairs at the lower right lead up to the Propylaea (C), the gateway to the sacred areas on the Acropolis.

a public meeting place. Nearby was the small temple of Athena Nike, built to honor Athena's role in bringing victory to the city. From the Propylaea, a pathway known as the Sacred Way led into holy areas of the Acropolis. It passed an enormous bronze statue of Athena, the Athena Promachus, erected to celebrate the Athenians' victory over the Persians. Along the Sacred Way there were small, columned buildings called treasuries, which contained offerings from other city-states to the gods for victories or other special events.

The path continued to the PARTHENON, the largest and most sacred structure on the Acropolis. Built of gleaming white marble, the Parthenon dominated the entire city and its surrounding countryside. Inside, the sculptor PHIDIAS erected a 40-foot-tall, gold-and-ivory statue of the goddess Athena. This work has disappeared.

North of the Parthenon was the ERECHTHEUM, another temple. This shrine to the gods of agriculture contained holy objects associated with the founding of Athens. A sacred olive tree grew in one of its courtyards.

* **odeum** hall used for musical or dramatic performances

* **amphitheater** oval or round structure with rows of seats rising gradually from a stage or central open space

The Acropolis had several other temples and buildings—including an altar to the god Zeus and some storehouses. The Theater of Dionysus, built in the 400s B.C., and the Odeum* of Herodes Atticus, built in A.D. 167, stand on the southern slopes of the Acropolis. Plays were given as part of religious festivals. The Theater of Dionysus, an amphitheater* that held 15,000 people, was designed so that even those seated at the back of the theater could easily hear the performers on stage.

The Acropolis remained the religious center of Athens for hundreds of years. In later centuries, people turned its temples into Christian churches or used them for other purposes. Remnants of the Acropolis still stand today, although in various stages of ruin. Even so, the Acropolis of Athens continues to inspire people with its commanding location and the great beauty and dignity of its architecture. (*See also* **Architecture, Greek; Mycenae; Religion, Greek; Temples.**)

ACTORS

See *Drama, Greek; Drama, Roman.*

ADONIS

* **underworld** kingdom of the dead; also called Hades

In Greek mythology, Adonis was a remarkably handsome youth who was loved by the goddess APHRODITE. He was popular throughout the Greek world, and colorful festivals took place in honor of his death and supposed rebirth.

According to legend, Aphrodite fell in love with Adonis when he was an infant. To keep him safe from harm, she hid him in a box and left him with PERSEPHONE, the goddess of the underworld*. After looking into the box, Persephone also fell in love with Adonis and refused to return him to Aphrodite. To settle the conflict between the goddesses, ZEUS decided that Adonis would spend spring and summer with Aphrodite and autumn and winter with Persephone. During the time when Adonis was with Aphrodite, crops and plants flourished. During his time with Persephone, vegetation died. The Greeks used the myth to explain the seasonal changes.

Adonis loved to hunt, but his passion for hunting eventually led to his death. Although Aphrodite warned him of the dangers of hunting, he ignored her advice. He was killed by a wild boar, probably Hephaestus (Aphrodite's jealous husband) in disguise. As Adonis lay dying, drops of his blood fell upon the soil and a beautiful flower—a red anemone—sprang from the spot. The blossoming of the anemone each year in the autumn symbolized his death.

See color plate 1, vol. 4.

The festival of Adonis, celebrated mainly by women, included various rituals, such as mourning his death, rejoicing at his symbolic rebirth each spring, and placing pots of herbs and flowers (called gardens of Adonis) on rooftops. At the end of the festival, worshipers flung the ceremonial plants, along with images of the dead Adonis, into the sea. (*See also* **Divinities.**)

ADOPTION

See *Family, Roman.*

AEDILE

* **plebeian** member of the general body of Roman citizens, as distinct from the upper class

* **cult** group bound together by devotion to a particular person, belief, or god

* **patrician** member of the upper class who traced his ancestry to a senatorial family in the earliest days of the Roman Republic

* **imperial** pertaining to an emperor or empire

An aedile was an annually elected official in ancient Rome. The position of aedile probably originated in about 490 B.C., when two plebeians* were elected to assist the tribunes, leaders of the plebeian assembly. At first, aediles were responsible for overseeing the temple of the goddess Ceres and the cult* associated with her.

In time, the responsibilities of aediles expanded to include various minor functions of government. Among the most important of these was the maintenance and repair of the city of Rome, including the temples and monuments, public buildings, bridges, sewers, streets, and aqueducts. Other duties included the supervision of traffic, food and water supplies, market practices, and religious observances. Aediles were also responsible for organizing public celebrations, such as games, parades, festivals, and funerals. As judicial officials, aediles could impose fines and other punishments for breaking laws.

By about 45 B.C., the office had grown into a college, or group, of six aediles, including patricians*. During the period of the Roman Empire, the office of aedile became a way for prominent plebeians to advance to the SENATE or other high office. Various towns and colonies throughout the Roman Empire also had officials known as aediles. The office disappeared about A.D. 200, and other imperial* officials took over the aediles' duties. (*See also* **Government, Roman; Patricians, Roman; Plebeians, Roman.**)

AEGEAN SEA

The Aegean Sea is an arm of the MEDITERRANEAN SEA. The Aegean is approximately 400 miles long and 200 miles wide, and is bordered by Greece on the north and west, ASIA MINOR on the east, and the island of Crete on the south. The Aegean has long served as a crossroads between the peoples of Europe and Asia. In ancient times, two great civilizations—the Minoan and the Greek—developed on the islands in the Aegean Sea. For these early civilizations, the sea provided numerous opportunities for trade and for contact with other cultures.

There are various theories about the origin of the name *Aegean*. The name may have come from Aegeus, the father of the Greek hero Theseus, or from Aegea, a mythical Amazonian queen. Both characters, according to legend, drowned themselves in the sea. The ancient Greek city of Aegae may also be the source of the sea's name.

The Aegean Sea is dotted with many islands. Their sheltered bays and natural harbors provided safe havens for traders and travelers in ancient times. However, pirates also found the islands useful as bases for attacking ships and coastal settlements.

AENEID

* **epic** long poem about legendary or historical heroes, written in a grand style

AN EPIC CRYSTAL BALL

Vergil's poems remained popular long after they were written, partly because of the belief that they could predict the future. In the Middle Ages they became known as the *Oracles of Vergil* and, along with the Bible, were used to tell fortunes. People of all walks of life would open the *Aeneid* and read the first passage of the poem they saw. This passage was regarded as an omen, or a prophecy of what was going to happen. King Charles I, who ruled England in the early 1600s, is said to have done this before his execution. The passage he read predicted the death of Aeneas. Evidence suggests that this superstitious practice may have begun as early as Hadrian's reign and persisted until the early twentieth century.

* **underworld** kingdom of the dead; also called Hades

Written by the Roman poet VERGIL in the 20s B.C., the *Aeneid* is an epic* that recounts the adventures of the Trojan prince Aeneas. In the *Aeneid,* Vergil combined myth, legend, and history to tell the story of the founding of Rome and to explain why Rome was destined to rule the world.

THE STORY OF AENEAS. Modeled on the *ILIAD* and the *ODYSSEY* of the Greek poet HOMER, the *Aeneid,* written in verse, consists of 12 books and almost 10,000 lines. Aeneas, the hero of Vergil's epic, also appeared in Homer's *Iliad,* which tells the story of a long war between Greece and TROY. In the *Aeneid,* Vergil takes up Aeneas's adventures after he escapes from the Greek conquerors of Troy to lead a band of followers to Italy. Vergil drew the material of his story from Homer, from Greek historians, and from earlier Roman writers who considered Aeneas the ancestor of the Romans.

From the start, the *Aeneid* shows through prophecies and conversations among the gods that Aeneas is destined to be the founder of a great civilization in Italy. First, however, Aeneas and his men must survive dangers and temptations on the journey to their destiny. Many of these obstacles are the work of the goddess Juno, the wife of Jupiter, who hinders Aeneas's journey because of her deep hatred for the Trojans.

As the poem opens, Aeneas and his men are caught in a terrible storm at sea. The storm drives them to CARTHAGE, a city on the coast of North Africa. There Aeneas has a love affair with Dido, the queen of Carthage, but he abandons her to continue his journey to Italy. The grief-stricken Dido kills herself, but not before cursing Aeneas and vowing that Carthage will be the enemy of his nation. Indeed, many years after the founding of Rome, Rome and Carthage fought a series of wars, which ended with the destruction of Carthage in 146 B.C.

Like Homer's hero Odysseus, Aeneas visits the gloomy underworld* of ghosts and spirits. During a dream, he goes to the world of darkness, beneath the earth, where he can talk to people long dead and to those not yet born. In the underworld Aeneas meets his father, who gives him a glimpse of the civilization that will be created by Aeneas's descendants. He tells Aeneas how the Romans should rule the lands they will one day conquer—by using their authority to establish peace and order.

Finally Aeneas and the Trojans arrive in Latium in western Italy, where they plan to settle. At first they are welcomed by Latinus, the king of the local people. Other Latins, however, view the Trojans as a threat, and war erupts. Aeneas defeats Turnus, the champion of these Latins, and weds Lavinia, the daughter of Latinus. Thus the Latins and the Trojans are joined to form a new people. Several hundred years later, Aeneas's descendant Romulus will found the city of Rome.

THE IMPORTANCE OF THE WORK. The *Aeneid* gave the Romans a history as heroic as that of the Greeks, and one that linked Roman military skills with legendary warriors. Vergil's epic celebrated the Roman virtues of responsibility, religious devotion, and order. It also glorified AUGUSTUS, Rome's first emperor, who ruled at the time the epic was written. Yet, according to legend, when Vergil was on his deathbed, he ordered the manuscript of the *Aeneid* burned—an order that was not followed. Some modern scholars think Vergil considered the *Aeneid* a failure, perhaps because its hero is troubled and brooding, or because the poem praises peace but does not establish the triumph of peace and justice over war and violence. (*See also* **Punic Wars.**)

AESCHINES

See *Oratory.*

AESCHYLUS

525–456 B.C.
GREEK TRAGIC DRAMATIST

* **literary convention** a practice or rule in drama, poetry, or other form of literature that has been agreed upon by custom

* **aristocracy** referring to the privileged upper class

* **dynasty** succession of rulers from the same family or group

* **extant** still existing, not lost or destroyed

* **patron** special guardian, protector, or supporter

eschylus was the first of a trio of great Greek tragic dramatists of the 400s B.C.—Aeschylus, SOPHOCLES, and EURIPIDES. Together they wrote about 300 plays, 33 of which still exist. Of these, 7 were written by Aeschylus. The works of all three writers became classics soon after their deaths. Aeschylus became known to Athenians as the father of tragedy and established the scenic as well as the literary conventions* of tragedy.

LIFE AND TIMES. Aeschylus's father was a member of the old Athenian aristocracy* from the town of Eleusis in ATTICA. Aeschylus was about 15 when the Pisistratid dynasty* was expelled, and the Athenians restored a democratic government. Then in 490 B.C., he fought with the victorious Greek army in the Battle of Marathon against the Persians. In Aeschylus's youth, Athenians began the tradition of holding competitions for local choral drama. In 484 B.C., six years after the Battle of Marathon, Aeschylus won his first competition.

From 480–479 B.C., Aeschylus lived through the Persian occupation of his homeland. His earliest extant* tragedy, *Persians,* dramatizes the impact of defeat on the Persian court in Susa. In 472 B.C., it was performed along with three other plays and won first prize. Aeschylus's patron* was PERICLES, who was then about 23 years old. In 468 B.C., four years after Aeschylus's *Persians* was performed, Sophocles won a competition, apparently over Aeschylus, with his first drama. From then on, the two poets frequently competed against each other.

During his life, Aeschylus made at least two trips to Sicily, where he, along with the poet PINDAR, enjoyed the patronage of Hieron, the tyrant* of Syracuse. Near the end of his life and following the production of his *Oresteia* in 458 B.C. in Athens, Aeschylus returned to Sicily. He died there at Gela two years later. The people of Gela buried him with many honors. If the story is correct that Aeschylus composed the inscription for his own gravestone, he chose to be remembered as a soldier rather than a poet.

THE PLAYS OF AESCHYLUS. Early Greek plays were written in the form of a tetralogy—a group of four plays designed to be performed one after another. The fourth play, called a satyr* play, was intended to provide comic relief from the three tragedies that had preceded it. Three of Aeschylus's seven plays—*Seven Against Thebes, The Suppliants,* and *Prometheus Bound*—come from different tetralogies, most plays of which have been lost. *Oresteia,* which includes *Agamemnon, Libation Bearers,* and *Eumenides,* is most often considered a trilogy*. Sophocles discontinued the format, and among existing Greek tragedies the trilogy is unique to Aeschylus.

Aeschylus's seven plays are in some ways very different from one another, but they all have a grandeur that is typical of his work. His characters and their actions are somewhat larger than life. His lyric* passages are longer than those in the plays of Sophocles and Euripides, and Aeschylus alone uses poetic narrative to present events that are essential to the story. Of all the Greek dramas, Aeschylus's plays are closest to the grand language and stylistic devices of the epic. He uses a literary vocabulary and a dense, and sometimes obscure, language with multiple meanings. Visual aspects in his plays—often pageantry characterized by splendor—are designed to reinforce the action.

Persians describes the humiliating defeat of Xerxes and his Persian forces in Greece, partly through the eyes of Xerxes' mother and his dead father, Darius I. Exposed for his folly and defiance of destiny, Xerxes loses his stature as a king and becomes a pitiable, ordinary mortal*.

Seven Against Thebes concerns the story of the house of Laius, father of OEDIPUS. The two sons of Oedipus fight over who shall inherit their father's rule in Thebes. They kill each other, thus fulfilling their father's curse.

In *The Suppliants,* the 50 daughters of Danaus have fled from Egypt and ask for sanctuary in Argos to avoid marriage with the 50 sons of their father's brother, Aegyptus. In the myth—and presumably in the lost sequel by Aeschylus—49 of the daughters obey their father's order to murder on their wedding night the husbands they have been forced to marry. Only one daughter, Hypermnestra, spares her husband, Lynceus, whom she loves.

In *Prometheus Bound,* Zeus's continuance as ruler of the Olympians depends on avoiding marriage with a goddess fated to bear a son who will overthrow his father. Prometheus knows the identity of the bride-to-be but will disclose the name only in return for his release from bondage. Zeus causes a catastrophic end for Prometheus because of his defiant refusal to reveal the secret.

The tragedy *Oresteia* focuses on the legendary story of the family of Agamemnon and Clytemnestra, the rulers of Argos. When Agamemnon returns home from the Trojan War and is murdered by his unfaithful

* **tyrant** absolute ruler

* **satyr** woodland deity that was part man and part goat or horse

* **trilogy** series of three dramatic works on a related subject or theme

* **lyric** poem expressing personal feelings, often similar in form to a song

* **mortal** human being; one who eventually will die

7

wife, Clytemnestra, their daughter Electra sends her brother Orestes into hiding, because she fears for his life. Returning from exile, Orestes murders his mother and her lover, for which deed he is driven insane by the Furies*. When Orestes goes to Athens and is acquitted by a jury of Athenian citizens, the Furies threaten to destroy Athens. Only after being purified by Apollo is he able to go home to Argos to take his place as the rightful heir of Agamemnon. Parts of the story are also told in dramas by Sophocles and Euripides. (*See also* **Drama, Greek; Persian Wars.**)

* **Furies** female spirits of justice and vengeance

AESOP

See *Fables.*

AETOLIA

Aetolia was an ancient district in the mountainous region of central Greece, directly north of the Gulf of Corinth. In ancient times, the inhabitants of the region belonged to various independent tribes and were ruled by minor kings. Known for their piracy, the Aetolians preyed on ships in the Gulf of Corinth and the Aegean Sea.

During the 400s B.C., the Aetolians joined together in a loose alliance of tribes. In time, this alliance developed into a political federation* known as the Aetolian League with its central government at Thermum. As the league grew in strength, it became one of the most important military powers in Greece, extending its influence across central Greece. The league also controlled cities in the more distant regions of the Peloponnese, Thrace, and ASIA MINOR.

Attempts to expand Aetolian territory led to conflicts with MACEDONIA during the 200s B.C. The Aetolians formed an alliance with Rome, and together they defeated the Macedonians in 197 B.C. However, when Rome kept the Macedonian region of Thessaly for itself, the Aetolians joined forces with SYRIA against their former ally. After Rome defeated Syria in 189 B.C., Aetolia was forced to surrender to Rome as well, bringing an end to Aetolian independence. Rome dissolved the Aetolian League and later incorporated Aetolia into the Roman province of ACHAEA. (*See also* **Federalism.**)

* **federation** political union of separate states with a central government

AFRICA

During ancient times, both the Greeks and the Romans established settlements along the northern coast of Africa. The Minoans of CRETE and the Mycenaeans of southern Greece had formed commercial and cultural ties with EGYPT as early as 1400 B.C. The Phoenicians, an ancient seafaring people from the eastern Mediterranean, colonized the city of Carthage about 750 B.C. In the late 600s B.C., the Greeks established trading centers in the Nile delta of Egypt and founded colonies along the Mediterranean coast of Africa.

One of the most important Greek settlements was Cyrene (in present-day Libya), which became a flourishing commercial and learning center. During this time, the Greeks also explored farther along the African coast, perhaps as far as the Atlantic coast of West Africa. ALEXANDER THE GREAT conquered Egypt about 330 B.C. and made it part of his empire. He founded the city of ALEXANDRIA in the Nile delta, and the city soon became one of the leading cultural centers of the Mediterranean world.

Roman influence in Africa began in 146 B.C. after Rome defeated the city of CARTHAGE in the PUNIC WARS. The Romans rebuilt Carthage, and the city and surrounding territory (an area that included much of present-day Tunisia) became the first Roman province in Africa. It was known as Africa Vetus or "Old Africa." During the rule of Julius Caesar, the Romans pushed westward into a region they called Africa Nova or "New Africa" (present-day Algeria).

Augustus Caesar extended Roman control in Africa southward to the Sahara. He also combined Africa Vetus and Africa Nova into a single province. During his rule, Roman colonization of North Africa increased dramatically. The most important Roman colony in Africa was Carthage, which developed into the second greatest city in the Western Roman Empire.

Under the emperor CLAUDIUS, the Romans advanced as far west as the Atlantic coast of northern Africa, creating two new provinces in A.D. 44 in the region of Mauretania (now Morocco). Thereafter, Roman territory in Africa continued to expand, reaching its greatest extent in the late A.D. 100s during the rule of SEPTIMIUS SEVERUS, the Roman emperor who came from Africa.

Africa proved to be a vital asset to the empire. The fertile coastal region, which the Romans enhanced with an extensive system of irrigation, became the "breadbasket" of Rome. Much of the best land was controlled by a handful of wealthy landowners. Africa provided marble, wood, precious stones, gold, and dyes.

Exports of agricultural and other products made Rome's African provinces very prosperous. Impressive buildings were erected in the towns and cities. As Roman culture flourished, the African provinces became leading intellectual centers and produced many notable individuals, such as the writer APULEIUS. Christianity also spread rapidly in Africa.

Africa provided the Roman Empire with much of its food supply. In addition to fish caught by fishermen, such as the ones depicted on this mosaic from the A.D. 400s, Africa produced corn, olives for olive oil, and wine. So fertile was the coast of North Africa that it became famous throughout the empire for its great wealth.

Many important church figures, including Tertullian, Cyprian, and St. Augustine of Hippo, came from Africa.

By the A.D. 300s, Roman control in Africa had begun to weaken as a result of local power struggles and the waning power of the empire. In the early 400s, the Vandals, a Germanic tribe, invaded Mauretania and later took Carthage, hastening the decline of Roman civilization in North Africa. (*See also* **Augustus, Caesar Octavianus; Caesar, Gaius Julius; Colonies, Greek; Colonies, Roman; Mycenae; Trade, Greek.**)

AFTERLIFE

The Greeks and Romans believed in the existence of life after death. However, neither civilization had specific religious teachings about the afterlife. Instead, many of the Greek and Roman ideas about the afterlife developed from ancient myths, the works of writers and philosophers, and the sayings of oracles*. These ideas varied widely and were often contradictory.

* **oracle** priest or priestess through whom a god is believed to speak; also the location (such as a shrine) where such utterances are made

Greek Ideas of the Afterlife. An important aspect of Greek belief in the afterlife was the idea of separation between a person's soul and his or her dead body. The Greeks called the soul *psyche* and the body *soma*. After death and burial, the soul was freed from the body and began a journey to the world of the dead. A barrier, usually a river, lay between the worlds of the living and the dead. The Greeks believed that the soul was given guidance during its journey. Often the guidance came from the god Hermes or from his assistant, the ferryman Charon, who helped souls cross the river that separated the two worlds.

For the Greeks, the world of the dead was a place of darkness beneath the surface of the earth. The god Hades ruled this underworld, which was also called Hades. Monsters guarded the entrance to Hades, and the dead souls faced such evils and terrors as grief, disease, fear, and hunger. The ferocious, three-headed dog named Cerberus guarded the ferry landing by the river that separated the underworld from the living world.

In Hades, the dead came before a judge who examined their past deeds and assigned appropriate punishments. The judge might sentence those who had committed minor wrongdoing to forever wander about the underworld in a mindless state, knowing neither great suffering nor great joy. Serious wickedness, on the other hand, was punished with severe beatings, heavy labor, starvation, and torture. In earliest Greek thought, all dead souls—both good and bad—lived in Hades. A description of how the early Greeks pictured the underworld is given in Book 11 of Homer's epic poem the *Odyssey*.

However, some Greeks believed that certain people, particularly heroes* and other virtuous individuals, would not be required to wander through the darkness of the underworld. Instead they would be mysteriously transported to the Isles of the Blessed, also known as Elysium or the Elysian Fields. This magical place was located somewhere beyond the wide river that encircled the earth. In the sun-drenched Elysian Fields, virtuous dead souls experienced great happiness and lived at ease among flower-filled meadows and beautiful landscapes. Originally restricted to

* **hero** in mythology, a person of great strength or ability, often descended from a god

* **cult** group bound together by devotion to a particular person, belief, or god

relatives of the gods and heroes, this idyllic afterlife was eventually expanded to include ordinary people who had lived good lives or to people who belonged to the cult* called the ELEUSINIAN MYSTERIES (worshipers of Demeter, the goddess of grain and fertility).

In the late 500s B.C., the philosopher PYTHAGORAS and others suggested that the human soul might not die completely after death. They believed that the soul was imprisoned within the body but eventually could be released and reborn in another body. Rather than as a reward, this rebirth was seen as a type of punishment because the soul had to suffer through more lives. A soul could be freed from the cycle of death and rebirth only by living a virtuous and disciplined life.

ROMAN IDEAS OF THE AFTERLIFE. The myths, philosophy, and religious views of the Greeks had a profound influence on early Roman ideas concerning the afterlife. Like the later Greeks, many Romans believed in the immortality, or everlasting life, of the soul. They also believed, to some extent, in the idea of reincarnation—the rebirth of the soul in a new body. These ideas are reflected in the works of various ancient Roman writers and in Roman rituals and burial practices for the dead.

The Romans believed strongly in the power of the dead to affect the living, so they maintained relations with dead ancestors through various rituals and public festivals. Among the most important of these festivals were the Parentalia, held each year in February, and the Lemuria, held each year in May. During the Parentalia, families visited the tombs of their ancestors and made offerings of food and wine. For the Lemuria, the father of a household followed certain rituals to keep his home and family safe from the ghosts of dead ancestors. The Romans attached great importance to rules regarding the treatment of the dead and to the rituals honoring them.

Like the Greeks, the Romans believed that souls traveled to another place after death. Some Romans thought that virtuous souls returned to a heavenly place after death to enjoy eternal happiness. Wicked souls, on the other hand, suffered great punishments and tortures. In Book VI of his epic, the *Aeneid,* the Roman poet VERGIL created a vivid description of the underworld that consisted of three different regions for the dead. Some of the dead stayed in an area in which they received neither punishment nor rewards. Others suffered in Tartarus, a place of eternal punishment. The more fortunate souls dwelled temporarily in Elysium until they were reincarnated or could return to the realm of eternal happiness.

During the early Roman period, ideas about the afterlife were not part of any organized religious beliefs or religious system. Although some people believed strongly in the notion of an afterlife, others dismissed the idea. During the period of the Roman Empire, however, the belief in immortality took hold as new religious cults gained popularity. These cults were usually dedicated to a particular god or goddess, who would become a follower's personal protector in life and guide for the soul after death. Because they offered their followers the hope of a peaceful and happy afterlife, and, more importantly, claimed to reveal hidden truths that would lead to a better and richer life on earth, some cults became known as mystery cults.

OUT WITH GHOSTS!

The Roman festival of Lemuria was held each year in mid-May. Its purpose was to rid the household of the *lemures,* or threatening ghosts. The Romans particularly feared the spirits of those who had died young. They believed that such spirits might be angry because their lives had been cut short. The poet Ovid described the ritual of Lemuria: The father rose at midnight, when ghosts were believed to prowl, and walked barefoot through the house. As he walked, he spit out nine black beans for the ghosts to eat or to protect the living from being carried off. At the same time, he said, "With these beans I redeem me and mine."

pagan referring to a belief in more than one god; non-Christian

Despite the teachings of these cults, a belief in an afterlife remained largely personal and individual. It was not until Christianity began to replace pagan* religious cults that the idea of the immortality of the soul and the promise of an afterlife became more widespread. (*See also* **Cults; Death and Burial; Religion, Greek; Religion, Roman.**)

AGAMEMNON

LEGENDARY GREEK KING

gamemnon, fabled ruler of MYCENAE, is a prominent figure in the epics of the Greek poet HOMER, and he is the subject of the play by AESCHYLUS that bears his name and begins the *Oresteia* trilogy. Homer depicts Agamemnon as a courageous man, but one who is easily discouraged and lacking in resolution. Aeschylus portrays him as a self-confident, but insensitive, man.

According to myth, Agamemnon and Menelaus were the sons of Atreus and suffered tragic fates because of a curse laid by the gods on their grandfather, Pelops. Agamemnon married CLYTEMNESTRA, and they had three children—ORESTES, ELECTRA, and IPHIGENIA. In Homer's story, Agamemnon, supreme commander of the Achaean forces heading for the TROJAN WAR, sails from the port of Aulis with a great contingent of troops aboard a hundred ships. Aeschylus adds another detail—when Agamemnon offends ARTEMIS by boasting that he is a better hunter than she, the goddess stills the wind, making it impossible for the fleet to sail. The priest Calchas counsels him to appease Artemis by sacrificing Iphigenia. He does so, and the winds blow again.

The nine-year war begins. Though a brave and able leader, Agamemnon unwisely quarrels with a rival chieftain, ACHILLES, over the possession of a captive princess, Briseis. Achilles refuses to fight and takes his troops out of the war. Achilles later allows his friend Patroclus to wear his armor and lead his troops in support of the Greeks. When the Trojan leader Hector kills Patroclus, Achilles in grief and rage returns to fight, slays Hector, is wounded, and dies. After long years of war, TROY finally falls.

After his long absence, Agamemnon returns to Mycenae, where Clytemnestra has taken Aegisthus as her lover. Aeschylus tells how, to avenge Agamemnon's sacrifice of Iphigenia, Clytemnestra kills him and his companion, Cassandra. Aegisthus is her willing accomplice in this deed. Aeschylus recounts in *Libation Bearers* (the second part of the *Oresteia*) that the pair are, in turn, killed by Orestes to avenge his father's death.

Agamemnon is portrayed quite differently by the ancient writers. Homer casts Agamemnon as a man of personal integrity, though lacking in determination and easily discouraged. In the *Odyssey,* he contrasts the unhappy homecoming of Agamemnon with the happy return of Odysseus to his faithful wife, Penelope. Aeschylus shows Agamemnon in a much less favorable light—blinded by his high opinion of himself, foolish in his boastfulness, and cruel enough to murder his own daughter. In modern literature, Agamemnon, as a father and husband figure, is the model for a central character in Eugene O'Neill's trilogy, *Mourning Becomes Electra* (1931), as well as in T. S. Eliot's play *The Family Reunion* (1939). (*See also* **Drama, Greek.**)

AGORA

The agora, a public gathering place in Greek city-states*, played a very important role in ancient Greece. In the agora, Greeks came together to trade goods, to learn about and discuss issues of common concern, and to make decisions about their community.

THE ROLE OF THE AGORA. The Greek agora served many functions. Most importantly, it was the center of political life in the community. The leaders of the POLIS, or city-state, met there in a governing council known as the boule. Any decisions made by the boule would be presented for approval at a formal meeting of citizens held in the agora. This decision-making process was the essential element of DEMOCRACY in Greece.

The agora also served as a place of worship. In ancient ATHENS, for example, the agora contained numerous altars, small shrines, and temples. Before entering these sacred places, Athenians had to purify themselves through various rituals. Anyone considered impure could be denied entrance to the agora. Those barred from the agora would also be excluded from participation in the decision making of the polis.

Lastly, the agora was a lively commercial and social center. It served as a public marketplace where merchants bought and sold goods and where citizens shopped. People also drew water at the agora's public fountains. As the main public area of the polis, the agora provided opportunities for citizens to gather and exchange information—and gossip—and for teachers to

* **city-state** independent state consisting of a city and its surrounding territory

The agora served as the political, commercial, and social center of a Greek city-state. It was there that citizens discussed the important issues of the day, traded their wares, and worshiped at the local shrine.

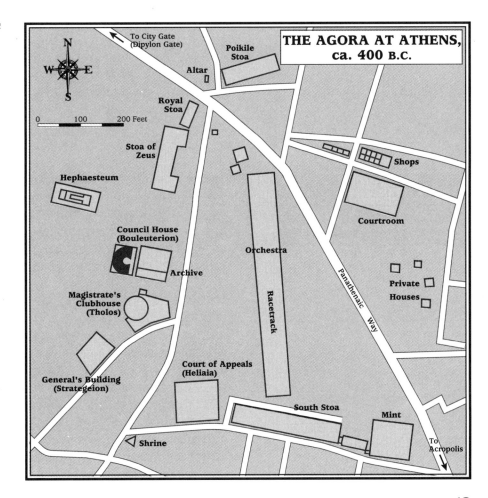

THE AGORA AT ATHENS, ca. 400 B.C.

hold informal outdoor classes. These commercial and social activities were an essential part of everyday life in ancient Greece.

BUILDINGS AND LAYOUT. In earliest times, the agora was simply an open space within a city. However, over the years the Greeks erected buildings, arranged in a complicated layout, in these public places. Some agoras covered one or more city blocks near the heart of the city. By the 400s B.C., agoras usually consisted of a number of public buildings, temples, and monuments to important citizens, as well as shade trees. While private homes were modest in size and design, structures in the agora tended to be quite large and lavish. By the 100s B.C., many Greek agoras had expanded in scope to include theaters and even racetracks.

An important feature of most agoras was the stoa, an open gallery* with a wall at the back and columns in front. In many cases, the agora was enclosed by several stoas, which provided shelter from sun and rain and space for merchants to set up shops. Students also met with their teachers in the stoas. In fact, the school of philosophy known as STOICISM was named after a particular stoa in Athens where that philosophy was taught. Between the stoas, or sometimes incorporated within them, were fountains, monuments, religious shrines, and public buildings such as law courts and government offices.

* **gallery** a roofed promenade, or place for strolling

The ancient Greeks enjoyed the life of the agora, but some of their enemies did not feel the same way. According to the Greek historian HERODOTUS, King Cyrus of Persia described the agora as the place where Greeks "gather together, swear oaths, and deceive each other." The ancient Romans created a similar open space, the Roman forum, as the focal point of urban society. (*See also* **Architecture, Greek; Cities, Greek; Forum; Government, Greek.**)

AGRICULTURE, GREEK

Farming was difficult in ancient Greece. Much of the country is mountainous, and only about one-fifth of the land can be easily cultivated. Moreover, the soil is generally of poor quality and the climate—with its hot, dry summers—is less than ideal for growing crops. Nevertheless, the ancient Greeks adapted their agriculture to the land and climate of the region.

* **archaeology** study of past human cultures, usually by excavating ruins

KNOWLEDGE OF ANCIENT GREEK FARMING. Most of our knowledge of ancient Greek farming has come from literature, archaeology*, and art. An early book on agriculture, HESIOD'S *Works and Days,* provides valuable details on farm activities, crops, and equipment. Another ancient writer, XENOPHON, wrote about different types of land, caring for the land, sowing and harvesting grain, and tending fruit trees. Studies of ancient farm tools and farm sites have provided important information about early Greek agriculture. Finally, images of traditional agricultural activities—such as plowing, sowing seeds, picking fruit, and taking produce to market—are found on ancient Greek pottery and paintings.

This small terra-cotta statue from the 500s B.C. shows a Greek farmer plowing with two oxen. Most farms in Greece were small, and farmers usually worked the land themselves with the help of a few slaves.

FARMS AND FARM LABOR. Because of the scarcity of good farmland and the hard work involved in farming, most Greek farms were small. These farms were generally owned and operated by individuals and their families, who sometimes had the help of a few slaves. More fertile regions, such as Thessaly in northern Greece, had larger farms that usually belonged to the estates of wealthy landowners. Many of these owners lived in a town or city and hired overseers to manage their estates. Slaves provided most of the labor on large estates, although free workers were also hired, especially at harvest time.

PRINCIPAL CROPS. Greek agriculture focused on a few basic crops, especially wheat, barley, grapes, figs, and olives. Farmers grew wheat and barley in the few fertile areas of Greece, notably in the plains of Argos and Olympia in the south.

Grapes, figs, and olives thrived in less fertile soils, and they could better withstand the extreme conditions of dryness and drought, which explains their importance in Greek agriculture. Farmers often planted these three crops next to each other, allowing the grapevines to grow up the olive and fig trees. The practice saved precious space and made efficient use of poor soils. Both grapes and olives had secondary uses. Grapes were made into wine, which was sometimes added to drinking water to improve its quality, and olives were pressed to make olive oil, an important export product. Many Greek farmers also had small garden plots where they raised vegetables and herbs for their own use and for selling in nearby towns and city markets.

Orchards flourished in many areas of ancient Greece. In addition to figs and olives, the Greeks grew apples, pears, cherries, peaches, plums, and dates, as well as a variety of nuts. The cultivation of these fruits and nuts depended largely on climate, with certain varieties growing best in particular regions.

LIVESTOCK.   The raising of animals was another important agricultural activity in ancient Greece. Many farmers kept cattle, sheep, goats, and pigs. Cattle served primarily as work animals. Milk came from sheep and goats, and these animals also provided wool and hair for making rope. Pigs and sheep provided meat.

Raising livestock depended on an adequate supply of food for the animals. In regions lacking suitable grazing land, farmers relied upon the other types of feed, such as harvested crops or food scraps from the farmer's table. Sheep and goats, which can survive in the least fertile areas, grazed over wide areas of Greece. The region of Arcadia, in the central part of the Peloponnese*, was known for its shepherds and sheep raising.

* **Peloponnese** peninsula forming the southern part of the mainland of Greece

Because honey was widely used as a sweetener, beekeeping was a common agricultural activity in ancient Greece. To increase the production of honey, the Greeks developed several methods for raising various types of bees. Many Greek towns passed laws to regulate beekeeping and levied taxes on activities related to beekeeping.

Farmers raised horses in the northern regions of Macedonia, Thrace, and Thessaly, which all had good pasture land. Horses, however, played no role in agriculture itself. The Greeks used them exclusively in battle or in ceremonial or festive events.

TECHNOLOGY.   Historians know relatively little about the agricultural methods or tools used by the ancient Greeks. It is known that they used irrigation on a small scale to provide water for certain crops. They also left land fallow* after a harvest.

* **fallow** land plowed and left unseeded for a season or longer so that moisture and organic processes can replenish the soil's nutrients

In most regions of Greece, the soil was light and easy to work. Fields, including fallow ones, were usually plowed three times a year—in spring, summer, and fall. Plowing loosened the soil, controlled weeds, and helped the soil retain moisture. The farmers used hand-held plows fitted with simple iron blades, pulled by oxen or mules. Today, Greeks living in remote areas use plows similar to those used by the ancient Greeks.

Because these light plows could only cut shallow furrows in the soil, Greek farmers sometimes had to use pickaxes or hoes to dig deeper furrows before planting crops. When a field was ready for planting, farmers sowed seeds either by throwing them from side to side or placing them in single rows. Then they covered the seeds with soil using a hoe or a rakelike tool called a harrow. Farmers pulled weeds by hand or used a sickle to cut the stems.

At harvest time, farmers cut the stalks of grain with sickles, tied them in bundles, and carried them away for threshing—the process of separating the grain from the stalks. For the threshing*, the stalks were placed on a stone or tile floor and then trampled by a team of mules or oxen. The harvested grain was stored for later use.

* **thresh** to crush grain plants so that the seeds or grain are separated from the stalks and the husks

During the early years in ancient Greece, simple farming methods provided enough food to meet the needs of individual families, as well as the inhabitants of neighboring villages. However, the growth of towns gradually created a greater demand for food. Greek farmers adopted crop rotation, which involves raising a series of different crops to keep the land in use without wearing out the soil. Such improvements in farm technology helped increase the production of food.

AGRICULTURE, ROMAN

* **province** overseas area controlled by Rome

Agriculture was of primary importance to the ancient Romans. Rome itself began as a farming community, and farming developed into a major economic activity throughout the Roman empire. Roman farmers adopted farming techniques developed in neighboring regions, such as Greece and North Africa. They also improved agricultural methods and spread these improvements to Roman settlements in the provinces*.

FARMS AND FARM LABOR. During the early years of the Roman Republic, agriculture consisted primarily of small family-owned farms. Largely self-sufficient, these farms sometimes used slave labor. The farmers often sold their surplus crops in town and city markets.

* **patrician** member of the upper class who traced his ancestry to a senatorial family in the earliest days of the Roman Republic

As Rome expanded, much of the land it conquered became the property of the Roman state. In the early republic, the patricians* (and in later years, the nobles) began taking over some of the public land, occupying more than the law allowed. Often they took the land without paying even the nominal rent tax. On this land, they eventually created huge agricultural estates known as latifundia. Unlike the self-sufficient family farms, the latifundia operated as profit-making businesses. They were owned by absentee landlords and worked mostly by large groups of slaves. During the period of the late republic, this type of estate farming dominated agriculture. In southern Italy, these estates became huge grazing ranches. Overgrazing, especially by sheep, caused such severe soil erosion in the region that the land has not fully recovered to this day. Although Italy contained some of the largest estates, large estates also existed in all provinces of the empire. The latifundia became essential in meeting the food needs of towns and cities.

Many farm owners were required to perform lengthy military service overseas. They could not easily farm their plots and were often eager to sell them. As a result, many small farms were sold to wealthy landowners, whose great estates became even larger. Some of the farmers who sold their land moved to the cities to find work. Others became farm laborers or tenant farmers, who leased land from the large estates and paid rent in both money and crops.

See color plate 9, vol. 1.

PRINCIPAL CROPS. The main crops in the Roman empire were grains (such as wheat and barley), grapes, olives, and figs. Fruits—such as apples, peaches, pears, plums and cherries—were also important crops. Roman farmers grew nuts, including almonds, walnuts, and chestnuts, and various vegetables and herbs.

Roman farmers planted grain primarily in lowland areas that had adequate rainfall or irrigation. The Po River valley of northern Italy and the regions of Etruria, Umbria, and Campania near Rome were all suitable for growing grain. Grain also grew well in the Roman provinces of EGYPT and AFRICA. In Roman times, before the advancing Sahara desert changed the landscape, the northern regions of Africa were more fertile and better watered than they are now. In fact, the fertile coastal region of the province of Africa became the granary* of Rome because of its importance in grain production.

Farmers grew grapes, olives, and other crops wherever climate and soil conditions were suitable. Grapes and olives usually grew well on the lower slopes of hills, while nut trees often occupied the higher slopes. In some regions of the empire, farmers specialized in particular crops. For example, Rome's eastern provinces became known for the production of rice, cotton, and hemp.

LIVESTOCK. The Romans raised many domestic animals—some for food and others for work. Throughout the empire, farmers used oxen, mules, and donkeys to help with plowing and other tasks. In some Mediterranean areas, cattle also served as work animals.

Sheep were the principal source of meat and milk in the Mediterranean areas, and they were a source of wool in other regions. Cattle also provided meat and milk as well as leather. Roman farmers made cheese from the milk of these animals. The Romans also used the milk of goats, and made ropes and sacks from the hair of certain types of goats. Pigs and poultry, raised throughout the empire, were important

* **granary** storage place for grain

The most important crops grown by Roman farmers were grains such as wheat and barley; grapes for wine; olives for olive oil; and figs. The Romans also raised livestock. Some domestic animals were used for food, while others, such as oxen, helped plow fields and perform other tasks.

ROMAN WINE MAKING

Wine making was an important activity in ancient Rome. Roman workers harvested the grapes, placed them in large vats, and stomped on them with bare feet to release the juice. The juice ran through pipes into tanks or pottery containers. The Romans drank some of the juice as new wine and boiled down the rest to use as a preservative or a thickener for thin wine. Then they removed the pulpy mush left in the vats and placed it in a special press to squeeze out the remaining juice. The juice from the pressing was allowed to ferment in jars, creating finer and more potent wines.

* **thresh** to crush grain plants so that the seeds or grain are separated from the stalks and the husks

sources of meat. The Romans also used the eggs, quills, and down of their poultry. They raised horses for riding, for use in battle, and for sporting events, but seldom used horses for farm work.

TECHNOLOGY. Historians know a great deal about Roman agricultural activities and technology. Much of this knowledge comes from the works of such ancient writers as CATO THE ELDER, Varro, Columella, and PLINY THE ELDER. In addition, archaeologists have studied ancient Roman farm tools. From these archaeological studies, historians have determined that Roman agriculture was complex and innovative.

The Romans approached agriculture as a science. They learned about different types of soils and chose crops to plant based on soil type and climate conditions. They improved the quality of soil by adding natural fertilizers, such as manure and the pulp from making wine and olive oil. They varied the size of their fields to suit the crop and the farming methods used. Many large farms had elaborate systems of crop rotation to keep soils fertile. The normal rotation cycle included a fallow period, during which time the land was left unplanted. Farmers usually continued to plow fallow fields two or three times a year to kill weeds and to help the soil retain moisture. After the fallow period, farmers would plant one season of a root crop, followed by a season of a grain crop, and finally a season of mixed grasses. In this way, the soil could replenish itself over time because not all plants took the same nutrients from the soil.

The Romans studied the drainage patterns of fields, dug trenches to drain wetlands, and devised ways to irrigate dry fields. They also built stone-walled terraces on slopes in order to make hillsides suitable for cultivation. To use the land more efficiently and to reduce the need for weeding, Roman farmers often cultivated several crops together. For example, they planted vegetables among grapevines or olive trees.

The Romans used a variety of farm tools designed to perform specific tasks. They made notable advances in the design of plows to suit certain soil and climate conditions. One of the most important of these was a wheeled plow, with a double-edged blade that could be used to turn over heavy soil. This was a great improvement over the ard, a wheelless plow with simple iron blades that could dig only shallow furrows in light soil.

Several Roman inventions made harvesting easier and more efficient. One of these was a new type of sickle for harvesting grain that eased the strain on the user's wrist. Another invention was a large, well-designed scythe for mowing tall grasses. A third remarkable invention was a harvesting machine that consisted of an enclosed wooden frame on wheels. The harvesting machine had metal teeth at the front, and the farmer used mules or oxen to push it through the field of grain. The metal teeth cut off the tops of the grain plants, which then fell into the wooden frame behind. For threshing*, the Romans used a *tribulum*—a weighted board, which was invented by the Greeks, that was fitted with sharp stones or metal rollers on the underside. They dragged the device across the grain on the threshing floor, and it easily separated the grain from the stalks and husks.

* **graft** to insert a shoot or bud from one kind of tree into a slit in a closely related tree so that it will grow there

In maintaining their orchards, the Romans improved the existing techniques for grafting* and devised some new ones. This not only improved the quality of fruit but also made it easier to introduce new varieties from other parts of the empire. The Romans also improved pruning tools and developed new ones to increase the efficiency of their work.

These new technologies and scientific methods spread throughout the Roman empire, replacing or improving the farming methods used by local people. As a result, the Romans helped improve agriculture and increase food production throughout much of Europe and North Africa. However, despite their innovations and scientific approach to agriculture, the Romans eventually faced problems of soil exhaustion from overusing the land. Bad weather sometimes caused crops to fail, resulting in occasional food shortages within the empire. (*See also* **Agriculture, Greek.**)

ALARIC

See *Visigoths.*

ALCIBIADES

ca. 450–404 B.C.
ATHENIAN POLITICIAN AND
MILITARY LEADER

* **city-state** independent state consisting of a city and its surrounding territory

Alcibiades rose to prominence in ATHENS during the period of the PELOPONNESIAN WAR, when the Greek city-states* of Athens and Sparta vied for dominance. But his personal ambition and unreliability led the citizens of Athens to cast him aside on two occasions.

Growing up in Athens, Alcibiades had many advantages. He was raised in the household of the Athenian statesman PERICLES, and he was the pupil and close friend of the philosopher SOCRATES. After Pericles' death in 429 B.C., Alcibiades became active in Athenian politics.

Eager to expand the power of Athens, Alcibiades succeeded in bringing Athens into an alliance against the city-state of Sparta. In 418 and 416 B.C., he led campaigns against the Spartans. Then, the following year, Alcibiades organized an expedition against Sicily with the intention of extending Athenian power into the western Mediterranean. At about the same time, the city was scandalized by a religious crime—the mutilation of statues of the god HERMES. Opponents of Alcibiades accused him of the crime, and soon after reaching Sicily, he was ordered back to Athens to stand trial. Instead, Alcibiades fled to Sparta, where he became a military adviser to King Agis II, the enemy of Athens. Alcibiades also persuaded Athens's allies to break their alliances with the city.

The Spartans began to have doubts about the trustworthiness of Alcibiades. Sensing the suspicions regarding his loyalty, Alcibiades traveled to ASIA MINOR, where he tried to regain his power base in Athens. His opportunity came in the form of an appointment as general of the Athenian fleet at Samos. After winning several victories, Alcibiades returned to Athens in 407 B.C. and was given command of Athenian forces in Ionia in western Asia Minor. However, this time, Alcibiades faced an alliance of the Spartans and the Persians and suffered defeat. In Athens, popular opinion turned against him. Alcibiades retired to Asia Minor, where he was murdered by Spartan agents.

The Greek historian THUCYDIDES discussed Alcibiades in his account of the Peloponnesian War, and the Greek biographer PLUTARCH wrote about Alcibiades' life. Alcibiades also appeared as a character in the *Symposium,* one of the philosophical dialogues of PLATO.

ALEXANDER THE GREAT

356–323 B.C.
KING OF MACEDONIA
AND WORLD CONQUEROR

A lexander III (the Great) was perhaps the most important military leader of the ancient world. A man of tremendous talent and single-minded determination, he established a mighty empire and spread Greek culture throughout the ancient world. His conquests included the PERSIAN EMPIRE as well as lands in central Asia and India.

EARLY YEARS. The son of King PHILIP II of MACEDONIA and his strong-willed wife Olympias, Alexander showed great promise from an early age. His parents encouraged him to believe that he could accomplish anything he desired. They also arranged for Alexander to study with the best tutors of the time, including the Greek philosopher ARISTOTLE. Through Aristotle, the intelligent and inquisitive Alexander learned about medicine, plants, animals, and geography. He also developed a profound attachment to Greek culture. He admired the plays of EURIPIDES and the works of the poet HOMER, especially the *Iliad.* He revered—and hoped to follow in the footsteps of—the legendary Greek heroes of the past.

A spirited and courageous youth, Alexander proved his skill as a horseman at age 12 by taming a very difficult stallion named Bucephalus. He also learned military strategy from his father. At age 16, while governing in his father's absence, he led a successful attack against rebellious tribes in Illyria, a region west of Macedonia. Two years later, Alexander

This detail from a first century A.D. mosaic depicts Alexander the Great at the Battle of Issus in 333 B.C. At Issus, Alexander's outnumbered troops soundly defeated the army of the Persian king Darius III. Although Darius escaped, Alexander continued to conquer Persian territory until he finally captured the Persian throne in 330 B.C.

See
color plate 10,
vol. 3.

* **envoy** person who represents a government abroad

BUCEPHALUS

Alexander's black horse, Bucephalus, was the most famous steed in history. Originally intended as a gift for Alexander's father, the horse was judged too wild and uncontrollable for riding. Alexander thought otherwise and took command of the horse. Discovering that Bucephalus was afraid of his shadow, Alexander pointed the horse towards the sun. He talked to the horse, stroked and calmed him. Alexander even taught Bucephalus to kneel down so he could mount him easily while wearing armor. Bucephalus was Alexander's horse for 20 years and accompanied him on his conquests. When Bucephalus died, he was honored with a magnificent funeral.

---

* **strait** narrow channel that connects two bodies of water

* **satrap** provincial governor in ancient Persia

* **pharaoh** ruler of ancient Egypt

* **oracle** priest or priestess through whom a god is believed to speak; also the location (such as a shrine) where such utterances are made

---

took command of the cavalry and played an important role in defeating the Greeks. This decisive victory gave Macedonia mastery over Greece. Afterward Alexander went to Athens as an envoy*.

In 336 B.C., Philip II was assassinated, and Alexander became king of Macedonia. Many historians believe that Alexander's mother may have been involved in the assassination plot. Philip had divorced Olympias and had taken another wife, and Olympias may have tried to protect her son's right to the throne. Most agree, however, that Alexander had no part in the murder. By age 20, he had inherited a strong kingdom, a well-trained army, and control of most of Greece. Alexander was ready to venture farther afield.

FIRST CONQUESTS.   Before he died, King Philip had begun planning an invasion of the Persian Empire. Alexander was determined to carry out this plan. First, however, he had to subdue rebellious tribes in the north and secure firm control over Greece. During the summer of 335 B.C., Alexander marched north with his army and established control over various tribes. Then he turned south toward the Greek city-state of THEBES, which had revolted against Macedonian rule. Alexander's troops destroyed the city, killed 6,000 of its people, and enslaved the survivors. Only the Theban temples and the house of the great poet PINDAR were spared because of Alexander's admiration for Greek culture. The destruction of Thebes shocked all of Greece, and other city-states quickly acknowledged Macedonian rule.

Alexander then turned his attentions toward Persia. In 334 B.C., his army of 40,000 Macedonian and Greek soldiers crossed the Hellespont (now known as the Dardanelles), one of the straits* separating Europe from ASIA MINOR. First Alexander defeated the local Persian satraps* at the Battle of Granicus. Then he marched along the coastline, liberating Greek colonies from Persian rule. Turning inland, Alexander quickly took control of the interior. While spending the winter at Gordium, the capital of the kingdom of Phrygia, he untied (or possibly just cut) the Gordian knot. This complex knot fastened an ancient royal chariot to a pole. According to legend, the person who loosened the knot would rule Asia. Alexander's success with the Gordian knot enhanced his rapidly growing fame.

The following year, Alexander led his army into SYRIA. Before long he came upon the troops of Darius III, the Great King of Persia. Although vastly outnumbered by the Persians, Alexander won a brilliant victory at the Battle of Issus. Darius escaped, and the survivors of his army scattered and fled.

Alexander marched to Tyre, an ancient port on the Mediterranean Sea that served as the base of the Persian navy. Located on an offshore island, Tyre had formidable defenses. Alexander's forces laid siege to the city for seven months before finally taking it in 332 B.C. Their victory destroyed Persian naval power in the Mediterranean.

From Tyre, Alexander moved into EGYPT. The Egyptians honored him for freeing them from Persian rule, and they accepted him as a pharaoh*. A sacred oracle* hailed Alexander as the son of Ammon, the Egyptian god of the sun. While in Egypt, Alexander founded ALEXANDRIA, which in time became one of the greatest Greek cities of the ancient world. It was one of the many cities named for Alexander.

THE DEFEAT OF PERSIA. With Persia's western territories under his rule, Alexander could focus on capturing Darius and conquering the central part of the Persian Empire. In an effort to halt Alexander's advance, Darius offered to give him all Persian territory west of the Euphrates River. But Alexander was determined to completely shatter the Persian Empire. In 331 B.C., he crossed the Tigris and Euphrates rivers and met Darius's army on the plains of Gaugamela (part of present-day Iraq). As in the Battle of Issus, the Persian forces vastly outnumbered Alexander's army. Nevertheless, Alexander's military genius overcame the Persians and led to another brilliant victory. Once again, Darius managed to escape.

Marching into the heart of Darius's empire, Alexander occupied the great Persian cities of Babylon, Susa, Persepolis, and Ecbatana. After looting the royal treasury at Persepolis, the sacred capital of Persia, Alexander burned the city to the ground as punishment for the Persians' destruction of ATHENS more than 100 years earlier. In the spring of 330 B.C., Alexander continued his search for Darius. Before he could capture the Great King, however, Darius was overthrown and assassinated by some of his own officers. The death of the Great King of Persia left Alexander free to assume that title.

Alexander's ambitious route of conquest greatly expanded the Macedonian empire. Spanning an area from Greece to India—a distance of over 3,000 miles—Alexander's conquests included such prized territories as Egypt and the Persian Empire.

THE MARCH EAST. Not content with his conquests of western and central Persia, Alexander continued to advance eastward into remote and uncharted territories. From 330 to 329 B.C., he led his army farther into central Asia, from the shores of the Caspian Sea to the snowy slopes of the Hindu Kush, one of the most rugged mountain ranges in the world. Along the way, he founded several cities and named them after himself.

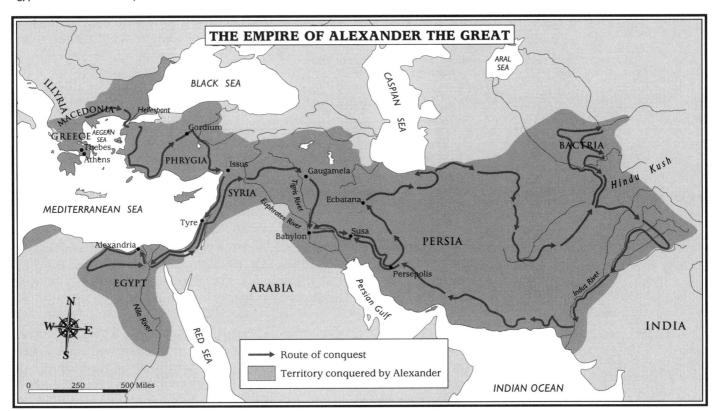

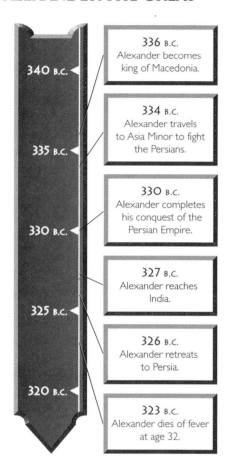

336 B.C.
Alexander becomes king of Macedonia.

334 B.C.
Alexander travels to Asia Minor to fight the Persians.

330 B.C.
Alexander completes his conquest of the Persian Empire.

327 B.C.
Alexander reaches India.

326 B.C.
Alexander retreats to Persia.

323 B.C.
Alexander dies of fever at age 32.

340 B.C.
335 B.C.
330 B.C.
325 B.C.
320 B.C.

* **dynasty** succession of rulers from the same family or group

In 328 B.C., he reached Bactria, the most distant region of the Persian Empire. It took Alexander three years to overcome the fierce resistance of the peoples of the region. To ensure future peace and encourage the spread of Greek culture and influence, Alexander had his soldiers establish military posts throughout central Asia. He also encouraged his troops to marry native women. Alexander set an example by marrying Roxane, a noblewoman of Sogdiana (present-day Uzbekistan).

Still unsatisfied with his conquests, Alexander was determined to push farther into unknown regions. In 327 B.C., he led his troops across the Indus River into INDIA, a kingdom whose spices and traders were known to the Greeks, but whose lands were hidden behind mystery and legend. During his march into India, Alexander sometimes met strong resistance and went to battle. In one of the greatest fights, he defeated King Porus, the most powerful ruler in the Punjab (an area in northwestern India). During this battle, Alexander's troops faced armored elephants for the first time. The experience frightened them and made them reluctant to continue their advance into unfamiliar territories.

The constant marching and combat took its toll on Alexander's troops. In 326 B.C., they refused to go any farther east. Faced with rebellion among the troops, Alexander decided to begin the long, difficult march back to Persia. Part of his army sailed down the Indus River and back to Persia along the coast. The remaining soldiers, led by Alexander, took a land route that passed through the desert of southern Persia. The march across the desert resulted in the greatest suffering and losses of Alexander's entire military campaign. Three-quarters of the troops died from thirst, hunger, and exhaustion.

Once back in Persia, Alexander found his kingdom in disorder. Satraps who had been left in charge during his absence had governed unwisely, and some had established private armies loyal to themselves. To restore order, Alexander executed several satraps and senior officials and replaced others.

In the autumn of 324 B.C., Alexander's boyhood friend and closest companion, Hephaestion, died at the city of Ecbatana. After a period of intense mourning, Alexander began a winter campaign in the mountains of northern Persia. He then returned to Babylon and prepared to sail for ARABIA, an area he had not yet conquered. Before he could leave, he became ill with a fever and died. Only 32 years old, Alexander had not named a successor. After his death, a son was born to Roxane, but the child did not live long.

Alexander's leading generals divided his empire and established kingdoms naming themselves as rulers. Of these kingdoms, the Ptolemy dynasty* of Egypt and the Seleucid dynasty of Syria and Persia lasted the longest. It was through these kingdoms that Alexander's legacy continued and Greek culture endured in his former empire.

GOALS AND ACCOMPLISHMENTS. During his brief lifetime, Alexander sought to create a politically unified empire and also to spread the Greek culture he so admired. The division of the empire into rival kingdoms after Alexander's death eliminated the possibility of a lasting, unified state. Yet he achieved his second goal. As a result of his conquests and the establishment of cities and colonies, Greek civilization took root in the conquered regions, and Greek became the language of education and commerce throughout the Mediterranean world. Moreover, a new Hellenistic or Greek-influenced culture dominated Persia, Egypt, and Asia Minor for years to come. (*See also* **Armies, Greek; Greece, History of: Hellenistic Age; Wars and Warfare, Greek.**)

ALEXANDRIA

Alexandria was a city in ancient EGYPT. It was founded in 331 B.C. by the king of Macedonia, ALEXANDER THE GREAT, who named the city after himself. Located at a crossroads of Asia, Africa, and Europe, Alexandria became one of the largest and most important cities of the ancient world. It was renowned as a prosperous commercial center and famous center of learning throughout the Greek and Roman periods.

Alexander the Great founded the city during his conquest of Persia, which controlled Egypt. For the location of his new city, he chose the site of a small fishing village on the Nile delta, the fan-shaped area in northern Egypt where the Nile River empties into the MEDITERRANEAN SEA. This location was well-suited for Alexander's military and commercial plans. It had a harbor large enough to accommodate many warships and merchant vessels, and it was connected to the interior of Egypt by the Nile River and various canals. According to tradition, Alexander helped select sites for the city's temples and AGORA (marketplace). When he left Egypt, Alexander chose a Greek named Cleomenes of Naucratis to be governor of Egypt. Alexander gave Cleomenes the responsibility for building and populating the new city. Cleomenes accomplished the second task by bringing people from nearby areas to live in Alexandria.

This detail of a floor mosaic from a Middle Eastern church shows the Egyptian city of Alexandria. Alexandria became one of the leading intellectual centers of the ancient world. Scholars from all over traveled to Alexandria to study at the Museum and the Library.

* **satrap** provincial governor in ancient Persia

* **dynasty** succession of rulers from the same family or group

* **portico** roof supported by columns, forming a porch or covered walkway

A LOST TREASURY OF KNOWLEDGE

The great Library of Alexandria contained much of the knowledge of the ancient Greek world. Its vast collection included books and documents on astronomy, geography, architecture, mathematics, medicine, biology, philosophy, and literature. In 48 B.C., a fire started during a battle between Egyptians and Romans that destroyed the library and almost all of its contents. It remains a terrible tragedy that much of the accumulated knowledge of the ancient Greek world was lost forever.

* **city-state** independent state consisting of a city and its surrounding territory

* **bureaucracy** large departmental organization that performs the activities of government

After Alexander's death in 323 B.C., the empire was divided among his generals and close companions. Egypt was left to Ptolemy, Alexander's boyhood friend and a general. Ptolemy became satrap* of Egypt and had Cleomenes executed. He then had himself crowned King Ptolemy I of Egypt, thus establishing the Ptolemaic dynasty*. Ptolemy had Alexander's body buried in Alexandria and continued the construction of the city. He later made Alexandria the capital of Egypt, and it remained the capital for almost 300 years.

During the rule of Ptolemy I and his successors, Alexandria became a center of HELLENISTIC CULTURE. The Ptolemies built royal palaces and elegant parks. They made Serapis the god of the city and built a temple in his honor. The Ptolemies respected Greek culture and helped shape the city along Greek ideals, especially the Greek interest in knowledge and learning. To support intellectual pursuits, the Ptolemies built a great museum and library. These became the city's most important and famous institutions.

The great Museum of Alexandria was not exactly like a museum today. Rather, it served as an institute for advanced study. The Museum had a large dining room, porticos*, and a tree-lined garden, where scholars presented ideas and debated philosophies. The Museum quickly developed into the most important center of Greek culture in the world. The Library of Alexandria, located near the Museum, became even more famous. It contained perhaps as many as half a million volumes, the largest collection of books in the world at the time. Famous and distinguished scholars served as the chief librarians, helping other scholars classify works, establish guidelines for research, compile dictionaries, and undertake a variety of other scholarly pursuits. The intellectual atmosphere of Alexandria, created largely by the Museum and the Library, attracted poets, writers, and scholars from all over the world. The classical works of Greek writers from HOMER to EURIPIDES were studied as the greatest models of literary achievement.

By 200 B.C., Alexandria occupied an area of about four square miles and had a population of about 500,000, making it the largest of all Greek cities. Its inhabitants included Greeks and Macedonians, Egyptians, Africans, a large Jewish community, and people from many other lands. Despite its diverse population, the city carefully preserved its Greek traditions and maintained close ties to the Greek city-states*. The government of Alexandria consisted of a principal minister who advised the king, a financial minister, a chief justice, priests from various religious groups, and military and naval officers. These officials directed a large bureaucracy* to carry out the day-to-day business of the city.

Alexandria had become an immensely wealthy city as a result of trade, which included exports of grain and other products from Egypt, spices from ARABIA, and other products from as far away as INDIA. Alexandrian merchants dominated most of the trade in the eastern Mediterranean region. The city's great port consisted of two large harbors. Situated at the entrance to one of these was a tall lighthouse with a blazing fire at the top to guide ships safely into the harbor. This lighthouse, known as the Pharos of Alexandria, was considered one of the seven wonders of the ancient world.

* province overseas area controlled by Rome

In 30 B.C., Egypt became a province* of the Roman Empire. Alexandria remained the capital of the province and continued to prosper. However, the city began to experience some political and social unrest resulting from its loss of independence under Roman control as well as from religious upheaval. Christianity, the new religion, spread rapidly in Alexandria. The city became an important center of Christian learning, and it produced many influential Christian thinkers.

Alexandria remained an important center of commerce, Christianity, and western culture until the A.D. 600s, when the Arabs conquered Egypt. Thereafter, the city declined in importance, and much of its great architecture and institutions eventually were destroyed. In modern times, Alexandria would prosper again. Today, with a population of over 3 million, Alexandria is the chief port and second largest city in Egypt. (*See also* **Cities, Greek; Harbors; Libraries; Persian Empire; Poetry, Greek and Hellenistic; Ptolemaic Dynasty; Trade, Greek; Trade, Roman.**)

ALPHABETS AND WRITING

The ancient Greeks believed that writing played an important part in the development of civilization. They associated the use of written language with order and democracy. Sometime around 600 B.C., for example, the Athenian politician SOLON had his new laws written on a large wooden tablet and placed on display so all could see them. This permanent posting of the laws made it clear that they were fixed and that they applied to everyone.

The Greeks used an alphabet, a set of symbols or letters representing various sounds, in their system of writing. They arranged letters of the alphabet to reflect the sound of spoken words, just as we do in English, Spanish, and other languages that developed in western Europe. The Greeks adapted their alphabet from the ancient PHOENICIANS of ASIA MINOR.

EARLY WRITING SYSTEMS. About 3,000 years ago, the Phoenicians developed a writing system that used several dozen symbols, each representing a syllable. This type of system, called a syllabary, differed significantly from other early writing systems. The Mesopotamians and Egyptians, for example, created hundreds of symbols that stood for words or ideas rather than merely sounds or syllables. The Phoenician syllabary was much easier to use than the earlier systems. A Phoenician only needed to learn about thirty symbols in order to read and write.

The Phoenician syllabary was not a true alphabet, however, because it did not have a symbol for every sound. In particular, it lacked symbols for vowel sounds. A Phoenician reader who saw the symbol for the sound "bp" would have to decide from the surrounding words and meaning whether the writer meant "bep," "bap," or "bop."

THE GREEK ALPHABET. The early Mycenaean civilization of ancient Greece also had a writing system based on syllables. Known today as Linear B, this writing system used at least 89 symbols to represent various combinations of consonants and vowels. However, Linear B was lost when the Mycenaean civilization was destroyed in the 1100s B.C.

The Roman alphabet is used to write English and many other modern languages. This chart shows how the alphabet developed over thousands of years.

EVOLUTION OF THE ROMAN ALPHABET					
Phoenician	Early Greek	Early Etruscan	Early Roman	Classical Roman	Modern Roman
aleph	alpha	A	A	A	A
beth	beta	B	B	B	B
gimel	gamma		C	C	C
daleth	delta	D	D	D	D
he	e(psilon)			E	E
waw	digamma			F	F
				G	G
zayin	zeta	I			
heth	(h)eta	B	HB	H	H
teth	theta				
yod	iota	I	I	I	I / J
kaph	kappa	K	K	K	K
lamed	lambda			L	L
mem	mu	M	M M	M	M
nun	nu		N	N	N
samekh	xi (chi)				
'ayin	o(micron)	O	O	O	O
pe	pi			P	P
sade	san	M			
qoph	koppa	Q	Q	Q	Q
resh	rho			R	R
sin	sigma			S	S
taw	tau	T	T	T	T
	u(psilon)	Y	V	V	U / V / W
	phi				
	chi (xi)	X	X	X	X
	psi	Y			
					Y
					Z

By the 700s B.C., the Greeks had learned about the Phoenician syllabary—probably through contacts with Phoenician traders—and had developed their own version of it. The Greeks adopted many of the Phoenician symbols but turned the syllabary into a true alphabet by adding symbols for vowel sounds. They also added new symbols for sounds used in Greek but not in Phoenician, and they dropped symbols for sounds not used in Greek. These changes made the Greek system more complete and accurate, as well as easier to use.

The letters of the Greek alphabet resembled the Phoenician symbols, and the Greek names for the letters echoed the Phoenician names. The Phoenician *aleph* and *beth* became the Greek *alpha* and *beta.* Each symbol represented the first sound in that symbol's name—alpha meant *a* and beta meant *b.*

At first the Greeks wrote from right to left. Then they changed to a continuous back-and-forth style in which one line read left to right and the next line read right to left. This type of writing was called *boustrophedon,* a word that described the way in which oxen plowed furrows back and forth across a field. After about 500 B.C., the Greeks settled on the system of writing from left to right. For hundreds of years, though, they used only capital letters and no punctuation. Signs for punctuation, lowercase letters, and cursive writing appeared much later.

Two versions of the Greek alphabet developed over the years. In 403 B.C., Athens adopted the Ionic alphabet. It became standard throughout Greece and was the ancestor of the modern Greek alphabet. The other version, the Chalcidian alphabet, spread to Italy.

THE ROMAN ALPHABET. By the 600s B.C., the ETRUSCANS, who lived in central Italy, had adopted the Chalcidian alphabet. They may have learned it from a Greek colony in Italy. The Etruscan alphabet had 26 letters—22 from the original Phoenician system and four that had been added by the Greeks.

In the 500s B.C., the Romans adopted the alphabet of their Etruscan neighbors, using only 20 letters. The Romans later added letters to represent additional sounds. The letter *g* was added to distinguish the hard "g" sound from the "k" sound of the Etruscan letter *c.* The letters *y* and *z,* which the Romans borrowed from the Greeks, were added in order to translate Greek into Latin more easily. By the time of the Roman Empire, the Latin alphabet consisted of 23 letters.

Like the ancient Greeks, the Romans began by using only capital letters. They carved beautifully formed inscriptions on stone monuments and tablets throughout their empire. Gradually, the Romans developed lowercase letters and cursive writing, which eventually came into use for everyday writing.

As the Romans extended their empire, people throughout most of Europe adopted their alphabet. Although the ability to read and write declined during the Middle Ages, the Latin alphabet was still the basis for almost all European writing. The English language, however, added three letters—*u, w,* and *j.* The Romans had no "v" sound in their language. The Romans had used the letter *v,* however, to represent both the vowel sound "u" and the consonant sound "w." In the Middle Ages, as people who used the "v" sound began to read and write in Latin, the vowel sound "u" came to be written as *u;* the letter *v* came to represent the consonant sound "v"; and a new letter, *w,* was used for the "w" sound. Also, the Roman *i* had represented both the vowel sound "i" and the consonant sound "j." The English added the letter *j* to distinguish between the two sounds. Thus, with only a few changes, the alphabet used by the Romans over 2,000 years ago has continued into modern times. (*See also* **Literacy.**)

> **Remember:** *Words in small capital letters have separate entries, and the index at the end of Volume 4 will guide you to more information on many topics.*

See map in Geography and Geology, Mediterranean (vol. 2).

The Alps are a large system of mountains in south-central Europe. About 500 miles long and 100 miles wide, the Alps begin near the Mediterranean coast of present-day France and Italy and curve in a great arc to the Balkan Peninsula. The name comes from *alpes,* the Latin word for the mountains.

Throughout much of the ancient period, the Alps were a formidable barrier between the Mediterranean cultures of Greece and Rome and the cultures that developed on the northern side of the mountain chain. The Romans referred to one section of the western Alps as the "Walls of Rome" because the mountains rise abruptly from the plains of Italy, forming a protective shield.

Although most of the Alpine region was a part of the Roman empire, few Romans lived there. For the Romans, the mountainous region's many passes and valleys served primarily as trade and invasion routes to western and northern Europe. HANNIBAL, the great Carthaginian general, also followed Alpine routes when he led his troops with horses and elephants across the mountains in a bold attack on Italy in 218 B.C. In the later years of the Roman Empire, barbarian forces from the north and east also used Alpine routes to invade Italy.

AMAZONS

THE GRAVES OF AMAZONS?

The Greek legends of Amazons may have been inspired by real women. Archaeologists in central Asia have recently discovered the graves of women buried with swords and daggers, indicating that they had been warriors. These women, however, were probably not as ferocious as the Amazons of myth. Scholars believe they carried weapons chiefly to protect their herds and their land.

* **hero** in mythology, a person of great strength or ability, often descended from a god

The Amazons, a mythical nation of women warriors, appear in many legends of the ancient Greeks. Called "man-haters" by the Greek playwright AESCHYLUS, Amazons were believed to live somewhere near the Black Sea on the edge of the known world.

Descended from Ares, the god of war, the Amazons were famed for their skill in battle. They fought with bows and arrows, axes, spears, and crescent-shaped shields. Although the Amazons lived in a society that was entirely female, they bore children after mating with men from other nations. However, they raised only their female offspring, sending away, killing, or making slaves of their male children.

The Amazons are featured in many of ancient Greece's enduring stories. In the Greek epic tradition that includes Homer's *Iliad,* the Amazons take the side of the Trojans in the Trojan War. The myth of HERACLES includes a description of his journey to the land of the Amazons. One of Heracles' labors was to take the girdle (belt) from Hippolyte, the queen of the Amazons. Another myth tells how the Greek hero* THESEUS kidnapped an Amazon queen, an act that led the Amazons to attack the city of Athens.

According to one story, the name *Amazon* came from a Greek word meaning "without breasts," because the Amazons were said to have cut off their right breast in order to draw their bows more easily. Another story suggested that the name meant "without grain" because the Amazons relied on hunting rather than agriculture for their food.

The legend of these female warriors continued into the modern world. Spanish explorers of the 1500s named the longest river in South America the Amazon. They were reported to have seen native women there who served as war captains, leading their men into battle. Even today, strong, powerful women are sometimes referred to as Amazons. (*See also* **Homer;** *Iliad;* **Myths, Greek.**)

AMBASSADORS

See *Envoys; Diplomacy.*

AMMIANUS MARCELLINUS

ca. A.D. 330–ca. 395
ROMAN HISTORIAN

Ammianus Marcellinus was the last great historian of the Roman Empire. His work, which continued the story of Rome at the point at which the historian TACITUS stopped, is the most important source of information about the period of the later Roman Empire. Ammianus wrote about a range of topics, including geography, culture, and the customs of foreign peoples.

Born to a noble Greek family in the city of ANTIOCH in the Roman province of SYRIA, Ammianus joined the army and served as an officer in both the eastern and western parts of the empire. While serving in GAUL, he met JULIAN THE APOSTATE, who would later be emperor of the Roman Empire. In A.D. 363, Ammianus accompanied Julian to Persia on a disastrous military campaign during which the emperor met his death. Ammianus left the army and spent time traveling through Greece, Syria, Egypt, and Palestine. Sometime after A.D. 378, he settled in Rome where he wrote his account of the Roman Empire.

Ammianus's history, *The Chronicle of Events,* consisted of 31 books covering the years from A.D. 96 to 378. Only the last 18 books, which cover the years from A.D. 353 to 378, survive. Written in Latin, the work provides a clear, impartial, and detailed account of the political, economic, and social history of the empire. Ammianus drew from his own experiences to create a vivid and dramatic picture of people, life, and events of the time. His biographies (including that of the emperor Julian, who played a central role in the history) are notable for their vivid descriptive passages and critical analysis. (*See also* **Rome, History of.**)

AMPHITHEATER, ROMAN

* **gladiator** in ancient Rome, slave or captive who participated in combats that were staged for public entertainment

* **tier** one of a series of rows arranged one above the other, as in a stadium

The Roman amphitheater was a roofless, oval-shaped arena used for spectator sports. Entertainment played an important role in Roman life, and the construction of amphitheaters in which to stage games and other events helped spread Roman culture throughout the Roman empire. The ruins of ancient Roman amphitheaters can still be seen today in towns in Europe and North Africa.

The earliest amphitheaters, which had been constructed of wood, were temporary structures. Designed specifically for fights between gladiators*, most were located near gladiatorial schools. The oldest permanent amphitheater to survive was built in the southern Italian city of POMPEII about 80 B.C. It featured an oval arena and was built up against the city wall on one side. Encircling the arena were rows of seats that rose in tiers* along the earthen banks. This seating arrangement enabled all spectators to have a good view of the entertainment. Stone walls supported the earthen banks beneath the seats. Most early amphitheaters were built on natural slopes or artificially constructed mounds of earth.

In time, Roman architects began building freestanding amphitheaters that did not rely on the natural landscape. These structures featured stone

The Romans constructed amphitheaters in cities and towns throughout the empire for their gladiatorial games. Many are still standing, as is this amphitheater in Arles, France. Its design is strikingly similar to that of modern sports stadiums.

* **vault** arched ceiling or roof

See color plate 12, vol. 2.

walls and vaults* to support the various levels of seating. In these structures, spectators gained access to their seats through interior corridors and staircases similar to those in modern stadiums. The design of the amphitheaters became more elaborate as well, with graceful arches covering the walkways, and statues and stone carvings adorning the walls.

Some of the later amphitheaters included rooms, cages for animals, storage areas, and passageways beneath the floor of the arena, along with pulley-drawn elevators that raised and lowered animals, people, and props through trapdoors into the arena. Some amphitheaters also had awnings over the seating areas to protect the spectators from the sun. The largest and most famous amphitheater of this type was the COLOSSEUM in the city of Rome.

Roman amphitheaters provided various types of sports and entertainment. Contests between gladiators, which included fights to the death, remained popular with spectators. Animal events often featured men hunting wild animals amid elaborate scenery or animals fighting one another. In another variation of the animal events, unarmed slaves and Christians were sent into the arena to face lions, bears, and other savage beasts. Such entertainment resulted in the deaths of thousands of people and animals.

In later years, the Roman emperors ended these bloody entertainments, and the Roman amphitheater declined in importance as people sought other, more acceptable, forms of amusement. However, the basic idea of the Roman amphitheater endured, and the modern stadium owes much of its purpose and design to these ancient structures. (*See also* **Architecture, Roman; Games, Roman.**)

ANACREON

See *Poetry, Greek and Hellenistic.*

ANAXAGORAS

See *Philosophy, Greek and Hellenistic.*

ANAXIMANDER

See *Philosophy, Greek and Hellenistic.*

ANAXIMENES

See *Philosophy, Greek and Hellenistic.*

ANIMALS

The Greeks and Romans shared their world with many different kinds of animals, and these animals served a variety of functions in private and public life. They provided food, served as beasts of burden and pets, and had featured roles in sporting events and other public spectacles. Animals also had important sacred, or religious, functions throughout the ancient world.

FOOD AND TRANSPORT. The major food-producing animals of ancient Greece and Rome were pigs, sheep, goats, cattle, and poultry. Pigs were an important source of food in both Greece and Rome. The meat of pigs formed a major part of the Roman diet, and bacon was a standard provision in the Roman army. In addition, the Romans used the dung and urine of pigs as fertilizer.

Farmers generally raised sheep and goats in areas where the landscape was too hilly for planting crops. The Greeks and the Romans raised sheep for wool and for meat. They used the milk from sheep and from goats to make cheese. Geese and chickens were also common farm animals.

Cattle were larger and more costly to keep than other livestock. Both the Greeks and the Romans used cattle as work animals to pull wagons or plows. The Romans ate beef and veal (the meat of calves).

Donkeys and mules, used by the armies to carry equipment and supplies, came from special farms called stud farms. The Roman army used so many mules as transport animals that large stud farms grew up throughout the empire.

PETS. Both the Greeks and the Romans kept animals as pets in their homes. Dogs were the most common pet—probably the small, white dog known today as the Maltese. Images of such dogs appear on Greek vases from the 400s B.C. Many Greek and Roman writings mention dogs, and inscriptions on ancient gravestones sometimes refer to an owner's affection for a dog.

The Greeks and Romans also kept tame birds. Especially popular were crows, magpies, and starlings, which can be taught to talk, and nightingales and blackbirds, which have beautiful songs. Both the Greeks and the Romans kept ferrets—small, weasel-like animals—to kill mice and rats. By the time of the Roman Empire, cats were beginning to replace ferrets as controllers of rodents.

The Romans raised fish in fish ponds, both for food and as pets. Some Roman estates had large outdoor enclosures called vivaria that housed birds and larger animals such as antelope, wild pigs, and deer.

ANCIENT EXTINCTIONS

Human threats to animal species began long ago. Ancient Greek and Roman writings and murals depicted lions, leopards, and hyenas roaming in Greece, hippopotamuses splashing near the mouth of the Nile, and marshes around the Mediterranean Sea teeming with birds. By the time of the late Roman Empire, however, hunting had greatly reduced the numbers of these animals and driven them into remote regions. The European wild ox, or auroch, was one animal driven to extinction. Hunters prized the animal for its strength and endurance in the chase. Romans used it for spectacles that featured scenes from classic mythology. (Zeus was sometimes depicted as an ox.) By A.D. 1000, only a few aurochs remained in central Europe. The animal became extinct in 1627.

ANIMALS

Romans kept cats as domestic pets starting in the first century B.C. Cats were useful animals to have around the household, since they captured mice, rats, and other vermin. However, as this mosaic from Pompeii shows, sometimes cats preyed on animals that were also useful to their owners.

* **trident** three-pronged spear, similar to a pitchfork

See color plate 4, vol. 1.

* **underworld** kingdom of the dead; also called Hades

The Romans liked exotic animals, too. Some Roman households had pet monkeys, and wealthy Romans kept showy animals such as flamingos from Africa.

GAMES AND SPORTS. In ancient Greece and Rome, HUNTING was a popular sport among the upper classes. These people hunted rabbits, deer, boars, and lions. Commoners hunted as well, but they did so to add meat to their diet and to destroy the wolves that raided their herds or the deer that ravaged their gardens.

Animals played a central role in one of the principal entertainments of the classical world—the public games. In Greece, the games were athletic competitions. In Rome the games were large, costly spectacles that often involved bloodshed. Greek competitions included horse and chariot races. The Romans held chariot races, but their games featured a variety of other animals as well.

In Rome and throughout Roman territory, people flocked to chariot races and often bet large sums on the outcome of a race. The horses used to draw the chariots were raised on stud farms and had special trainers. Fans knew the names of winning horses and followed their careers closely. The Romans treated racehorses well, but they were not as kind to other animals used in the games. Sometimes, they sent animals into arenas to face professional fighters called gladiators, who used nets, spears, swords, and tridents* against the animals. At other times, fierce animals fought unarmed people—generally slaves, criminals, or prisoners of war—in the arena. The crowd also watched animals fight each other. Starved wolves or lions might be turned loose in an arena with a herd of deer.

At first, the Romans displayed exotic animals such as ostriches, camels, and elephants as curiosities at circuses and in parades. Starting around 50 B.C., however, they began to use these imported creatures in hunts and combats. Tigers, leopards, lions, bears, bulls, and elephants fought animals or teams of trained hunters. Ostriches, deer, gazelles, and goats faced both animal and human enemies. Even rarer animals—hippopotamuses, rhinoceroses, and crocodiles from Egypt—appeared from time to time. The emperor NERO flooded an arena so that he could show polar bears catching seals.

Far-ranging networks of hunters and shippers provided animals for the Roman arenas, stripping entire regions of their wildlife. Enormous numbers of animals perished. Thousands died in the 100 days of games held to celebrate the opening of the Roman Colosseum. Although one crowd supposedly burst into tears and protested the slaughter of a herd of elephants, for the most part there seems to have been little opposition to the cruelty that was part of the games.

SACRED USES OF ANIMALS. From earliest times, certain birds and animals were thought to create links between the human world and the world of the gods and spirits. The Greeks and Romans honored their gods with blood sacrifices, or offerings of animals. They looked for perfect animals to use in the sacrifice. Worshipers offered light-colored animals to gods of the heavens and dark-colored animals to gods of the underworld*. The sacrifices followed strict rituals, which generally involved cutting the animal's throat and burning its meat on an altar. In some cases, the worshipers then devoured the meat. Many sacrifices occurred in fulfillment of vows, either by individuals or by a representative of the state. For example, a worshiper might vow to sacrifice 12 white roosters to ensure the occurrence of a desired event. Common sacrificial animals included bulls, cows, horses, roosters, sheep, and goats.

Another sacred use of animals was in divination or augury—the interpreting of omens* to predict future events. Trained observers practiced augury, reading great significance in such things as the flight of birds or the roll of thunder. There were complicated rules for augury. For example, a raven croaking on the right was a good omen, but a crow's caw was a good sign only if it came from the left. Another type of divination, called haruspicy, involved looking for omens in the entrails (inner organs) of sacrificed animals. (*See also* **Agriculture, Greek; Agriculture, Roman; Augur; Games, Greek; Games, Roman; Omens.**)

* **omen** sign, good or bad, of future events

ANTIGONE

MYTHICAL GREEK PRINCESS

See
color plate 8,
vol. 3.

ntigone, an important figure in Greek drama, was the daughter of OEDIPUS (the king of Thebes) and Jocasta (his mother and wife). Perhaps better than any character, she has come to symbolize personal courage and strength in behaving according to her conscience, even when that action was in opposition to the laws of the state. Two of the tragedies of Sophocles—*Oedipus at Colonus* and *Antigone*—are the chief sources of Antigone's inspiring story.

The first tragedy tells how Oedipus, blinded by a self-inflicted wound and banished from Thebes, is guided during his exile by his loving and devoted daughter, Antigone, until he chooses to die. His two sons, Eteocles and Polynices, quarrel over who will succeed to the throne, and the prediction is made that the brothers will murder each other.

In the second tragedy, Creon, the brother of Jocasta, becomes king. Creon orders that his dead nephew Eteocles, whom he favored, be buried with full honors, while Polynices, whom he declared a traitor, be denied burial. Antigone defies the edict and buries her brother Polynices, for which she is brought before Creon. He rules that she be locked in an underground vault and left to die—even though she is betrothed to Creon's son, Haemon. The king is unmoved by Haemon's appeal for Antigone's life, until the prophet Tiresias tells Creon that he has angered the gods. (The gods forbid both the exposure of the dead and the underground burial of the living.) Accordingly, the king relents, allowing the burial of Polynices, and calling for the rescue of Antigone. But his change of mind is too late; Antigone has hanged herself. In sorrow and anger, Haemon kills himself in the presence of Creon and Eurydice, the queen. Eurydice takes her own life, and Creon is left a ruined man, having lost both his family and the throne.

Antigone has inspired writers through the ages. It asks the timeless question of when should an individual be guided by the higher, unwritten laws of conscience, and when by the laws of state. The French playwrights Jean Cocteau (in 1922) and Jean Anouilh (in 1942) each wrote an adaptation of *Antigone,* both of which were translated into English. Anouilh wrote his play during the German occupation of France in World War II. In this version of the story, Antigone is portrayed as a woman speaking out against tyranny. (*See also* **Aeschylus; Drama, Greek; Euripides; Sophocles.**)

ANTIOCH

ntioch, now the city of Antakya in southern Turkey, was once the capital of ancient SYRIA. Seleucus I, a general in the army of ALEXANDER THE GREAT and founder of the Seleucid dynasty, established Antioch about 300 B.C. He named the city after his father, Antiochus.

Located at a crossroads of trade routes between Asia and the Mediterranean Sea, Antioch grew quickly into a prosperous commercial and trade center. In 64 B.C., the Romans annexed the region around Antioch, and the city became the capital of the new Roman province of Syria. Antioch continued to grow and prosper, becoming one of the most important Roman cities in Asia. The Romans built temples, baths, aqueducts, and other great public buildings in Antioch. One of the distinctive features of the city's architecture, a street lined by a marble colonnade*, was copied in cities throughout Asia Minor.

* **colonnade** series of regularly spaced columns, usually supporting a roof

About A.D. 47, Antioch also emerged as an early center of Christianity. The apostle Paul used the city as headquarters for his missionary activities, and the term *Christian* was first used in Antioch to describe the disciples of Jesus.

Antioch reached the height of its greatness and prosperity in the A.D. 300s. It became known for its beautiful architecture and its centers of learning. At the time, the city's population exceeded 200,000. However, in the A.D. 500s, several earthquakes and fires and an outbreak of plague* struck Antioch, devastating the city's population. Later the Persians invaded, and the city never fully recovered. In A.D. 637, Antioch was conquered by the Arabs. (*See also* **Aqueducts; Baths, Roman.**)

* **plague** highly contagious, widespread, and often fatal disease

ANTONIUS, MARCUS

ca. 82–30 B.C.
ROMAN MILITARY OFFICER
AND POLITICIAN

* **quaestor** Roman financial officer who assisted a higher official such as a consul or praetor

* **tribune** in ancient Rome, the official who protected the rights of plebeians from arbitrary actions by the patricians, or upper classes

arcus Antonius, better known as Mark Antony, was one of the most important military and political leaders in the last days of the Roman Republic. A friend and supporter of Julius Caesar, Antony was a courageous soldier and skilled administrator. But as he rose to the highest levels of power, his quick temper and fondness for pleasure brought him trouble.

Born into a prominent Roman family, Antony had a reputation as a wild youth. About 58 B.C., he began a military career, serving with distinction in Egypt and Palestine and then joining Julius Caesar in GAUL. On his return to Rome, Antony held the offices of quaestor* and tribune*. As tribune, he opposed the Senate decree that attempted to take away Caesar's armies and weaken his power. In the civil war that followed, Antony fought along with Caesar, commanding troops at the battle in Greece and defeating POMPEY, Caesar's former friend turned rival. Antony and Caesar then served together as consuls* of Rome.

* **consul** one of two chief governmental officials of Rome, chosen annually and serving for a year

The assassination of Julius Caesar in 44 B.C. abruptly changed the political situation in Rome. Antony seized Caesar's property and claimed to be his successor. He also aroused public sentiment against Caesar's assassins, BRUTUS and Cassius, who fled Rome. Soon, however, a rival for power emerged—Caesar's adopted son and heir, Octavian (Octavianus AUGUSTUS). At first, Octavian joined forces with Antony's opponents in the Senate, led by the great statesman CICERO. Their armies defeated Antony in northern Italy in 43 B.C. Antony withdrew to Gaul but returned shortly to Rome with a new army.

Octavian made peace with Antony. They joined with Aemilius Lepidus to form the Second Triumvirate, a government in which the three leaders shared power. Antony ruled the eastern provinces and Gaul, Octavian took control of Italy and Spain, and Lepidus governed Africa. Antony had his enemies in Rome, including Cicero, killed, and in 42 B.C. he defeated Brutus and Cassius at the Battle of Philippi in Macedonia. Both Brutus and Cassius committed suicide.

While in his eastern provinces, Antony met CLEOPATRA, the queen of Egypt. He became involved in a passionate relationship with this foreign ruler, which resulted in his losing support in Rome. At the same time, his alliance with Octavian began to crumble. In an effort to halt the further deterioration of the friendship, Antony returned to Rome and married Octavian's sister in 40 B.C. Three years later, though, he left his Roman wife and returned to Cleopatra. Antony proclaimed himself and Cleopatra co-rulers of Egypt and other Roman provinces in the east.

The Romans grew increasingly critical of Antony and his foreign lover. Octavian used Antony's loss of popularity to increase his own power. He claimed that Antony planned to subject Rome to foreign rule and published Antony's will to prove this charge. In his will, Antony left large territories to his illegitimate children by Cleopatra and named Caesarion, Cleopatra's son by Julius Caesar, as Caesar's heir. Judging the terms of the will as disloyal to Rome, the Roman Senate stripped Antony of his power and position.

Octavian then declared war on Cleopatra. The war reached a climax in September 31 B.C., when Octavian's navy defeated the forces of Antony and Cleopatra at the Battle of Actium off the coast of Greece. The couple fled to the city of Alexandria in Egypt. A year later, Antony and Cleopatra committed suicide. Octavian, taking the name Augustus, became the first emperor of Rome. (*See also* **Caesar, Gaius Julius; Consuls; Quaestor; Rome, History of: Roman Republic, Late; Senate, Roman; Tribunes.**)

APHRODITE

* **mortal** human being; one who eventually will die

Aphrodite was the goddess of love, beauty, and fertility in Greek mythology. To her followers, Aphrodite represented the power of physical love and desire. She was a popular goddess, worshiped throughout the Greek world. She also inspired many works of art and literature. The myrtle was Aphrodite's special tree, and the dove was her sacred bird. In Rome, she was known as Venus.

Two myths tell about the birth of Aphrodite. In one, she emerged fully grown from the foam of the sea (*aphros* in Greek) and washed ashore. In another story, told by the poet HOMER, she was the daughter

This famous statue of Aphrodite, known as the Venus de Milo, was carved around 150 B.C. near the Maeander River in Asia Minor. It was discovered in 1820 on the island of Melos in the Aegean Sea and is now in the Louvre Museum in Paris.

of ZEUS, the supreme ruler of the gods, and the goddess Dione. Aphrodite married Hephaestus (called Vulcan by the Romans), the blacksmith to the gods.

Aphrodite had several lovers, including Ares, the god of war, and the handsome youth ADONIS. Despite Aphrodite's efforts to protect Adonis from harm, he was killed by a wild boar (probably Aphrodite's jealous husband) while hunting. Aphrodite's love for the mortal* Anchises of TROY resulted in the birth of a son, called Aeneas, who became a great Trojan warrior and the subject of Vergil's epic poem, the AENEID.

Aphrodite's connection with the city of Troy appears again in a story known as the Judgment of Paris. According to the story, a golden apple marked "for the fairest," or most beautiful, was left at a wedding banquet by an uninvited guest, the goddess of Discord. The goddesses HERA, ATHENA, and Aphrodite each claimed the apple. To settle the dispute, Zeus sent the goddesses to Paris, the handsome Trojan prince.

Each goddess offered Paris a special gift to win his favor. Hera said she would make him a great ruler; Athena offered to help the Trojans in battle; and Aphrodite promised to give him the most beautiful woman in the world. Paris chose Aphrodite and presented the golden apple to her. Keeping her promise, Aphrodite helped Paris take the beautiful Helen away from her husband, King Menelaus of Sparta. This led to the Trojan War, which the Greeks fought to bring Helen back.

During the Trojan War, Aphrodite supported Troy, and sometimes came to the city's aid. In the ILIAD, Homer describes a battle in which Menelaus seized Paris by the helmet and started to drag him away. Aphrodite rescued Paris by loosening the bindings of his helmet so that it fell off. Then she enclosed him in a mist and transported him home to safety.

According to some legends, Aphrodite's birth in the sea occurred near the islands of Cythera and Cyprus. These islands were sacred to Aphrodite, and each had important temples dedicated to the goddess. One of the *Homeric Hymns* describes Aphrodite as having arisen from the "delicate foam" and carried on the "breath of the wet wind" to Cyprus.

Aphrodite's beauty inspired great works of art, among them a statue at Cnidus made by PRAXITELES in about 350 B.C., and another famous statue, known as the Venus de Milo, which dates from the 150s B.C. In addition, several Greek poets described Aphrodite's extraordinary beauty and her influence in matters of love. (*See also* **Divinities; Mars.**)

APOLLO

* oracle a priest or priestess through whom a god is believed to speak; also the location (such as a shrine) where such utterances are made

The god Apollo commanded the highest respect in Greek culture. The Greeks considered him a symbol of light and often called him Phoebus, which means shining. They also saw him as a source of reason and truth. Greek city-states consulted Apollo's oracles* on questions of policy, and individuals sought advice from the god on personal matters. Apollo's replies, delivered through the oracles, carried great authority.

The son of ZEUS and the goddess Leto, Apollo was usually described as a figure of youth and beauty. He and his twin sister, ARTEMIS, were born on the island of DELOS, a place revered by the Greeks. The Romans also worshiped Apollo, the son of Jupiter and Latona and brother of Diana.

The town of DELPHI was particularly important to Apollo. According to legend, a dragon named Python once guarded Delphi. Apollo killed the dragon and established an oracle on the spot. Although Apollo had oracles in various other places, his temple at Delphi became the most important religious center in ancient Greece.

Apollo was protective of his priests and priestesses. The plot of Homer's epic poem the ILIAD is set in motion when a Greek warrior, AGAMEMNON, seizes the daughter of Chryses, one of Apollo's priests. When Chryses prays to Apollo for help, the god comes storming down from Olympus. With his arrows, Apollo sends a plague into the Greek camp to punish Agamemnon. Apollo stops the plague only when the girl is returned home safely.

Various myths tell of Apollo's loves and adventures. He loved a nymph* named DAPHNE who fled from his attentions and, to avoid him, changed herself into a laurel tree. In sorrow, Apollo wore a crown made from the laurel. When Apollo loved the maiden Cassandra, he gave her the gift of prophecy—the ability to tell the future. Cassandra would not accept Apollo's love, but he could not force her to return his gift. In his anger, Apollo declared that no one would ever believe her prophecies. So Cassandra kept her special gift, but it was useless.

Coronis was another young woman who became the object of Apollo's attentions. When Coronis lost interest in Apollo and fell in love with someone else, Apollo punished her with death. But Coronis was expecting Apollo's child, so he rescued the child from her body. The child, named ASCLEPIUS, became a legendary physician.

Apollo was fond of a youth named Hyacinthus. Once when the two were playing a game of discus*, Apollo accidentally hit Hyacinthus in the forehead, wounding him badly. Full of grief, Apollo tried without success to save his friend. Blood streamed from the boy's head and, where it landed, a purple flower—the hyacinth—bloomed. Its reappearance every spring served as a reminder of the dead Hyacinthus.

In addition to prophecy, Apollo had a number of other functions. Both he and his son Asclepius were associated with medicine and healing. Apollo also loved music and poetry, and he was often portrayed holding a lyre*. In other places, Apollo appeared carrying a bow, showing his connection to archery. Although Apollo, like other gods, could show anger when offended, he generally represented a sense of order in Greek society. (*See also* **Oracles; Religion, Greek.**)

Apollo was one of the most popular of the great Greek gods. People throughout the Greek world consulted Apollo's oracles, particularly at his shrine at Delphi. This sculpture, known as the Apollo Belvedere, is a Roman copy of a Greek statue from the 300s B.C. It is currently in the Vatican Museum.

* **nymph** in classical mythology, one of the lesser goddesses of nature

* **discus** a heavy, circular plate hurled for distance as a sport

* **lyre** stringed instrument similar to a small harp

APPIAN WAY

The Appian Way (Via Appia in Latin) was the oldest and longest of the ancient Roman roads. With superior engineering skill, the Romans constructed all-weather roads that were better than any built until the nineteenth century.

The Appian Way began in the city of Rome and was the main route southward out of the city. It ran southeast for 132 miles and then at Capua headed eastward across Italy for 234 miles, ending at the port of Brundisium (modern Brindisi) on the Adriatic Sea.

Like all the main Roman roads, the Appian Way was paved with durable rock such as basalt, granite, or porphyry. To build the road, surveyors first planned the route. Next, workers carefully dug a deep bed into which they placed naturally rounded stones surrounded by clay or earth. Finally, they laid huge paving stones on top and fitted them together closely to form a smooth surface. Most of the Appian Way was about ten feet wide, which allowed two carriages traveling in opposite directions to pass each other. At certain places, the road measured as much as twenty feet in width, and near the gates of Rome it widened to thirty feet.

Construction of the Appian Way began in 312 B.C. under the rule of Appius Claudius Caecus, the censor* for whom it is named. The road was completed by 244 B.C. Portions of the Appian Way—with roadside tombs, distance markers, and bridges—can still be seen today. (*See also* **Roads, Roman.**)

* **censor** Roman official who conducted the census, assigned state contracts for public projects (such as building roads), and supervised public morality

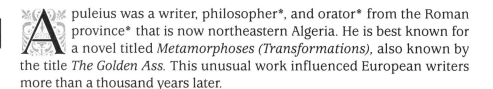

APULEIUS

BORN ca. A.D. 120
ROMAN WRITER

* **philosopher** scholar or thinker concerned with the study of ideas, including science

* **orator** public speaker of great skill

* **province** overseas area controlled by Rome

Apuleius was a writer, philosopher*, and orator* from the Roman province* that is now northeastern Algeria. He is best known for a novel titled *Metamorphoses (Transformations),* also known by the title *The Golden Ass.* This unusual work influenced European writers more than a thousand years later.

LIFE. Apuleius was born near the North African city of CARTHAGE in a town called Madauros. Like his father, Apuleius became a town senator. He traveled widely as a young man and spent time as a student in both ATHENS and ROME. Unlike many other Latin writers, he was proud of his provincial origin and preferred to be called a Madauran rather than a Roman.

Apuleius spent most of his life in North Africa. He met his wife in the A.D. 150s at the place that is now Tripoli in LIBYA. He achieved fame as a poet and philosopher in Carthage, where he became chief priest of the province. Carthage and Madauros erected statues in his honor. Where and when he died is not known.

STYLE AND PHILOSOPHY. At the time that Apuleius was writing, both Greek and Roman culture were dominant in the Mediterranean region. For this reason, Apuleius skillfully wove Greek and Latin themes and language into his works. His style was extravagant and bawdy*, incorporating poetic images and a mixture of old-fashioned expressions and popular slang. His work was also full of clever puns, alliteration*, scholarly references, and scenes of great beauty. Yet Apuleius often wrote for audiences who were not well educated. His surviving works include introductions to Greek philosophy and culture for provincial Latin readers.

One of Apuleius's works—a speech called the *Apology* (Greek for "speech in defense of")—was his reply to charges made against him by his wife's family. Her family had claimed that Apuleius bewitched her into marrying him. In this speech, he used some ideas from the Greek philosopher PLATO, whom he greatly admired. Apuleius defended himself

* **bawdy** humorously indecent

* **alliteration** repetition of consonant sounds at the beginning of words or within words

by using Plato's distinction between passion and noble love, which witchcraft could not affect. The speech exemplifies Apuleius's vivid style and his interest in philosophy.

A METAMORPHOSIS. Of all his surviving work, however, *The Golden Ass* is the most interesting to modern audiences. At first it appears to be a simple story about a young man named Lucius, who sets out to visit a friend. What gives the work its richness are the many stories embedded within it. As the story unfolds, Lucius reaches his friend's house in northern Greece. Pamphile, the friend's wife, is skilled in magic, and Lucius sees her use a magic ointment to transform herself into an owl, the symbol of wisdom. Lucius then asks Pamphile's maid to help him obtain some of the magical ointment so that he, too, can become an owl. Lucius learns that the magic can be reversed by eating roses. Unfortunately, the maid brings the wrong ointment and instead of an owl, he becomes an ass—the symbol of stupidity and lust. At that moment, three real thieves break into the house and capture him to carry their loot for them.

Now an ass, Lucius remains captive in the thieves' cave, together with a bride whom the thieves have also kidnapped. The thieves' housekeeper looks after them until, eventually, the bride's husband arrives. He pretends to be another thief, tricks the thieves, gets them drunk, and kills them. At this point, Lucius escapes, but finds himself unable to shed his animal form. After still more adventures, he finally meets the Egyptian goddess Isis, who helps him find rose petals to eat so that he can become human again. Shaken by all of his adventures, Lucius's story ends with his conversion to the worship of Isis.

The tales within the main story concern a wide range of subjects—the exploits of the thieves, love, witches, and even the philosopher SOCRATES. They are narrated by a host of colorful, mischievous characters who tell their tales with bawdy humor and satire*. The storytellers include: Lucius's companions on his journey to northern Greece, his friend, his friend's wife Pamphile, the thieves and their housekeeper, and others who own him while he is an ass.

The centerpiece of the work is the long tale of CUPID AND PSYCHE, told by the thieves' housekeeper. In this tale, the goddess Venus sends her son, Cupid, to punish Psyche for being her rival in beauty. Instead of punishing Psyche, Cupid falls in love with her. The housekeeper tells this story supposedly to comfort the kidnapped bride and reassure her that a happy ending is on its way. However, in one of the book's many unexpected twists, the bride and her husband in fact meet a terrible fate. After their reunion, they encounter a man who becomes a rival for the bride's love. He kills the husband, and the bride kills herself.

At first glance, *The Golden Ass* seems to be a romantic tale with entertaining stories and a surprising ending. For readers who dig deeper, however, it becomes a work about Plato's mystical view that much of the world is an illusion, full of constant change and misunderstanding. Apuleius's style would later influence the medieval writers Giovanni Boccaccio and Geoffrey Chaucer, both of whom also wrote major works comprised of collections of narrated short stories. (*See also* **Literature, Greek; Literature, Roman.**)

* **satire** literary technique that uses wit and sarcasm to expose or ridicule vice and folly

AQUEDUCTS

Aqueducts are channels, built above or under the ground, that carry water from a source to areas where the water is needed. The word aqueduct comes from two Latin words: *aqua,* meaning water, and *ducere,* meaning to lead. In the 500s B.C., the Greeks constructed simple aqueducts in Athens and on the island of Samos. It was the Romans, however, who became the greatest aqueduct builders in the ancient world. Their knowledge of engineering enabled them to improve their construction techniques and to erect elaborate aqueduct systems throughout their vast empire.

The first Roman aqueduct, the Aqua Appia, was built in 312 B.C.—the same year construction began on the first Roman road, the Via Appia, or APPIAN WAY. (Both projects were named for the Roman official in charge of public works, Appius Claudius Caecus.) The Aqua Appia carried water to Rome from natural springs about ten miles outside the city. When this aqueduct could no longer provide enough water for the city, the Romans added a second one in 272 B.C. Known as the Aqua Anio Vetus, the new aqueduct brought water from the Apennines, a mountain range east of Rome. Over the next five centuries, nine additional aqueducts were constructed around Rome. Some parts of them are still in use. The Romans also built aqueducts throughout the empire in Greece, Italy, Spain, France, North Africa, and Asia Minor.

The major portion of most Roman aqueducts consisted of underground conduits, or tunnels. In the early systems, these conduits were made entirely of stone lined with mortar*. After the Romans learned how to make concrete from volcanic ash, they used concrete to build aqueducts. The Aqua Tepula, built in 125 B.C., was the first aqueduct constructed of poured concrete. The Romans also made pipes of clay, lead, and bronze to carry water through the concrete conduits.

The Roman system of aqueducts relied on gravity, allowing water to flow from higher elevations to lower ones. Roman engineers took advantage of natural slopes in the terrain. If aqueducts had to cross ravines, or narrow valleys between hills, the Romans erected great stone bridges to carry the water across. These bridges, with their distinctive

* **mortar** mixture of lime, cement, sand, and water that is placed between stones to hold them together

Built during the reign of the emperor Augustus, this aqueduct, the Pont du Gard, supplied water to the ancient city of Nemausus (present-day Nîmes, France). The finely engineered aqueduct had such a slight incline that water fell less than 60 feet as it flowed the 30 miles from its source to the town.

ARCHES, were the most striking features of ancient Roman aqueducts. Two of these beautiful bridge aqueducts survive today in Segovia, Spain, and in Nîmes, France.

When the water from an aqueduct reached a city, it went first to a system of brick-and-concrete tanks called *castella,* or castles. From there, the water was channeled to public baths and fountains and to private customers. Some of the water was used to flush out the city sewers. A city official called an AEDILE had responsibility for overseeing the water system, including the aqueducts. In times of drought, water supplies to private homes were cut off. Public fountains, on the other hand, were always supplied with water.

Aqueducts were expensive to build and maintain. For this reason, Romans generally built them to supply water to large cities. Smaller cities and towns throughout the Roman empire had to rely on local wells and springs or on simple underground pipelines for their water supply. As the Roman Empire began to decline in the late A.D. 300s and 400s, its system of aqueducts began to deteriorate as well. In the centuries that followed, Roman aqueducts were neglected and most fell into ruin. (*See also* **Construction Materials and Techniques; Waterworks.**)

ARABIA

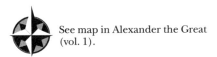

See map in Alexander the Great (vol. 1).

* **dynasty** succession of rulers from the same family or group

* **province** overseas area controlled by Rome

* **frankincense and myrrh** fragrant tree resins used to make incense and perfumes

The name *Arabia,* which means "island of the Arabs," refers to a large peninsula in southwestern Asia bounded by the Persian Gulf, the Red Sea, and the Indian Ocean, and to the region northwest of the peninsula, including parts of modern-day Syria and Jordan. In ancient times both Greece and Rome tried to control Arabia, attracted by its strategic location at a crossroads of land and sea routes linking Asia, Africa, and the Middle East.

Greek knowledge of the region was scant until the time of ALEXANDER THE GREAT, who died in 323 B.C. before he could launch his plan for conquering Arabia. By this time, an Arab people known as the Nabataeans had migrated from present-day Jordan into northwestern Arabia. The Nabataean kingdom prospered, and its capital of Petra became an important trading center. In the 200s B.C. the Ptolemaic dynasty*, Greek rulers in Egypt, established settlements in parts of western Arabia. They called the fertile southwestern coast Arabia Felix (happy or lucky Arabia), the northwestern part of the peninsula Arabia Petraea (stony Arabia), and the interior region Arabia Deserta (desert Arabia).

The Romans first attempted to gain a foothold in Arabia in 25 B.C., when the emperor AUGUSTUS sent an unsuccessful expedition there. However, in A.D. 106 the emperor TRAJAN took control of the Nabataean kingdom, and it became Rome's Arabia province*. The province became wealthy because important caravan trade routes ran through it. Merchants paid high tolls and taxes to transport precious goods such as frankincense and myrrh* from southern Arabia and silk, pottery, and other products from India and Asia. In the late A.D. 200s, the emperor DIOCLETIAN made the southern part of Roman Arabia into a new province called Palestine. Both Arabia and Palestine remained prosperous until they were conquered by the Arabs in the 600s.

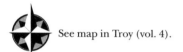

ARCHAEOLOGY OF ANCIENT SITES

Archaeology is the study of the physical remains of the past—such things as ancient graves, ruins of buildings, works of art, and objects used in everyday life. These ruins and artifacts* provide vital clues to the past, offering archaeologists the opportunity to learn about the cultures and societies of ancient peoples.

DIGGING FOR TREASURES OF ANCIENT ROME. The field of archaeology emerged in Europe during the A.D. 1500s, a period of cultural rebirth known as the Renaissance. At that time, many Europeans became very interested in the past, particularly in the ancient civilizations of Rome and Greece. Attention focused first on the ruins of Roman civilization that were uncovered in Italy. People began to excavate* among the ruins of the Roman Forum and other sites in and around the city of Rome. The primary goal of this effort was to find works of art from the ancient world that could be collected by individuals and museums. As it happened, the discoveries provided creative inspiration as well as the artworks themselves. Renaissance artists used ancient objects as models for new works of art, and Renaissance architects were influenced by the design of ancient Roman buildings.

In the A.D. 1700s, archaeologists explored the sites of POMPEII and Herculaneum, Roman cities in Italy that had been buried in ash during the volcanic eruption of Mt. Vesuvius in A.D. 79. Again, the primary purpose of the excavations was to obtain valuable works of art, but the cities unearthed in the digging brought other gifts from the past. The archaeologists found remarkably well-preserved remains of homes, shops, public buildings, streets, and gardens as well as sculptures, wall paintings, and even remains of grains and wine. These discoveries revealed a great deal about the lives of the cities' ancient inhabitants and changed the way people thought about the past.

In the years that followed, archaeology increasingly focused on the importance of ruins and artifacts as a window to the past, providing crucial information about ancient history. At the same time, archaeology became more of a science with certain principles and procedures. Archaeologists learned to dig slowly and carefully and to make extremely detailed records of their findings, including the precise location of every fragment of pottery or other artifact unearthed. This scientific approach enabled archaeologists to piece together a clearer and more accurate picture of the past.

ON THE TRAIL OF ANCIENT GREEK LEGENDS. In the late 1800s and early 1900s, archaeological excavations uncovered important ruins of early civilizations in Greece and on the island of CRETE. The inspiration for these explorations came from stories and legends in ancient Greek writings such as the *Iliad,* the epic poem written by HOMER.

In the 1860s, an amateur German archaeologist named Heinrich Schliemann began a search for the ancient city of TROY. Although many people thought that Troy existed only in legend, Schliemann had read Homer's descriptions of Troy and believed it had been a real place. Determined to find the long-lost city, Schliemann used the *Iliad* as his guide and in 1870 began excavating a large mound on the northwestern coast of ASIA

* **artifact** ornament, tool, weapon, or other object made by humans

* **excavate** to uncover by digging

See map in Troy (vol. 4).

MINOR (present-day Hissarlik in Turkey). There the archaeologist uncovered not one but a series of cities, buried one on top of the other. He also found gold jewelry and other treasures that convinced him that he had found Troy. Over the next century, other excavations confirmed Schliemann's belief.

Schliemann next set out in search of ancient MYCENAE. Again using Homer's epics as a guide, he explored a site in Greece and uncovered massive fortifications and royal tombs. This discovery provided the first look at Mycenaean culture, the ancestor of Greek civilization.

In 1900, British archaeologist Sir Arthur Evans began excavating a site on the island of Crete in search of the house of the legendary King MINOS of Knossos. Evans's explorations revealed an ancient palace and other ruins, the first evidence of the ancient Minoan civilization that flourished from about 3000 to 1400 B.C. The work of Schliemann and Evans uncovered vital information about the earliest Aegean civilizations and provided a framework for historians and archaeologists studying the history of ancient Greece.

MODERN ARCHAEOLOGY. In the last hundred years, archaeologists have unearthed a wealth of information about ancient Greece and Rome. Through their work, experts now know a great deal about how the people of these civilizations lived, worked, traded, and worshiped. Unlike the archaeologists of earlier centuries who focused on individual works of art or buildings, many archaeologists today explore broad topics such as the economic and social interactions of different ancient cultures. They also work with biologists, historians, sociologists, and other specialists to study all aspects of the civilizations. In addition, modern technology helps researchers find new information by analyzing traces of ancient food, accurately dating ancient artifacts, studying skeletal remains to determine the cause of death, and investigating underwater shipwrecks or submerged ruins. Through their work, archaeologists continue to uncover secrets about the ancient world as they reexamine old sites and discover new sites that have remained hidden beneath the surface of the earth. (*See also* **Architecture, Greek; Architecture, Roman; Art, Greek; Art, Roman.**)

DIGGING UP THE PAST

Archaeologists have found that many famous sites of the ancient world were not destroyed, but merely buried. Much of modern Athens, for instance, is built on top of the ancient city. In early 1997, workers digging the foundation for a new art museum in Athens uncovered what is believed to be the school Aristotle founded, the Lyceum. Scholars recognized the Lyceum from descriptions of it made by ancient authors. Other important findings may be waiting underground, but the needs of the modern city do not allow for a thorough examination of what might be there.

ARCHES

* **vertical support** upright beam or column that serves as a base in construction

The arch, one of the basic architectural forms, is a curved structure that spans an opening. Arches can be functional—for example, they can support a wall—or they can be decorative. The Romans used arches extensively in the construction of AQUEDUCTS, AMPHITHEATERS, BRIDGES, and domed temples.

For centuries, the peoples of the ancient Middle East and Mediterranean used vertical supports* topped by horizontal beams in the construction of doorways and gates. The Greeks also developed a corbeled (or stepped) arch. The Lion Gate at Mycenae in Greece is an example of this early form of arch. Corbeled arches were built with rows of blocks on either side of the opening, each jutting out a little farther over the row below until the two sides met in the middle at the top of the arch.

A true arch consists of vertical supports with blocks arranged in a semicircle across the opening. The Egyptians used the arch as early as

ARCHES

Several Roman emperors constructed triumphal arches to celebrate their military victories. The Arch of Titus, which stands in the Roman Forum, celebrates the defeat of the Jewish revolt in A.D. 70.

See color plate 2, vol. 2.

2700 B.C., mainly in tombs and other small structures. The Mesopotamians used arches for their city gates. Although the Greeks understood the principle of the arch, they did not combine it with other architectural elements until the 300s B.C.

The early Romans learned about arches from the ETRUSCANS, their neighbors in central Italy. The Etruscans taught the Romans how to build bridges, drainage systems, and aqueducts, all using arches. The Romans further developed the arch, using wedge-shaped blocks (called *voussoirs*) to form a curve across the top of the arch. The curved section rested firmly on two vertical supports. The last stone to be inserted was the keystone, the topmost center stone. The pressure of the other stones against the keystone helped to support the arch. This arch, which was stronger than earlier types of openings, led to the development of the vault*.

Working in mortar*, concrete, and stone, the Romans built thousands of structures that featured arches and vaults. Their creative use of these elements revolutionized architecture. Several famous examples of Roman arch and vault technique can be seen today. They are the Pont du Gard in southern France (a huge aqueduct dating from the early first century A.D.), the exterior of the COLOSSEUM, and the Arch of Constantine commemorating the emperor's victory over Maxentius in A.D. 312. Sculpted scenes of the emperor's campaign decorate the sides and top of this triumphal* arch. (*See also* Aqueducts; Architecture, Roman; Constantine.)

* **vault** arched ceiling or roof

* **mortar** mixture of lime, cement, sand, and water that is placed between stones to hold them together

* **triumphal** refers to the ancient Roman ceremony during which a victorious general enters the city

ARCHIMEDES

ca. 287–212 B.C.
GREEK MATHEMATICIAN

* **Hellenistic** referring to the Greek-influenced culture of the Mediterranean world during the three centuries after Alexander the Great, who died in 323 B.C.

Archimedes is considered to be the greatest mathematician of the ancient world. He played a major role in the development of mathematics after EUCLID, making significant contributions to geometry and physics. Archimedes is also remembered for several ingenious inventions.

LIFE OF ARCHIMEDES. Archimedes was born about 287 B.C. in the Greek colony of SYRACUSE on the island of SICILY. The son of an astronomer, Archimedes studied in ALEXANDRIA in Egypt, an important center of Hellenistic* culture. According to historians, Archimedes designed one of his most famous inventions while in Alexandria—a mechanical device for raising water from the Nile River into canals for the irrigation of nearby farm fields. Known as Archimedes' screw, the device consisted of a screw-shaped spiral enclosed in a cylinder. When the bottom of the device was placed in water and the cylinder rotated, water traveled up the spiral and flowed out the top. Modern versions of Archimedes' screw are still in use in some parts of Egypt.

After completing his studies in Alexandria, Archimedes returned to Syracuse, where he continued his work in mathematics and science. In about 214 B.C., the Romans attacked Syracuse and began a siege that lasted more than two years. During that time, Archimedes helped defend the city by inventing several war machines and weapons. One of

Archimedes was one of the greatest mathematicians in history. He died during the Roman conquest of his home city of Syracuse in 212 B.C. According to a famous story, Archimedes was immersed in a mathematical problem during a battle and was killed by a Roman soldier. This copy of a Roman mosaic from the A.D. 100s depicts this story.

these was a catapult, a device for hurling stones, arrows, and other objects. Another was supposedly a system of mirrors that could concentrate the rays of the sun and set Roman ships on fire. Even so, the Romans defeated Syracuse in 212 B.C.

According to legend, Archimedes was working on a mathematical problem and drawing figures in the sand when the Romans entered the city. Absorbed in his work, Archimedes ignored the questions of a Roman soldier, who became angry and killed him. The Romans knew of his reputation and allowed him to be buried with honors. Archimedes had designed his own tomb—a sphere inside a cylinder, to commemorate the mathematical discovery that the sphere occupies two-thirds of the space of the cylinder.

ARCHIMEDES' ACHIEVEMENTS. Archimedes was famous in his own time primarily for his clever inventions. In addition to the Archimedes' screw and various weapons, he also invented a compound pulley*. According to a story recounted by PLUTARCH, King Hieron of Syracuse overheard Archimedes' boast: "Give me a point of support and I shall move the world." When Hieron asked for a demonstration, Archimedes attached a pulley to a ship loaded with men and cargo. Then, by gently pulling on the ropes attached to the pulley, he moved the ship toward him as easily as if it were running along the surface of the water.

Although best known for his inventions, Archimedes' contributions to mathematics and physics are perhaps more significant. In geometry, Archimedes calculated an approximate number for pi (π), the value that represents the ratio of the circumference of a circle to its diameter. Archimedes also explored the properties of complex curved figures and determined how to calculate their areas and volumes.

Archimedes wrote many works on mathematics and science, discussing his various principles and providing proof of their accuracy. Only nine of these works have survived. One of those, *On Floating Bodies,* is the first known work in the field of hydrostatics, a branch of physics dealing with the properties and characteristics of fluids. *On Floating Bodies* discusses the physical law of nature that has come to be known as Archimedes' principle. According to Archimedes' principle, an object immersed in a fluid is buoyed, or kept afloat, by a force equal to the weight of the fluid displaced by the object. This important scientific principle explains how and why objects float.

A story is told of how Archimedes came to discover this principle. King Hieron had ordered a new crown of solid gold, but he suspected that the craftsman had cheated him by mixing silver with the gold. Hieron asked Archimedes to determine if the crown contained solid gold. At first, Archimedes could not think of a way to do this. The answer came to him suddenly one day as he was bathing. He noticed the water level of his bath changed as he sat down in the water. Archimedes realized that the amount of water displaced by an object depends on its weight and volume. By measuring the amounts of water displaced by equal quantities of silver and gold, he would be able to determine whether or not the crown was made of solid gold. As the story continues, Archimedes was so excited by his discovery that he jumped out of

* **compound pulley** mechanical device with a series of wheels and rope that is used to transmit force from one object to another

Remember: Consult the index at the end of volume 4 to find more information on many topics.

his bath and ran naked through the streets shouting "Eureka," which means "I have found it" in Greek.

Like many scientific discoveries from the ancient world, the importance of Archimedes' principle and his other discoveries was not evident until many years later. After the rediscovery of his works during the Renaissance*, Archimedes' ideas profoundly influenced the development of both mathematics and physics. (*See also* **Mathematics, Greek; Science; Technology**.)

* **Renaissance** period of the rebirth of interest in classical art, literature, and learning that occurred in Europe from the late 1300s through the 1500s

ARCHITECTURE, GREEK

* **classical** in Greek history, refers to the period of great political and cultural achievement from about 500 B.C. to 323 B.C.

The ancient Greeks developed a monumental and highly distinctive architectural style. This style reached its peak in the 400s B.C., and came to be known as classical* architecture. Architects of this period combined design ideas used on the Greek mainland with elements from the Aegean islands and ASIA MINOR. They created graceful and impressive building designs still visible in the remains of their temples and monuments. Their work, and that of Greek builders, influenced the architecture of other cultures, especially Rome.

The remains of this round temple at the Greek city of Delphi provide an excellent example of the Doric order of Greek architecture. The three thick, plain, deeply grooved columns are typical of Doric structures.

See color plate 1, vol. 2.

* **mortar** mixture of lime, cement, sand, and water that is placed between stones to hold them together

* **entablature** in classical architecture, the horizontal part that rests on the columns

* **capital** top part of a column or pillar

Columns were a dominant feature of early Greek architecture. The Doric, Ionic, and Corinthian orders shared some basic features of layout but could be distinguished from one another by certain details in design.

ARCHITECTURAL ORDERS

Greek architecture developed specific styles known as orders. The word "order" refers to the standard parts of a structure and their arrangement in buildings. The three orders developed in Greece were called Doric, Ionic, and Corinthian. All three orders used rows of columns along the building's exterior that rested on a platform and supported the roof. The design, arrangement, and decoration of the columns and other details distinguished one order from another.

DORIC ORDER. The basic order and the first to develop was the Doric order, which appeared in the early 500s B.C. At first, the Greeks constructed their buildings of wood. However, as the Doric order evolved they began to use stone, which they fitted together without mortar*.

The Doric order had three main divisions: a stepped platform, columns, and an entablature*. The shaft of the Doric column had grooves known as flutes. At the top of the shaft was the capital*, which supported the entablature. The entablature was the most complex part

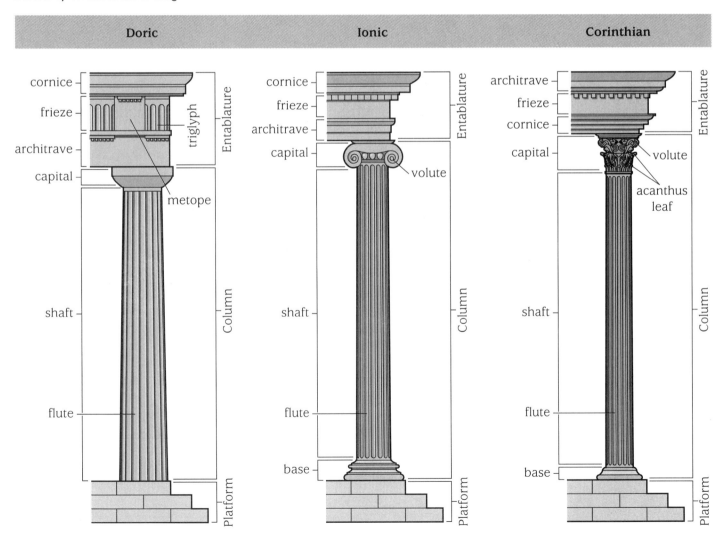

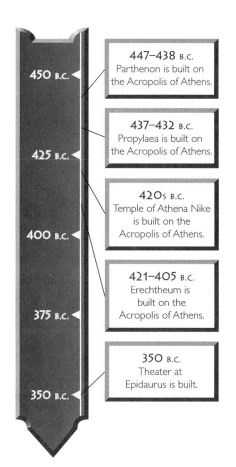

450 B.C.

447–438 B.C.
Parthenon is built on
the Acropolis of Athens.

425 B.C.

437–432 B.C.
Propylaea is built on
the Acropolis of Athens.

420s B.C.
Temple of Athena Nike
is built on the
Acropolis of Athens.

400 B.C.

421–405 B.C.
Erechtheum is
built on the
Acropolis of Athens.

375 B.C.

350 B.C.
Theater at
Epidaurus is built.

350 B.C.

of the Doric order. It included the architrave (a row of stone blocks resting on the columns), the frieze (a horizontal band, often ornamented with sculpture or carvings), and the cornice (an ornamental, horizontal molding at the top of a wall or building). Two surviving examples of the Doric order are the PARTHENON on the ACROPOLIS of Athens and the Temple of Poseidon in Paestum, Italy.

IONIC ORDER. The Ionic order originated in the islands of the Aegean and in Asia Minor and was lighter and more ornate than the Doric order. The Ionic column rested on a carved base and had a more slender and graceful shaft than the Doric column. The Ionic capital included a large double scroll, called a volute.

The earliest Ionic columns may have been used simply to support statues. Around 570 B.C., a large Ionic temple dedicated to the goddess Hera was built on the island of Samos. Its scale was colossal—over 50,000 square feet. The people of Ephesus, presumably in rivalry, built an even larger temple to Artemis. Several years later, the people of Samos rebuilt their temple to Hera larger still. In the late 400s B.C., architects used the Ionic order in the temple of Athena Nike and in the Erechtheum, both located on the Acropolis of Athens.

CORINTHIAN ORDER. The Corinthian order developed in the late 400s B.C. It evolved from the Ionic order but differed from both the Doric and Ionic orders in the style of its capital. The Corinthian capital looked like an upside-down bell decorated with carvings of the curly leaves of the acanthus plant. The plant seemed to sprout from the top of the column shaft. Initially, Greek architects used the Corinthian capital only for interiors, but its use soon spread to the exteriors of large buildings. The Romans liked the Corinthian order so much that they used it in their most important monuments.

GREEK CITIES AND BUILDINGS

Many Greek cities grew gradually, without a plan for the placement of streets and buildings. Beginning in the late 500s B.C., city plans came into use, particularly in new settlements that were built as colonies. Some city plans consisted of a grid of streets, with an orderly arrangement of building sites. The AGORA, or marketplace, was a central feature of the city. Regardless of the shape of the city, the most important structure was the temple, built to honor and worship a significant god. While earlier peoples of the Aegean, such as the Minoans and Mycenaeans, created huge structures of stone, the Greeks surpassed them by constructing elaborate buildings.

TEMPLES. The temples of the ancient Greeks were their most outstanding architectural accomplishment. A temple was a freestanding building with a large, main room called a *cella* and a porch called a *pronaos*. Inside the *cella* was the statue of the favorite god of the city or region. Columns rose from a stepped platform to support stone beams and a low-pitched roof. The roof gables formed

* **pediment** triangular space formed by a low-pitched roof
* **terra-cotta** hard-baked clay, either glazed or unglazed

A FAMOUS TOMB

The most famous building of the Hellenistic period was not a temple but a tomb. It was the tomb of Mausolus, who served in the 350s B.C. as a governor of the Persians. Mausolus's widow, Artemisia, built the tomb at Halicarnassus in Asia Minor.

The building rose in three stages to a height of about 134 feet. A wide base supported Ionic columns. Above the columns rose a pyramid crowned by a chariot containing statues of Mausolus and Artemisia. Decorations showed chariot races and mythological battle scenes.

The tomb of Mausolus inspired other funeral monuments. In fact, the English word *mausoleum* means "an outsized tomb."

---

triangle-shaped pediments*. Builders used large, carefully shaped blocks of stone for the main structure. They built the ceiling of wooden beams and covered the roof with terra-cotta* tiles supported by wooden rafters.

The Greeks decorated their temples with carvings and colorful paint. Moldings in various shapes displayed continuous decorative patterns. Builders usually painted elements such as the frieze, cornice, moldings, and ceilings in blue or red, and also used black, green, and gold paint.

CIVIC BUILDINGS. Greek architects also produced buildings for the central marketplace. The stoa, a long, freestanding porch or covered walkway, was a typical structure of the agora. A stoa could be straight or L-shaped. It could have a single or double aisle, and it could be with or without rooms. Doric or Ionic columns decorated the stoa.

Some Greek cities had a *prytaneum*, a building for entertaining state guests. This building might contain city offices and a hearth where a fire burned at all times. In some places, there was also a treasury building in which the city's dedications to a particular god or goddess were held. Treasuries had inner rooms and a porch of columns, and they were usually smaller and more square than temples. Other urban buildings included theaters and concert halls. Theaters consisted of a stage area; a circular orchestra for dancing, singing, and reciting; and a semicircular seating area for the audience. Some cities had a stadium for races. Spectators stood on embankments and looked down into the racing area.

PRIVATE HOMES. The Greeks lavished attention on their public buildings but spent little on private homes. Early houses were simple, one-room buildings of wood or stone, with a porch on one side. However, when private homes became more elaborate in the late 400s and 300s B.C., architects began to build dwellings with several rooms facing south onto a court and a special room for dining.

THE ATHENS OF PERICLES. The Acropolis was a fortified hill above the city of Athens. In 480 B.C., the Persians attacked the city and destroyed the temples and statues on the Acropolis. By 448 B.C., the Athenians had begun to rebuild the Acropolis under the leadership of PERICLES. This was the most ambitious building project in the history of Greek architecture. The rebuilt Acropolis marked the high point of Greek artistic endeavor.

The greatest building on the Acropolis was the Parthenon, dedicated to Athena, the patron goddess of Athens. The architects Ictinus and Callicrates built the Parthenon in the Doric style, with some Ionic features, between 447 and 438 B.C. Certain refinements contributed to the greatness of the Parthenon. The stepped platform and the entablature are slightly bowed or arched so that the center is a bit higher than the ends. The columns tilt inward very slightly, and every capital was slightly modified. The complex curves and variant dimensions were unlike the true horizontals and right angles of most temples. They created a vibrant and continually interesting picture in the viewer's eye and gave the Parthenon a sense of life.

Soon after the building of the Parthenon, Pericles commissioned a huge gateway, the Propylaea, at the western end of the Acropolis. The architect Mnesicles began building the Propylaea in 437 B.C. using Doric and Ionic elements. Next to the Propylaea was the Temple of Athena Nike, designed by Callicrates in the 440s and built later, probably between 427 and 424 B.C. This temple belonged to the Ionic order. Opposite the Parthenon was another temple, the ERECHTHEUM, named after Erechtheus, a legendary king of Athens. The Erectheum was completed in 405 B.C. It is one of the best examples of elaborate Ionic architecture in Athens.

HELLENISTIC ARCHITECTURE. During Greece's Hellenistic* era, Greek culture spread to the east, and many new cities were settled. The growth of cities created a tremendous demand for public buildings, such as council chambers, markets, theaters, sports arenas, and elaborate private homes. As a result, the design of city buildings became more varied.

Individual citizens paid for many buildings during this period. The most important patrons, however, were kings, who built imposing monuments to project an image of their power. The wealthy kings of PERGAMUM in Asia Minor, for example, built a royal capital with numerous public buildings in the Doric style. When the emperors of Rome undertook ambitious building projects, they looked to Hellenistic-style buildings for architectural inspiration. (*See also* **Architecture, Roman; Cities, Greek; Columns, Types of; Construction Materials and Techniques.**)

* **Hellenistic** referring to the Greek-influenced culture of the Mediterranean world during the three centuries after Alexander the Great, who died in 323 B.C.

ARCHITECTURE, ROMAN

See color plate 9, vol. 2.

The ancient Romans developed a distinctive architectural style that displayed the variety, power, and wealth of their culture. At first, Roman buildings and other structures were modeled largely on the architectural styles and traditions of the Greeks. However, Roman builders soon discovered new CONSTRUCTION MATERIALS AND TECHNIQUES that helped them implement more complex designs.

The most important idea that Roman builders borrowed from the Greeks was the use of the three Greek orders, or styles, of building. These styles were known as the Doric, Ionic, and Corinthian orders. Each order used a particular type of COLUMN and had other special features, such as a horizontal base and detailed roof structure. The Romans adopted these orders as well as the Greek method of using stone blocks for construction.

BUILDING TECHNOLOGY

Beginning in the 300s B.C., the Roman government undertook vast building projects, including TEMPLES, civic buildings, ROADS, BRIDGES, and AQUEDUCTS. This surge in construction gave builders the opportunity to improve building technology.

CONSTRUCTION MATERIALS. The Romans discovered new types of construction materials that gave them greater design flexibility. No longer were they limited to the cut blocks of stone used by the Greeks. In the 200s and early 100s B.C., the Romans developed concrete, which they made by mixing stone fragments with mortar*. Builders molded concrete into shapes that were too heavy or too awkward to produce in stone. Concrete also replaced timbers in structures such as ceilings, where wood had been a fire hazard. At first, Roman builders used wooden armatures, or frameworks, in which they poured the concrete. Later, they replaced these with stone or brickwork. Once the concrete cured, or hardened, it bonded with the brick or stone outer layer and was stronger than stone.

Another material that contributed to the development of Roman architecture was MARBLE. By the A.D. 100s, the Roman empire had expanded to include regions with good sources of marble and other fine building materials. Gray and pink granite from Egypt, yellow marble from North Africa, green and white marble from Euboea in the Aegean Sea, and white marble from Greece became readily available throughout the Roman empire. Builders used these colorful stones to decorate important buildings.

CONSTRUCTION DESIGN AND TECHNIQUE. Improvements in construction technique also enabled the Romans to explore new design possibilities. Their most important innovation was the development of the ARCH, a curved structure resting on two supports and spanning an opening, such as a doorway. As an alternative to the Greek style of vertical columns supporting horizontal beams, the arch brought greater variety to Roman building styles. Arches also enabled the Romans to build vaults*. They formed high vaulted ceilings by crossing arches. Vaults could be linked to create very large structures. In 193 B.C., Roman builders

The Pantheon in Rome, a temple dedicated to all the gods, was built during the reign of the emperor Hadrian in the A.D. 100s. The massive dome of the structure was 142 feet across, and it remained the largest such dome ever built until modern times.

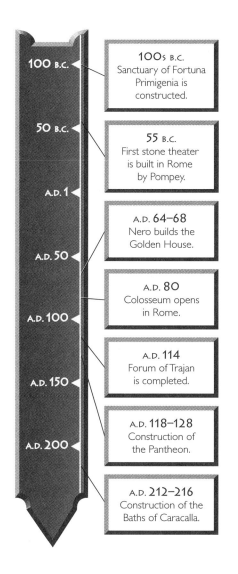

100 B.C.

100s B.C.
Sanctuary of Fortuna
Primigenia is
constructed.

50 B.C.

55 B.C.
First stone theater
is built in Rome
by Pompey.

A.D. 1

A.D. 64–68
Nero builds the
Golden House.

A.D. 50

A.D. 100

A.D. 80
Colosseum opens
in Rome.

A.D. 114
Forum of Trajan
is completed.

A.D. 150

A.D. 118–128
Construction of
the Pantheon.

A.D. 200

A.D. 212–216
Construction of the
Baths of Caracalla.

* **Roman Republic** Rome during the period
from 509 B.C. to 31 B.C., when popular
assemblies annually elected their governmental
officials

* **sanctuary** place for worship

constructed a huge warehouse to store the city's grain. It had 50 vaults, each nine yards wide, joined by interconnecting arches.

As the Romans extended their control over other regions, they came into contact with other cultures and occasionally adopted foreign architectural designs. One such feature was the Syrian arch. In this design, the traditional horizontal roof structure of Greek architecture is broken by a central arch rising from a pair of columns.

One of the most striking Roman architectural features was the dome. Building on their experience with arches, the Romans experimented with curved structures that could support weight. Eventually, they developed the dome. By the A.D. 100s, the Romans had begun to build great monuments with massive domed ceilings.

ROMAN BUILDINGS

As Rome's power increased, the Romans enlarged their cities, conquered foreign cities, and established new colonies. The demand for new buildings continued through the end of the Roman Republic* and remained strong during the period of the Roman Empire. Changes in Roman society gradually created a need for different types of buildings, such as elegant palaces for powerful rulers, BATHS, and AMPHITHEATERS for popular pastimes. Roman architects continually met the challenges that new kinds of construction projects demanded.

THE ROMAN REPUBLIC.   From the 300s B.C. until 31 B.C., architects of the Roman Republic developed the Roman style. Buildings still contained many Greek elements, but new features, such as concrete vaults, appeared. These new features showed up in many public buildings, such as the sanctuary* of Fortuna Primigenia, built in the late 100s B.C. at Praeneste, southeast of Rome. The architect designed a vast complex of buildings on a hillside, using concrete to make platforms on the uneven ground and to construct sloping and curving vaults. Greek and Roman elements blended in such designs as vaults resting on rows of columns.

The Roman theater featured another stylistic innovation. The Greeks often built theaters at the base of a hill, with seating arranged on the natural slope. The Romans used concrete to build artificial slopes. The slopes were supported by vaults under the seating area. Here the architects installed corridors and stairways to help the spectators reach their seats. As a result, the Romans could build theaters in flat locations, such as the center of a city. When the Roman general Pompey built Rome's first theater in 55 B.C., he added another new feature—a small temple dedicated to Venus at the top of the auditorium so that the goddess could watch the entertainments.

During this period, the Romans also built heated public baths. They installed efficient hot-water heating systems to control the temperature of the bathing pools and used concrete vaulting to construct the large bath chambers.

THE ROMAN EMPIRE.   Roman architecture continued to thrive during most of the Roman Empire until the A.D. 300s. Roman architects no

* imperial pertaining to an emperor or empire

* imperial pertaining to an emperor or empire

* basilica in Roman times, a large rectangular building used as a court of law or public meeting place

longer relied on Greek models for the basic structure of their buildings. They did, however, continue to use Greek elements for decoration.

One new type of building was the imperial* palace. In the A.D. 60s, the emperor Nero built the Golden House, a magnificent palace with an artificial lake and a private park. According to writers of the day, the palace had a revolving dome decorated with gold and jewels and dining rooms in which the ceilings "rained" perfumes and flowers. The palace also had some unusual shapes, such as an eight-sided room and a five-sided courtyard.

A palace built for the emperor Domitian several decades later had separate official and private quarters. There was a basilica* and an audience chamber, each containing a recessed area for the emperor's throne.

One of the greatest monuments built in the city of Rome during the early empire was the COLOSSEUM. This massive amphitheater held about 50,000 spectators and had an elaborate system of corridors and stairways. It was the model for other amphitheaters in Italy and the Roman provinces.

The emperor Trajan completed a new FORUM—a public meeting place used for public assemblies, judicial proceedings, and other events—in Rome in A.D. 114. With a statue of Trajan at its center, the forum had a basilica, an imposing column with carved decorations, and two libraries. Four years later, under the emperor Hadrian, work began on another Roman monument, the temple known as the PANTHEON. The most remarkable feature of the Pantheon was its huge concrete dome. The dome covered a vast open interior 142 feet wide and a marble floor in a checkerboard pattern.

Public baths reached a new level of luxury in the early A.D. 200s with the construction of the Baths of Caracalla in Rome. This elaborate structure was built of concrete under a layer of bricks. In addition to the bathing pools, the Baths of Caracalla included a swimming pool, games courts surrounded by columns, libraries, large lecture halls, and beautiful gardens. The bath building faced southwest so that the afternoon sun shone into the heated rooms.

The great building projects of the emperors produced techniques and innovations that changed Roman architecture. Roman builders preserved some elements of Greek architecture, but by inventing and using new designs, improving construction methods, and discovering new materials, the Romans advanced beyond their Greek models, creating a style that was distinctly their own. (*See also* **Architecture, Greek; Cities, Roman; Houses; Palaces, Imperial Roman; Theaters.**)

ARES

See *Mars.*

ARGONAUTS

See *Golden Fleece.*

ARISTOCRACY

See *Class Structure, Greek; Class Structure, Roman; Government, Greek; Government, Roman.*

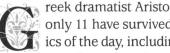

ARISTOPHANES

ca. 445–385 B.C.
GREEK COMIC DRAMATIST

* **classical** in Greek history, refers to the period of great political and cultural achievement from about 500 B.C. to 323 B.C.

* **satire** literary technique that uses wit and sarcasm to expose or ridicule vice and folly

* **bawdy** humorously indecent

* **chorus** in ancient Greek drama, a group of actors whose singing or dancing accompanies and comments upon the action of a play

Greek dramatist Aristophanes wrote about 40 comic plays, of which only 11 have survived. His plays dealt with many of the leading topics of the day, including politics, philosophy, and literature. They are the only complete examples of Greek comedy from the classical* period.

Little is known about Aristophanes' life. He may have been born on the Greek island of Aegina. His first play was produced in ATHENS when he was only 18, and he won several important prizes when he presented his plays at competitions. Aristophanes often used public figures as characters in his plays, but his mocking portrayal of the Greek politician Kleon led to a lawsuit against the young playwright.

GREEK OLD COMEDY.   Greek comedy may have had its origins in the entertainment at local festivals. The first formal performances of comedy were staged in Athens in 486 B.C., and plays from this early period—including those of Aristophanes—belong to a style known as Old Comedy. Old Comedy often included a substantial element of fantasy. The plays used satire* to comment on figures from mythology and Greek politics. The language was informal and even bawdy*, with numerous references to bodily functions.

Old Comedy contained certain structural features. For example, it used choruses* of animal characters, such as birds, frogs, or wasps, to comment on the action or themes of the play. The chorus often spoke for the playwright, and at some point in the middle of the play the chorus addressed the audience directly. The Greeks called this speech to the audience the *parabasis*. In addition, Greek comedy of this period often interrupted the story to remind spectators in the theater that they were watching a play.

EARLY PLAYS.   Aristophanes' earliest surviving play, *Acharnians,* won first prize in a competition when the poet was barely 20 years old. Like some of his other comedies, *Acharnians* features a bold hero whose fantasy comes true. The play is about Dikaiopolis, a crusty old farmer who wants Athens to make peace with the city of Sparta and end the PELOPONNESIAN WAR. Angry at the misery caused by six years of conflict, Dikaiopolis negotiates his own private treaty with the Spartans. The rest of the play shows him justifying his plan and enjoying the benefits of peace—food, wine, and lovemaking.

Many of the themes of Aristophanes' later plays appear in this early work. Some of these themes involve contrasts—between war and peace, city and country, or old and young people. Another theme is the role of comedy in the community. Aristophanes suggests that the comic playwright has certain civic responsibilities, such as advising the Athenians on public issues and commenting on the literature of the day. In his role as literary critic, Aristophanes makes EURIPIDES, the Greek dramatist, into a comic character in *Acharnians.*

Four other early plays of the 420s B.C. develop Aristophanes' favorite themes. In *Knights,* the playwright again makes fun of the politician Kleon, thinly disguising him as a blustering bully. In the play, Kleon tries to trick an

REPEAT PERFORMANCE

In contrast to today's theater, ancient Greek plays ordinarily had only one performance. However, Aristophanes' *Frogs* made such a favorable impression on the judges of a drama competition that they gave the playwright a unique honor: a second performance of the play the following year. The judges based their decision on the play's solemn plea for civic peace and harmony. They seem to have agreed with Aristophanes, who believed that part of his job was to offer sound advice to the city.

ARISTOPHANES

PLAYS OF ARISTOPHANES

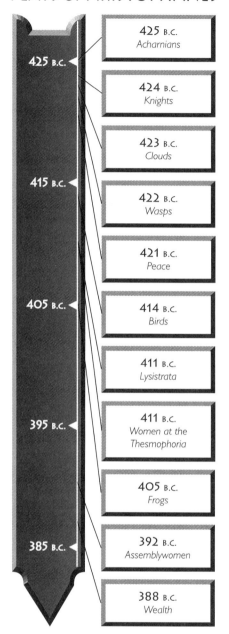

425 B.C.
Acharnians

424 B.C.
Knights

423 B.C.
Clouds

422 B.C.
Wasps

421 B.C.
Peace

414 B.C.
Birds

411 B.C.
Lysistrata

411 B.C.
Women at the Thesmophoria

405 B.C.
Frogs

392 B.C.
Assemblywomen

388 B.C.
Wealth

425 B.C.
415 B.C.
405 B.C.
395 B.C.
385 B.C.

* **parody** work that imitates another for comic effect or ridicule

* **underworld** kingdom of the dead; also called Hades

old man named Demos, who represents the Athenian people. However, an even trickier character, a lowly sausage seller, outsmarts Kleon.

Clouds is a satire of the "new learning" promoted by the SOPHISTS, a group of Athenian philosophers in the late 400s B.C. In the same play, Aristophanes draws a comic portrait of the philosopher SOCRATES. Although Socrates' approach to education was quite different from that of the Sophists, his unusual behavior and appearance made him irresistible to Aristophanes as a comic target. The first production of *Clouds,* however, was not a success. It is the only surviving play of Aristophanes without a happy ending, which may explain its failure.

After *Clouds,* Aristophanes wrote *Wasps,* which ridicules the Athenian jury system. His next play, *Peace,* a celebration of the joys of peacetime, was produced just a few weeks before the conclusion of a truce between Athens and Sparta.

LATER CAREER. *Birds* is the longest and perhaps the greatest of the surviving plays of Aristophanes. Disgusted with debts and taxes in Athens, two old men set out for the land of the birds. One of the men, the tramp Pisthetairos, persuades the birds to make him their leader. Before the play ends, he has overpowered the gods as well. The gods agree to let him marry Basileia, the beautiful woman who represents Zeus's power and authority, and the play ends with the wedding. Pisthetairos achieves the ultimate comic fantasy: supreme power.

Lysistrata is probably the best known and certainly the most frequently performed play of Aristophanes. It is one of several comedies in which Athenian women—controlled by men in real life—play a leading role. Comedy loves to turn reality upside down. In *Lysistrata,* the women decide to force the men of Athens to arrange a lasting peace with Sparta by refusing to have sexual relations with their husbands until the men take action. Lysistrata, the heroine of the play, is courageous, funny, and imaginative—one of Aristophanes' most memorable characters.

In *Women at the Thesmophoria,* Aristophanes combines comedy and literary parody*. The women of Athens are angry at Euripides because of the unflattering portrayal of female characters in his plays. Euripides sends one of his male relatives, disguised as a housewife, to plead his case with the women. The fun at Euripides' expense continues in *Frogs,* in which the god Dionysus visits the underworld* and judges a poetry contest between Euripides and the earlier playwright AESCHYLUS. Euripides loses the competition.

Aristophanes' last two surviving comedies, *Assemblywomen* and *Wealth,* appeared in the 300s B.C. They clearly signal changes in the format of Old Comedy. Neither play has a parabasis, and the chorus plays only a small role in *Wealth.* In *Assemblywomen,* the women disguise themselves as men and take over the assembly with humorous results. *Wealth* explores the relationship of justice to prosperity and poverty. In this play, the outrageous, biting tone of Old Comedy seems to have almost disappeared.

ORIGINALITY AND INFLUENCE. Aristophanes boasted, often through his choruses, of his new and original ideas. Most likely these boasts were tongue-in-cheek. Like most dramatists, he doubtless borrowed ideas from

58

earlier and from contemporary playwrights, just as he often recycled his own successful material.

On a deeper level, however, Aristophanes created comic stories of lasting power. Unlike the writers of tragedies, who drew their material from Greek legends, comic writers had to invent new plots. Aristophanes succeeded admirably in creating meaningful and enjoyable dramas. (*See also* **Drama, Greek.**)

See color plate 8, vol. 3.

ARISTOTLE

384–322 B.C.
GREEK PHILOSOPHER
AND SCIENTIST

* **philosopher** scholar or thinker concerned with the study of ideas, including science

* **dialogue** text presenting an exchange of ideas between people

Aristotle was one of the great philosophers* of ancient Greece. He was interested in an extraordinary number of subjects and he wrote important works on many of them. He created methods of philosophical study that are still used. He also conducted systematic research in such fields as animal anatomy and Greek political systems. His written works covered these subjects as well as psychology, astronomy, physics, and literature. His work had an enormous influence on later generations of scholars through the Middle Ages to modern times.

ARISTOTLE THE TEACHER. Aristotle was born in Stagira in Macedonia in northern Greece. His father was a doctor and court physician to Macedonia's King Amyntas II. Aristotle's interest in animal studies and his knowledge of dissection may have been influenced by his father's profession.

At the age of 17, Aristotle traveled to ATHENS and entered Plato's Academy. PLATO was an important Greek philosopher whose writings shaped the development of Western thought, and the Academy was a school for philosophers that Plato founded. Aristotle remained there as a student and associate for 20 years. During this time, he wrote several dialogues* that became famous in the ancient world. Only fragments of these works have survived.

When Plato died in 347 B.C., Aristotle left Athens for northern Asia Minor. There he met Pythias, the woman who became his wife. He also began his biological research, studying marine species in the Aegean Sea off the island of Lesbos. In 342 B.C., he returned to Macedonia to become tutor to the 13-year-old son of King PHILIP II. That son later became ALEXANDER THE GREAT, the Greek conqueror who brought all of Persia as well as parts of India under his control.

As Alexander's teacher, Aristotle wrote several other works that have not survived, including *Monarchy.* It would be interesting to know what advice he gave to Alexander on this subject. But when discussing monarchs in his later work, *Politics,* he notably omitted mention of Alexander as a worthy example. He also did not stay with Alexander's court beyond his teaching appointment.

Soon after Philip died, Aristotle returned to Athens and founded his own school—the Lyceum—where he taught for 12 years. Then, in 323 B.C., Alexander the Great died, and there was a wave of anti-Macedonian feeling in Athens. Apparently fearing for his life, Aristotle returned to Macedonia, where he died a year later of a stomach ailment.

ARISTOTLE'S WORKS.

Nearly all of Aristotle's surviving works date from his years at the Lyceum. They seem to be lecture notes that he developed for teaching there, and they were kept at the Lyceum when he left for Macedonia. The notes then changed hands several times over the next two hundred years. It was not until the first century B.C. that various editors organized the works in the form known today.

Aristotle's works fall into groups of texts on related subjects. In his works on logic*, which include *Categories, On Interpretation, Prior Analytics*, and *Posterior Analytics,* he discussed the process of reasoning and constructing valid arguments. In *Metaphysics,* he drew a distinction between matter (the material substance of objects in the world) and form (the special nature of an object that gives it an identity).

Aristotle wrote several works on the natural sciences, including *Physics,* which considers such subjects as time, space, movement, and change in nature. *On the Heavens* sets forth his views on astronomy. In a series of works, including *On the Soul,* he discussed various aspects of human psychology. He also wrote texts on weather and on the biology of animals.

In two of his works on ethics*, *Nichomachean Ethics* and *Eudemian Ethics,* Aristotle wrote about morality and human behavior. He considered human society in a wider context in *Politics,* where he discussed citizenship and systems of government, such as democracy and monarchy. He also produced works on art, including *Rhetoric,* which is about persuasive public speaking, and *Poetics,* which concerns poetry and drama.

ARISTOTLE'S METHOD.

Aristotle was not a scientist in the modern sense. Although his studies of animals involved much firsthand observation, he did not base his work solely on observed facts. For his work in philosophy, he used human beliefs and interpretations—both his own and those of other people—as raw material.

Typically, Aristotle's lectures would start with a careful and respectful review of other people's opinions about a topic. Then he would investigate and compare these opinions, exploring where they differed and how parts of them might fit together. One of his strengths as a thinker was his ability to approach questions from many different directions. Finally, he would try to develop a logical and consistent view, rejecting some ideas but saving as many as he could. The result would be a construct* of ideas that Aristotle called "scientific understanding." This technique led him to break new ground in many subjects.

His thoughts about matter and form provide an example of this method. One of the issues that philosophers have always discussed is the nature of objects and events. What makes one object a chair and another a person? How much do they have to change before they cease to be a chair or a person? How do we know when that has happened? The answers at first seem obvious, but careful thought shows that they are based on complicated assumptions.

When Aristotle wrote, there were two schools of thought about matter and form. The earliest Greek philosophers focused on the materials of which objects were made and the ways in which the materials

* **logic** principles of reasoning

* **ethics** branch of philosophy that deals with moral conduct, duty, and judgment

* **construct** working hypothesis or concept

Aristotle was one of the greatest and most important philosophers in history. A student of Plato and tutor to Alexander the Great, Aristotle studied a wide range of subjects. His works in such fields as logic and political theory remained influential through the Middle Ages and into the modern age.

ARISTOTLE'S LASTING INFLUENCE

Aristotle's work influenced the thinking of writers, philosophers, and scientists for many centuries after his death. His ideas became particularly important during the Middle Ages. In the A.D. 800s, his works were translated into Arabic and studied by Islamic and Jewish scholars. Latin translations made in the 1100s and 1200s launched a surge of interest in Aristotle in the West, enabling Christian theologians, such as Thomas Aquinas, to use Aristotle's ideas about the human soul. In the 1620s, the philosopher Francis Bacon was influenced by Aristotle. Even later, in the 1800s, the naturalist Charles Darwin expressed his admiration for Aristotle's work in biology.

* **syllogism** form of argument in which two true statements (premises) lead to a third statement (conclusion) that must also be true

changed. Aristotle argued that this was not enough—changes could occur even if the materials remained identical. For example, when an animal dies it becomes a heap of matter that is no longer an animal, even though it consists of the same materials. Similarly, if a chair is pulled apart and made into something else, the materials are the same, but the object has changed. Thus, the identity of an animal or a chair is not defined by its materials alone.

The other school of thought was that of Aristotle's teacher Plato. Plato's solution to the problem was that there must be something nonmaterial about an animal, a chair, or indeed a human being. Plato called this a form, something that incorporates all the properties of an object but exists on an ideal plane. He argued that forms were in fact more real than objects, and objects appeared only when forms were in some way projected onto matter.

Aristotle did not fully agree with Plato's theory of forms. He accepted that the idea of form was needed for identifying an object. But he saw no reason to conclude that forms had a reality apart from their existence in objects. Further, he noted that some properties of a particular form were unimportant for identifying an object, while others were vital. For example, a person who becomes tanned by the sun remains the same person, but a statue, however lifelike, never becomes the person it represents. Continuing this line of argument, Aristotle developed ideas on how we perceive and think that are still relevant and are similar to some theories of modern psychology.

LOGIC.   Aristotle's most important contribution to human thought is often said to be his analysis of formal logic, described in his text *Prior Analytics*. Formal logic shows how arguments can be presented in syllogisms*, built from premises. Premises are basic understandings that lead to conclusions. The conclusions, in turn, become the premises for other conclusions. This analysis has never been improved.

Of course, Aristotle's answers were not always accurate. A very influential argument that is now known to be false is his theory of four elements. He argued that all materials are made up of one or more of the following elements—fire, air, water, or earth. As might be expected, he gave logical explanations for this idea, but the premises, or basic principles on which his argument rested, were incorrect.

GOOD LIVING.   For all Aristotle's focus on logic, however, his thinking was not rigid. He accepted that some subjects, such as politics and ethics, are practical matters that are by nature inexact.

In *Nichomachean Ethics,* Aristotle tried to explore what is really meant by "good living." He concluded that good living cannot be defined by a logical system that always works out. Instead, the real world creates situations where different values sometimes come into conflict. He saw rules for behavior as only summaries of the practical wisdom of others. In an effort to live a good life, individuals must apply careful reasoning and develop their own judgment. Aristotle's philosophy recognizes these complexities of human life, even while it strives for order and reason. (*See also* **Philosophy, Greek and Hellenistic; Science.**)

ARMIES, GREEK

See color plate 13, vol. 4.

Each ancient Greek city-state* had its own army. Few cities, however, could afford to maintain a full-time army of professional soldiers. As a result, most Greek military forces consisted of citizens trained to take up arms in times of crisis. These citizen-soldiers had to supply their own weapons and armor. At first, most soldiers came from the upper classes because only the wealthy could afford the necessary arms. By the mid-600s B.C., military equipment had become less expensive, allowing craftspeople and small landowners to acquire arms and join the ranks of the military.

Greek armies were relatively small, perhaps no more than 10,000 men. In most armies, the soldiers elected their officers, and the overall command alternated among several generals chosen by popular vote.

TRAINING. In most city-states, young men began military training at age 18. While serving in the army, they received pay and a living allowance. After one or two years of training, the soldiers returned to civilian life, but they could be called for military service until the age of 60. In time of war, these retired soldiers might be required to report for service at a moment's notice and bring along enough food—barley meal, onion, and cheese—for three days.

Military training in SPARTA was different from that in other city-states. Basically a military state, Sparta required male citizens from the upper classes to begin military training as early as age seven and to remain soldiers all their lives. Sparta's highly trained soldiers were generally considered the best in Greece.

ORGANIZATION. Greek armies consisted mostly of infantry, or foot soldiers. Some infantrymen were hoplites, heavily armed spear carriers. Others were peltasts, who were more lightly armed and more mobile. Military groups tended to be divided by social class, according to the cost of equipment. The peltasts usually came from the lower classes because the equipment they required—javelins and simple shields of woven twigs—was not expensive. The cavalry stood at the high end of the scale in terms of cost. Because horses were expensive and scarce, few Greek armies included a cavalry. The cavalries that did exist consisted mainly of young men from the wealthy, landowning families.

One of the most important infantry units was the phalanx, a tightly massed formation of hoplites. Bearing shields and spears, these soldiers advanced and fought as a single unit. Keeping the phalanx in formation took great discipline.

RISE OF PROFESSIONAL SOLDIERS. Greek armies changed during the 300s B.C. when Asian rulers hired Greek soldiers to serve in their armies. Greek soldiers were highly valued because of their great discipline and battle skills. The chance to work in foreign armies led to the rise of a class of professional soldiers in many Greek city-states. Mercenaries*, also known as soldiers of fortune or free lancers, fought for anyone who paid them. As Greek city-states began hiring mercenaries to supplement or replace the citizen troops, Greek armies became more professional.

The greatest changes in Greek armies occurred in MACEDONIA under kings PHILIP II and his son ALEXANDER THE GREAT, both of whom ruled in the 300s B.C. Philip created a large professional army of highly trained soldiers and mercenaries recruited from all classes of society. He also added new groups of infantry and expanded the cavalry. Alexander adopted his father's changes and introduced the lancers, a new form of cavalry that was used mostly for scouting and pursuing retreating enemy troops. With the expanded use of cavalry, which could advance more quickly than the infantry, Macedonian armies became stronger, more flexible, and more capable of pursuing and destroying an enemy.

Macedonian armies, with as many as 60,000 men, were much larger than the armies of the Greek city-states. The Macedonian army was based on a phalanx of about 4,000 men, divided into smaller units that were trained to maneuver separately or together. Other infantry and cavalry groups coordinated their actions with the phalanx, increasing its effectiveness.

The Macedonian armies were the most formidable fighting forces in the Mediterranean world. The great power of these armies and their ability to move quickly over long distances allowed Philip and Alexander to expand their kingdoms and to create huge empires. (*See also* **Wars and Warfare, Greek; Weapons and Armor.**)

ARMIES, ROMAN

See color plate 11, vol. 1.

The Roman armies were the most highly organized and disciplined fighting forces of their time. These powerful legions enabled Rome to conquer neighboring and distant peoples, building an empire that spanned much of Europe and reached into Asia and northern Africa. When the conquered lands became part of the Roman empire, the armies defended Rome's far-flung frontiers and maintained peace throughout the Roman world. Yet the significance of the Roman armies went far beyond their military role. When Roman soldiers traveled to distant parts of the empire, they carried with them Roman ideas, customs, and culture. After military service, many soldiers settled in these distant lands, forming colonies of Roman army veterans. As a result, the armies played an important role in the spread of Roman civilization.

CITIZEN-SOLDIERS OF EARLY ROME. The earliest Roman armies consisted of Roman citizens who owned property. The Romans considered military service a basic responsibility of citizenship, and male citizens between ages 17 and 46 could be called to serve whenever Rome needed soldiers. They served until the crisis was over, and then returned to civilian life. During their years of eligibility, men served a maximum of 16 years as foot soldiers in the infantry or 10 years in the cavalry. Later military reforms changed the maximum amount of service to 20 and then 25 years.

Soldiers had to provide their own WEAPONS AND ARMOR. The wealthiest citizens, who could afford horses and equipment, served in the cavalry. Those of lesser means did their military service in the infantry. The poorest citizens, who could not afford to equip themselves, often did not serve at all. Citizen-soldiers received only a small payment for their time and service. Their main income came from their farms or business interests. (Regular military pay was not introduced until 406 B.C.) Each soldier did receive an allotment, called a *salarium,* for the purchase of salt. The modern word *salary* is derived from the Latin *salarium.*

RISE OF A PROFESSIONAL ARMY. In the early years of the Roman Republic, armies generally fought in areas near Rome. They regularly returned home after each campaign to attend to their property and businesses. However, beginning with the PUNIC WARS against CARTHAGE, Roman armies often stayed abroad for a year or longer, and the citizen-soldiers became reluctant to serve.

In 107 B.C. the politician and army commander Gaius MARIUS had difficulty recruiting men who were willing to be away from home for long periods. He solved the problem by ending the property requirement for military service and opening the army to volunteers. Romans from the poorer classes flocked to join the armies, attracted by the possibility of long-term careers and booty* from overseas conquests. These new soldiers formed Rome's first permanent, professional army.

* **booty** riches or property gained through conquest

THE ROMAN LEGIONS. Roman armies were composed of forces called legions. By 31 B.C., Rome had sixty legions. The emperor AUGUSTUS reduced the number of legions to twenty-eight, totaling about 300,000 men. Each legion had a name—referring to a province*, an emperor, or a god—and a number. If a legion was destroyed in battle, its name was never used again.

* **province** overseas area controlled by Rome

A standard legion contained 4,200 soldiers. It was made up of four types of infantry—*triarii,* the oldest legionnaires*; *principes,* the seasoned veterans; *hastati,* the younger soldiers; and *velites,* the youngest, poorest, and most lightly armed troops. Each of these groups was divided into units of 60 or 120 men called maniples, the basic fighting units of the army. Because of its size, the maniple could maneuver quickly in any type of terrain. Maniples were further divided into centuries. In later years, a unit called the cohort, containing 300 to 600 legionnaires, replaced the maniple as the basic unit within the legion. Each cohort contained two centuries, and ten cohorts made up a legion.

* **legionnaire** member of a legion

In addition to infantry, each legion included a cavalry of between 120 and 300 men. These mounted soldiers rarely fought in battle, serving primarily as scouts and messengers. Cavalries that did fight usually consisted of foreign troops. Each legion also had military engineers, surveyors, stonemasons, and other experts to select sites for army camps and to supervise the building of roads, defensive walls, forts, and bridges.

Overall command of the Roman armies was held by two CONSULS, civilian officials who served for one-year terms, which might be extended during emergencies. In time of war, one consul was chosen, often by lot, to lead a particular campaign. An army could also be commanded by a praetor*, if a consul was unavailable. Next in the chain of

* **praetor** Roman official, just below the consul in rank, in charge of judicial proceedings and of governing overseas provinces

The Column of Trajan, erected in Rome in A.D. 114, celebrated the emperor Trajan's victory in the Dacian Wars. This detail of the reliefs that decorate the column shows Trajan addressing his troops, while other soldiers chop down trees with axes.

See color plate 9, vol. 2.

command were the legates, often members of the Roman SENATE. A legate was someone to whom the commander might delegate some of his power.

Each legion was led by six TRIBUNES, who rotated command daily so that no one officer became too powerful. Below the tribunes were the centurions, the backbone of the army. They were responsible for disciplining the soldiers. A large staff of clerks in each legion took care of keeping records, overseeing supplies, handling documents, and various other tasks.

Remember: *Consult the index at the end of volume 4 to find more information on many topics.*

* **imperial** pertaining to an emperor or empire

* **palisade** wooden fence made of stakes or pointed sticks as a barrier against invaders

FOREIGN TROOPS.   From the early days of the Republic, Rome made use of the armies of allied states to help defend its territories. These groups of non-Romans, known as the *auxilia,* or auxiliaries, generally patrolled distant frontiers and supported the legions in battle. The men who joined the auxiliaries were promised full Roman citizenship after 25 years of service.

The *auxilia* resembled legions in both organization and chain of command. Their infantry units were divided into cohorts, which in turn were divided into centuries. The commanding officers of the *auxilia* came both from Roman legions and from the ranks of the *auxilia.*

Some *auxilia* contained expert units, such as Syrian archers or Spanish cavalry, that made use of the special skills of particular peoples. The Roman legions often called on these expert auxiliary units for help.

THE PRAETORIAN GUARD.   During the Roman Republic, the principal commander of a legion often selected a group of soldiers to act as his private bodyguards. This guard was known as the praetorian cohort, after the *praetorium*—the commander's tent. Following the model of the praetorian cohort, the emperor Augustus established a special force called the Praetorian Guard. These guards were charged with protecting the emperor and received better pay and benefits, and often better training, than ordinary soldiers.

Some soldiers of the Praetorian Guard were based in Rome, where they patrolled the imperial palaces and other major buildings. Others were stationed in towns around Rome. In time, this special force of between 4,500 and 9,000 men became a threat to imperial* power. Although the Praetorian Guard had no direct role in government, its members could force an emperor from power if he lost their support and loyalty. In A.D. 41, some members of the guard aided in the conspiracy to murder the emperor CALIGULA, and then placed his uncle CLAUDIUS on the throne. Later emperors weakened the guard by reducing its numbers and stationing its soldiers away from the imperial palace. Some emperors replaced the Praetorian Guard with individuals loyal to them. In the early A.D. 300s, the emperor CONSTANTINE I abolished the Praetorian Guard.

TRAINING AND ARMY LIFE.   Intensive training and strict discipline gave Roman armies their great strength. Soldiers trained rigorously, marching and running long distances with heavy packs on their backs and practicing for many hours with their weapons. Discipline was very severe. Soldiers who broke rules were harshly punished.

Army camps, known as *castra,* were highly organized. The camps were laid out like cities, with parallel streets that formed a square or a rectangle. Located at the ends of the two main crossing streets were the four principal gates that were used to enter or leave the camp. The camp was surrounded by a ditch, and a palisade* was built on the excavated soil. Because all camps had the same layout, every soldier knew exactly where to pitch his tent and where to store horses, baggage, and supplies. Temporary camps could be taken down easily and moved quickly—important features when the army was on the move and needed to construct camp on a new site every day.

In time, Rome built more permanent camps and forts throughout the empire. These military bases defended the frontiers and sheltered local peoples in times of danger. They also attracted Roman traders and colonists, who established communities around the military bases and brought Roman civilization to remote regions. Several modern European cities grew around the sites of permanent Roman camps.

When Roman soldiers retired they received a payment and a plot of land, often in the province where they had served. Former soldiers who settled on these plots helped to populate the Roman provinces and to extend Roman culture and ideals to the far corners of the empire. Eventually, however, soldiers became a cause of instability in the Roman empire. As more and more foreign troops joined the Roman armies and served in distant provinces, their loyalty to Rome weakened, and Rome's control of its provinces declined. (*See also* **Armies, Greek; Naval Power, Roman; Wars and Warfare, Roman.**)

ARMOR

See *Weapons and Armor.*

ART, GREEK

* **mosaic** art form in which small pieces of stone or glass are set in cement; also refers to a picture made in this manner

* **classical** in Greek history, refers to the period of great political and cultural achievement from about 500 B.C. to 323 B.C.

The styles and techniques the ancient Greeks developed in painting, mosaics*, and sculpture have had an enormous influence on the art that followed. Borrowed and adapted by the ancient Romans and spread throughout the Roman empire, the art of classical* Greece became the model for great painters and sculptors throughout the history of Europe.

PAINTING

Ancient Greek artists painted on a variety of surfaces, including stucco-lined walls, wood panels, stone pillars and tombs, and pottery. Painters who worked on larger objects, such as walls and panels, were known as monumental painters. They were greatly respected and honored by the ancient Greeks. Unfortunately, little of their work survives. Much of what is known about the evolution of Greek painting comes from examples of painted pottery, especially vases.

MONUMENTAL PAINTING. Ancient writers, especially PLINY THE ELDER and PAUSANIAS, describe the work and reputation of the wall and panel painters of classical Athens. Known for his skill at portraying emotion, Polygnotos of Thasos, the first great painter of this period, painted murals of famous battles on several important buildings in Athens. Other artists in the 400s B.C. developed techniques that made paintings seem more realistic. Agatharchos, for instance, developed a system of perspective—a way of giving a painting the appearance of depth and distance—perhaps while painting scenery for the plays of AESCHYLUS.

Artists further refined these techniques in the 300s B.C., the "golden age" of Greek painting.

Paintings on the inside and outside of tombs and on stelae* provide more evidence regarding ancient Greek painting. Archaeologists have uncovered tombs in MACEDONIA dating from the early 300s B.C. The paintings on these tombs feature rich colors, skillful shading, and dramatic expression.

EARLY GREEK VASE PAINTING.   Greek painted pottery dates back to the 900s B.C. These early vases, painted in a style known as Geometric, were decorated with bands of geometric patterns, such as diamonds, triangles, and zigzags. Some pottery incorporated small, simple silhouettes of horses and people as part of these ornamental bands. Later, painters from Athens and the Greek city of Corinth experimented with more ambitious illustrations, including scenes from Greek mythology, such as PERSEUS beheading Medusa and the exploits of HERACLES. Specializing in small, red-clay vessels for holding oils, the Corinthian painters engraved fine decorative details onto dark painted silhouettes. Other colors, mainly reds and whites, were then added. The masterpiece of this style is the Chigi Vase, a small wine pitcher on which a fierce battle is depicted.

In the late 600s B.C., Corinthian painters added their refined engraved work to the larger pottery vessels popular in Athens, producing the "black-figure" style that became the dominant style throughout Greece. In this style of painting, details were created by a sharp instrument that

* **stelae** engraved pillars used as gravestones

This amphora—a large jar with two handles—was painted around 530 B.C. by Exekias, the greatest of the Greek black-figure vase painters. Now in the Vatican Museum, the amphora shows Achilles and Ajax, two great heroes from Homer's *Iliad*, playing a game during a pause in the battle.

See color plate 12, vol. 4.

cut through the black glaze of the figures to the lighter clay color of the vase. Although at first illustrating mythological subjects in ornamental bands, or friezes, black-figure painters experimented with scenes of fewer and larger figures. Exekias, one of the finest of all Greek vase painters, is the artist of a famous amphora*, now in the Vatican Museum, that depicts the Greek heroes Achilles and Ajax hunched over a game board.

* amphora large, oval jar with two handles and a wide mouth

THE RED-FIGURE STYLE. Around 525 B.C., an artist known as the Andokides Painter invented the "red-figure" style of pottery painting, essentially reversing the technique of the black-figure style. In red-figure painting, the background of the illustration was painted black, leaving the reddish color of the clay for the figures. Details, such as facial features, could then be painted on, rather than engraved, making individual figures stand out more than the silhouettes of black-figure painting. Red-figure painting was particularly appropriate for depicting scenes of daily life, such as athletes exercising, music competitions, and school scenes. Between 520 and 480 B.C., the great age of red-figure painting, many fine painters produced increasingly experimental and personal work. One of the finest examples of this period is the great krater* by Euphronios, now in the Metropolitan Museum of Art in New York City. On one side, it shows the death of the epic hero Sarpedon and, on the other side, ordinary soldiers arming themselves.

* krater jar or vase with a wide mouth and a large, round body that is used for mixing wine and water

The best Athenian vase painters of the 400s B.C. were influenced by the art on public buildings, especially the relief* sculpture of the great buildings on the ACROPOLIS. These artists also imitated the styles of the monumental painters of the period, with scenes from mythology and legend again becoming popular. In an offshoot of the red-figure style, painters of *lekythoi* (narrow jugs used for scented oil in funeral rites) covered pottery with delicate multicolored freehand drawings—usually of mourners at a tomb—on a white background.

* relief method of sculpture in which the design is raised from the surface from which it is shaped

Vases with red-figure painting were also produced in the Greek cities of southern Italy and Sicily, although they were not as fine as Athenian painting. By the end of the 300s B.C., the style disappeared as painted pottery became less important.

MOSAICS

Mosaics made of rounded pebbles set in a layer of cement were used as flooring as early as the 1000s B.C. Beginning in the 400s B.C., however, artists created elaborate illustrations and designs using this technique. Many places in Greece had floors decorated with mosaics, but the finest early examples were from the city of Olynthos in Macedonia. Found in private homes, usually on the floors of dining rooms, these mosaics contained a central rectangular or circular panel depicting a scene from Greek mythology, surrounded by an ornamental border. Later artists attempted to imitate the effects of the painting of the time by using smaller pebbles and a greater variety of colors. The masterpiece of the art of pebble mosaic was created in two large buildings at Pella, the capital of Macedonia, in the late 300s B.C. In addition to mythological

* **terra-cotta** hard-baked clay, either glazed or unglazed

topics, these mosaics depict a lion hunt and a deer hunt, subjects associated with the Macedonian leader ALEXANDER THE GREAT.

In the 200s B.C., artists invented the tessellated mosaic, which is a mosaic made from small cubes of stone, glass, and terra-cotta*. The technique was so refined that as many as 30 tesserae, or cubes, could fit into a square centimeter. Since these mosaics decorated private homes, most depicted pleasant subjects such as scenes from drama or mythology. A particularly fine tessellated mosaic, found in the House of the Masks on the island of DELOS, portrays the god DIONYSUS riding a leopard.

SCULPTURE

Most surviving early Greek sculpture consists of small terra-cotta or bronze statues, usually of animals, that were used for decorative or religious purposes. In the 600s B.C., inspired by Near Eastern and Egyptian culture, the Greeks experimented with new styles and techniques. In the "Daedalic" style (named after DAEDALUS, the mythical inventor and artist), human figures were molded in terra-cotta or carved from ivory or stone. Rigid standing figures with arms pressed against the sides, Daedalic sculptures had flat-top heads and triangular faces that were flanked with horizontally arranged waves of hair.

The typical Greek sculpture of the 500s B.C. were *kouroi,* which were large stone figures of nude young men, and *korai,* similarly large statues of clothed young women. At first very blocklike in form, like the Egyptian statues on which they were modeled, the kouroi and korai gradually became more anatomically realistic. All Greek stone statues were originally brightly painted, including facial features, hair, and skin.

The Greeks had long used bronze to make small statues, but by the classical period, they created large bronze figures using a method called the lost-wax technique. The lost-wax technique consisted of coating a clay model with wax. The wax-covered figure was then covered with material that hardened around the wax, which was then melted. Molten bronze was poured into the space where the wax had been. Once the bronze had cooled and hardened, the clay model in the center was removed, and the result was a hollow bronze sculpture.

Sculptures in the 400s B.C. displayed a sense of movement and a more natural depiction of the body than that of the rigid kouroi. Athletes became popular subjects for sculpture, such as the Discus Thrower by Myron. Also, sculptors began to explore states of consciousness in their work, giving their statues facial expressions and postures that showed concentration, fatigue, or dismay.

The most famous sculptor of the period was PHIDIAS. A friend of the Athenian leader PERICLES, Phidias supervised all the artwork on the ACROPOLIS in Athens. His most famous works, such as a colossal statue of the goddess ATHENA in the PARTHENON, have not survived, although statues on the building itself indicate his artistic vision. The figures on these sculptures combined serene expressions with an impression of movement. Phidias trained many sculptors, who later traveled throughout Greece spreading his style.

Later sculptors worked in a variety of styles. Polykleitos the Elder, of the city of Argos, was famous for the perfect proportions and harmonious

ALEXANDER THE GREAT'S PERSONAL SCULPTOR

Alexander the Great would allow only his court sculptor, Lysippos of Sikyon, to create his image. According to the Greek biographer Plutarch, Lysippos captured Alexander's likeness exactly, portraying the king with his head tilted dramatically to one side, his mouth slightly open, and with melting eyes. This was the expression, according to Plutarch, that Alexander's friends liked to imitate.

See color plate 10, vol. 2.

beauty of his figures. Praxiteles, a well-known Athenian sculptor of the 300s B.C., created playful work, such as a sculpture of the god Hermes dangling a bunch of grapes in front of the infant Dionysus. Lysippos of Sikyon, the court sculptor of Alexander the Great, produced realistic portraits of public figures in a style that became popular in the 200s B.C. By the late 100s B.C., many Greek sculptors had moved to Rome to set up workshops. Roman sculpture was highly influenced by Greek work and was, in fact, usually made by Greeks. (*See also* **Architecture, Greek; Architecture, Roman; Art, Roman; Crafts and Craftsmanship; Gems and Jewelry; Mosaics; Sculpture, Greek; Sculpture, Roman.**)

ART OF LOVE

See *Ovid.*

ART, ROMAN

* **Hellenistic** referring to the Greek-influenced culture of the Mediterranean world during the three centuries after Alexander the Great, who died in 323 B.C.

* **booty** riches or property gained through conquest

* **Roman Republic** Rome during the period from 509 B.C. to 31 B.C., when popular assemblies annually elected their governmental officials

The art of ancient Rome was indebted to several influences. Probably earliest was the art of the Etruscans, whose civilization arose in central Italy in the eighth century B.C. Before about 400 B.C., Etruscan art itself had owed much to the art of Greece, the Middle East, and native cultures of Italy.

The art of the Hellenistic* age, especially that of the Greek colonies in southern Italy and Sicily, had a direct influence on Roman art. After the Roman conquest of Greece, much Greek art, particularly sculpture, came to Rome as booty*. Also at that time, many Greek artists had traveled to Italy to find work. During the late Roman Republic* and the Roman Empire, wealthy Romans amassed art collections containing not only booty but also works they had commissioned from Greek artists. Distinctive Roman styles gradually developed, and they, in turn, influenced artists throughout the empire.

PAINTING

Panel paintings on wood that had come from Greece as the result of conquest were carried in victorious processions through Rome, later turning up in private collections. Very few panel paintings have survived. They are known to us mainly through descriptions in literature. Wall paintings, or murals, replaced the panel technique, sometimes as decoration, sometimes to depict people or scenes.

* **excavate** to uncover by digging

* **masonry** brick or stone work

First Pompeian Style. Among the most important mural paintings are those found on the surviving walls of houses in Pompeii and Herculaneum, which were buried and preserved when the volcano on Mt. Vesuvius erupted in A.D. 79. The ruins were discovered in the late 1700s and have been thoroughly excavated*. The name "First Style" has been given to colorful decorations on plaster walls, which were made to imitate masonry*, marble, or alabaster (a mineral). This style of painting started in the Hellenistic Greek world and spread to Italy and Sicily by the 200s B.C. Roman villa owners also had other masterpieces of Greek

The eruption of Mt. Vesuvius in A.D. 79 buried the Roman towns of Pompeii and Hercula- neum, killing thousands of people, but pre- serving intact wonderful examples of Roman art and architecture. This wall painting from Pompeii depicts a scene from the myth of Iphigenia.

* **mosaic** art form in which small pieces of stone or glass are set in cement; also refers to a picture made in this manner

painting copied for them, giving us an insight into the high quality of such Hellenistic art. An example is the famous mosaic* from the House of the Faun in Pompeii. Created in the 100s B.C., it depicts a scene from Alexander the Great's victory over the Persians. The mosaic was copied in remarkably fine detail (in color and form) from a lost painting of the early 300s B.C.

SECOND STYLE OF WALL PAINTING. During the early first century B.C., a second style emerged, one that imitated the architectural forms of columns and arches, beyond which the illusion of distant land- scapes and buildings was created. (The modern name for this style, which at first sight appears real, is *trompe l'oeil,* meaning "trick of the eye" in French.) During the years of the Roman Empire, fancy decora- tion became stylish, with paintings of fantastic scenes, imaginary pic- ture galleries, and popular Egyptian motifs.

OTHER STYLES. The third style of wall painting favored surface effects and even more fantastic subjects, expressed also in stucco wall and vault* decoration in relief* and often painted in strong colors. A house in Pompeii of the first century A.D. is a good example of this phase, with elaborate representations in bright colors of formal gardens, pavilions, and villas.

* **vault** arched ceiling or roof
* **relief** method of sculpture in which the design is raised from the surface from which it is shaped

Emerging later in this century, another style returned Roman art to architectural illusionism. Smaller rectangular pictures were painted in the center of a wall, often with visual effects that suggested depth. Decorations in the palace of the emperor NERO in Rome featured elaborate plant forms intertwined with animals.

In the last years of the empire, the great creative period of wall painting was largely exhausted. Painters copied the styles, motifs, and ideas of earlier times. Much of the best work being done at that time was in the provinces* of the empire.

MOSAICS

Roman mosaics were closely related to Hellenistic painting because they were often copied from wall or panel paintings, which are now lost. The technique, however, was further developed by Roman artists. The tesserae, or tiny cubes, made of colored marble or other stone, tile, or glass, were refined in size and more varied in colors. A gold tessera was made by coating a glass cube with a thin layer of gold, which in turn was covered with glass to protect it from wear and tarnishing. Mosaic was used principally for floors, not only in private homes but in public buildings as well. Decorations of walls and vaults were also sometimes embellished with mosaics or made entirely of them. The Roman provinces made major contributions to the art of floor mosaics, particularly North Africa and Sicily. One of the most remarkable discoveries in the African style, from a fourth-century Sicilian villa, is known as the Great Hunt and measures 15 by nearly 200 feet. It shows the hunting and capture of wild animals for the Roman circuses, with such realistic details as a leopard sinking its teeth into the neck of a gazelle. Such narrative mosaics influenced the work in other provinces, including Spain, Syria, and Palestine. The tradition of wall and vault mosaics was carried forward in early Christian and Byzantine* church decoration.

SCULPTURE

Possibly the earliest Roman sculpture that has come to light reflects the influence of Etruscan work. It is a bronze figure of the she-wolf who, according to legend, nursed ROMULUS AND REMUS, the founders of Rome. It is thought to date from the sixth century B.C. Nevertheless, Greece became the strongest influence on Roman sculpture by way of the Greek colonies in southern Italy and in Asia Minor. Roman sculptors borrowed from the Greeks in technique and style and sometimes made outright copies. Statues excavated in Italy and presumed to be Roman may actually be the spoils of war, copies of Greek statues, or works by Greek sculptors made for Roman patrons. Marble, the material of choice for fine Greek sculpture, was first imported into Italy from quarries in the eastern Mediterranean. However, the best marble, discovered in the Augustan period, came from quarries in Liguria, in northwest Italy. Other materials used for sculpture were limestone, bronze, tufa (a volcanic rock), and terra-cotta (hard-baked clay like that

* **province** overseas area controlled by Rome

* **Byzantine** referring to the Eastern Christian Empire that was based in Constantinople

See
color plate 9,
vol. 2.

* **frieze** in sculpture, a decorated band around a structure

GREEK OR ROMAN?

Whether a work of art should be considered Greek or Roman is still debated by scholars. Among the works so questioned are three in the Vatican museums in Rome. The Apollo Belvedere, a marble statue of the Greek god, is a Roman copy of a Greek original in bronze. Also in the Vatican is a headless and limbless work called the Belvedere Torso, made in the first century B.C. by a Greek sculptor for a Roman patron. Laocoön and His Sons (a marble sculpture of a Trojan priest and his two sons being crushed by serpents) is the work of three Greek sculptors for an imperial Roman patron in the first century A.D.

* **sarcophagi** ornamental coffins, usually made of stone

used to make pottery). The taste of wealthy collectors of sculpture, however, favored whatever appeared to be the most "Greek," whether or not it was actually from Greece. Therefore, marble was most favored.

During the years of the Roman Republic, families often commissioned sculpture to be placed on tombs, with portraits of family dignitaries on friezes* or in the round. Such use of images had not been customary in classical Greece. Thus Roman sculptors made an important original contribution—they portrayed the individual faithfully, whereas the Greek sculptor aimed at creating an idealization of the human figure. Later, during the Roman Empire, there were highly original Roman sculptures that honored rulers and represented both history and propaganda. An example is the Column of TRAJAN in Rome. The monument celebrates that emperor's conquest of Dacia (modern Romania) in the early 100s A.D. Spiraling around the marble column, nearly 100 feet in height, is a continuous frieze depicting, in realistic detail, episodes of the Dacian campaign against the barbarians. Trajan is always the focal point and shown as the prime strategist and master of the conquest.

Religion, represented by the gods and goddesses, was also a common theme. A bronze statuette (about 20 inches high), found in Herculaneum and dated to the first century B.C., depicts the dual deity Isis-Fortuna. Details are drawn from the Egyptian goddess Isis and the Roman goddess Fortuna. This superb work from two very different sources of inspiration was probably used for worship in an Isis cult. A six-foot marble statue of the emperor AUGUSTUS, wearing armor over his toga, was found in the villa of the emperor's wife, Livia, near Rome. Dated to the reign of TIBERIUS in the first century A.D., it is believed to be a copy, made as a memento for Livia, of a bronze statue that was cast during the reign of Augustus. A small cupid and dolphin beside the right leg is a reference to the goddess Venus, and on the breastplate are relief figures of Apollo and Diana, who, according to Roman belief, gave favor to Augustus's naval victory over Mark Antony and Cleopatra in 31 B.C.

In the second and third centuries A.D., wealthy Roman citizens began buying carved marble sarcophagi* to contain the bodies of their deceased family members inside the tomb. Workshops specializing in such sculpture emerged in the larger cities of the empire, especially near the marble quarries. The carvers used a great variety of motifs, decorated with subjects from Greek mythology, and sometimes identifying the deceased with a particular Greek hero. Other themes were drawn from daily life, battle scenes, or cults such as those of DIONYSUS and of MITHRAS. Another favorite was the mythical hero HERACLES, who visited HADES and returned to the mortal world. Among the finest surviving funereal sculptures is the Ludovisi Battle Sarcophagus, which dates to the A.D. 200s. Rising above a tangle of fighting troops and barbarians is the triumphant figure of the victorious young leader on horseback.

GEMS. In antiquity, precious stones were thought to have magical and medicinal powers, and they were used as ornaments and as seals. The Etruscans used the scarab (beetle) as a model for seals and gems, and the Romans followed that tradition. There was a wide choice of

* **imperial** pertaining to an emperor or empire

subjects for gems in the years of the republic and later in the imperial* court. The cameo, with decoration or figures in relief, was highly prized. The emperor Claudius commissioned a large cameo of sardonyx, an orange-red mineral, showing a scene of his triumphal invasion of Britain in A.D. 43, during which he declared Britain a province of the Roman Empire. (*See also* **Architecture, Greek; Architecture, Roman; Art, Greek; Crafts and Craftsmanship; Cults; Gems and Jewelry; Sculpture, Greek; Sculpture, Roman.**)

ARTEMIS

* **nymph** in classical mythology, one of the lesser goddesses of nature

In Greek mythology, Artemis was the patron goddess of hunting and the protector of children and wild animals. These roles emphasized her strong connection with nature. She is often portrayed wandering through forests armed with her bow and arrows, and accompanied by a group of nymphs*. In Roman mythology, Artemis was known as Diana.

The daughter of ZEUS and the goddess Leto, Artemis was the twin sister of APOLLO. Artemis and Apollo were fiercely loyal to their mother. Niobe, the queen of Thebes, proclaimed herself superior to Artemis's mother because she had many sons and daughters while Leto had only two children. Artemis and Apollo took Niobe's boast as an insult to their mother and killed all of Niobe's children. Niobe's grief at her loss was so intense that she turned to stone. The gods carried her to a mountainside where the craggy stone remained, flowing with tears.

Artemis prized her solitude and occasionally punished those who intruded. Actaeon, a great hunter, once accidentally came upon Artemis while she was bathing. The goddess was so distressed that Actaeon had seen her naked that she turned him into a deer. Actaeon's hunting dogs then attacked and killed the deer.

The mighty hunter, Orion, faced a similar fate. When Orion attempted to seduce Artemis (or perhaps one of her companions), Artemis sent a scorpion to sting his heel. Upon his death, Orion was placed in the sky as a constellation. Artemis made sure the scorpion received the same honor.

In another myth, the Greek leader AGAMEMNON shot one of Artemis's sacred deer just as his army was about to set sail for Troy. As a protector of animals, Artemis became furious and stopped the wind from blowing so that the Greek ships were forced to delay their departure. She refused to restore the wind until Agamemnon sacrificed his daughter.

ASCLEPIUS

* **underworld** kingdom of the dead; also called Hades

Asclepius, the son of APOLLO, was the Greek god of healing. According to legend, he challenged the authority of ZEUS (ruler of the gods) and HADES (lord of the underworld*) by saving too many people from death. Because of Asclepius's curative power, people frequently sought his help.

The worship of Asclepius spread throughout Greece and later to Rome, and many temples were built in his honor. The most important

75

temple was at EPIDAURUS in the Peloponnese in southern Greece. The ruins there include a small building and altar dating from the late 500s B.C.

People often came to the temples of Asclepius seeking cures for various illnesses. First, these sufferers washed themselves with water from a natural spring near the temple. Then, they dressed in plain white robes—without rings, belts, or even shoes. Next, the worshipers made an offering to the god, usually fruit or cakes. Then they went to sleep in a special room. They believed that the god visited and healed them as they slept.

Accounts of the healing experience survive in temple inscriptions and also in literature. These accounts describe Asclepius as a bearded figure who appeared to patients in their dreams or when they were in a transitional state between waking and sleeping. In some cases, Asclepius used medications, while in others he performed surgical procedures. One report details how the god cut open a man's stomach, removed an abscess, and then stitched him up again. Often the cures involved sacred snakes that licked the patients in their sleep. The symbol for Asclepius—the *caduceus,* a staff or wand with one or two serpents wrapped around it—became the symbol for the medical profession. (*See also* **Hippocrates.**)

ASIA MINOR

* strait narrow channel that connects two bodies of water

See map in Geography and Geology, Mediterranean (vol. 2).

Asia Minor, also called Anatolia, is a large rectangular-shaped peninsula that straddles Europe and Asia. Often referred to as the "mother of nations," Asia Minor was the home of several great ancient civilizations, including the Hittites in about 1300 B.C. and the Lydians in about 700 B.C. Here, too, stood the famous cities of TROY, EPHESUS, and PERGAMUM. Today the nation of Turkey occupies the area once known as Asia Minor.

Asia Minor was bordered by three seas—the Black Sea on the north, the AEGEAN SEA on the west, and the MEDITERRANEAN SEA on the south—and separated from Europe by the straits* of the Bosporus and the Dardanelles. Asia Minor's geographic location at the crossroads of Europe and Asia provided great opportunities for trade. At the same time, the region's lack of natural defenses made it an easy target for invasion.

Beginning in the 900s B.C., the Greeks established several colonies along the western coast of Asia Minor and introduced their culture to the region. They later established trading relations with the Lydians, who allowed the Greek colonies to govern themselves even though the colonies lay within the Lydian empire. In the 500s B.C., Cyrus the Great of Persia conquered the region and ended the independent status of the Greek colonies. This and other actions by the Persians eventually led to war between Persia and Greece. In the PERSIAN WARS, (499–479 B.C.), the Greeks defeated King Xerxes and drove the Persians from the Greek cities.

In 334 B.C., ALEXANDER THE GREAT of MACEDONIA won the rest of Asia Minor for the Greeks when his armies swept in and seized the region from the Persians. In the aftermath of Alexander's conquest, Greek culture spread throughout Asia Minor in a process known as Hellenization. Following Alexander's death in 323 B.C., Asia Minor broke into several small states, and civil war raged in the region for many years.

Rome conquered Greece in 146 B.C., and Asia Minor became part of the Roman empire a few years later. The Romans reunited the various states in the region and formed the imperial* province of Asia. The Roman province enjoyed great prosperity. The apostle Paul, a native of the city of Tarsus in the southern part of Asia Minor, made the region an early center of Christianity. After A.D. 395, Asia Minor became part of the Eastern Roman Empire, also known as the Byzantine Empire. The region continued to prosper until the early 600s, when the first of many Arab and Turkish invasions began. (*See also* **Colonies, Greek; Rome, History of: Roman Empire, Christian Era; Trade, Greek.**)

* **imperial** pertaining to an emperor or empire

ASSYRIA

Assyria was an ancient kingdom on the upper reaches of the Tigris River. (The area is now divided between the countries of Turkey and Iraq.) At its height in the mid-600s B.C., the great Assyrian empire extended from the lowlands of SYRIA in the west, to the mountains of Persia (present-day Iran) in the east. The name *Assyria*—Greek for "country of Ashur"—came from Ashur (Assur), the name of both a god and the early capital city.

Arriving in the region about 2000 B.C., the Assyrians had formed a state by 1300 B.C. They began a period of expansion about 1000 B.C., building an ever-growing empire by a series of conquests. In 612 B.C., however, the Babylonians and Medes overwhelmed the Assyrians and destroyed their empire, including their last capital city, Nineveh.

Assyria became a battleground in the 300s B.C., first between the Persians and the Greeks under ALEXANDER THE GREAT, and then between the Romans and the Parthians. Although Alexander incorporated the region into his empire, it broke away after his death. The Roman emperor TRAJAN claimed Assyria as a Roman province* in A.D. 116, but his successor, HADRIAN, abandoned it a few years later. The Roman emperors who followed tried to regain control of Assyria. Instead, the country fell into the hands of the Parthians in the late A.D. 200s and then the Sasanians gained control. Assyria remained under Sasanian control until the Arabs conquered the region in the A.D. 600s. (*See also* **Persian Empire; Rome, History of: Roman Empire.**)

* **province** overseas area controlled by Rome

Astronomy is the study of the heavenly bodies—the sun, moon, planets, and stars. Astrology is the belief that the position and movement of those heavenly bodies influence life on earth. Today, astronomy is a science, while astrology is considered an occult, or magical, practice. The two were not always sharply separated, however. In ancient times, they often were closely linked and regarded with equal respect.

Both astronomy and astrology had their roots in the skywatching practices of the ancient Babylonians and other civilizations of the ancient

* **celestial** relating to the heavens

Near East. Babylonian astronomers watched as the heavenly bodies seemed to rise, move across the sky, and set. They saw that these motions occurred in cycles or patterns that were repeated daily, monthly, yearly, or at longer intervals. From their observations, they created orderly systems of timekeeping. Their calendars advised people when to plant and sow crops and when to hold religious celebrations. Certain celebrations were linked to celestial* events, such as solar and lunar eclipses or the longest and shortest days of the year. The Babylonians also began the practice of giving names from myth or legend to various constellations, or groups of stars. Greek and Roman astronomers later adopted this practice.

A SCIENCE OF THE SKIES. The early Greeks watched the sky very closely. Greek farmers used the positions of the sun and stars to plan and organize agricultural chores for each season. Greek sailors used the stars to guide their navigation. The Greeks' main contribution to astronomy, however, was their effort to explain what they saw. They did more than merely observe and record the movements of the heavenly bodies. They sought to understand *why* and *how* those bodies moved in such an orderly and predictable way. In doing so, the Greeks transformed stargazing into a science.

Greek astronomers spent little time wondering about what the planets were made of or how they came into existence. Instead, they wanted to find a logical, orderly system for predicting the movements of the sun, moon, and planets. They looked to mathematics and geometry to help discover such a system. In the 300s B.C., a mathematician named Eudoxus proposed a theory about the movement of the sun, the moon, and the planets. Eudoxus suggested that each heavenly body was fastened to the inside of a series of concentric spheres, with the Earth at the center. The spinning of the spheres made the planets move. Eudoxus's theory failed to explain all celestial movements, however, and other Greek thinkers tackled the problem.

Around 270 B.C., the mathematician and astronomer Aristarchus correctly suggested that the sun, not the Earth, is at the center of the planetary system. He also suggested that the Earth moves around the sun like the other planets, and that it rotates, or spins, on an axis. Most ancient thinkers did not believe that the Earth moved, so they rejected Aristarchus's ideas.

More than a century later, in about 150 B.C., the astronomer Hipparchus developed a theory of celestial movement based on the geometry of circles. He suggested that the sun and the moon moved around the Earth in circular paths, or orbits. To explain why celestial movements are not perfectly regular or symmetrical, Hipparchus theorized that the Earth was not exactly at the center of the orbits, or that the orbits themselves moved in complicated patterns. Hipparchus also compiled a star catalog that listed 850 stars and gave the location of each in the sky.

The most influential astronomer of the ancient world was PTOLEMY, who lived and worked in the A.D. 100s. A keen observer, Ptolemy accepted Hipparchus's theory and used his own observations to expand it.

OUTLAWING ASTROLOGY

Ancient Romans were free to study astrology, but professional astrologers were not always free to cast horoscopes. During the time of the Roman Empire, it was treason to cast the emperor's horoscope, for to "know" his time of death might prove a political advantage. Astrologers were particularly feared during times of internal strife and disorder. Roman authorities drove them out of Rome and the Italian provinces at least nine times between 139 B.C. and A.D. 93. Each time, however, they returned to satisfy the Romans' love of divination.

Astrology, or the belief that the sun, moon, planets, and stars influence human affairs, was widespread among the ancient Greeks and Romans. Even great astronomers and mathematicians such as Ptolemy and Hipparchus believed that the movement of the planets foretold future events. This altar, currently in the Louvre Museum in Paris, was used in ancient astrological practices.

He developed an elaborate theory that explained celestial movement as a series of interlocking circular orbits. Ptolemy's system was detailed and difficult to understand, and it was based on some inaccurate notions, including the idea that the sun revolves around the Earth. Nevertheless, the system enabled astronomers to account for and predict the movement of all known heavenly bodies at any moment. Ptolemy also produced a star catalog that listed over 1,000 stars. His view of the universe was accepted by astronomers throughout the Mediterranean world, and it remained the foundation of astronomy for more than 1,000 years after his death.

FORETELLING THE FUTURE.   One reason that the sun, the moon, the planets, and the stars attracted so much attention in the ancient world was that these heavenly bodies were believed to have an affect on human lives and earthly events. This notion, the basis of astrology, was widespread among ancient peoples of the Near East. Beginning in the 300s B.C., astrology spread throughout the Greek and Roman civilizations.

In ancient Greece, astrology was based on the belief that the heavens and the Earth were connected in some mysterious way. This idea eventually had a great effect on Greek culture and philosophy. For example, the followers of STOICISM, who believed that each person's destiny is determined from birth, supported the astrological notion that celestial movement shapes human lives. The astronomers Hipparchus and Ptolemy also believed in astrology.

Astrology took many forms. Among the most popular and well-known aspects of astrology was divination, or fortune-telling. Astrologers most commonly performed divination by calculating, or casting, horoscopes. A horoscope supposedly revealed the pattern of a person's life based on the position of the stars and planets at the time of his or her birth. Astrologers often were called upon to cast horoscopes for newborn royal or noble infants.

Casting horoscopes required considerable astronomical knowledge and mathematical skill. As a result, many astrologers also were astronomers. Astrology actually may have helped to create the science of astronomy. It certainly helped keep astronomy alive, since both astronomy and astrology used the same framework of observation and theories about the heavens.

Astrology as a means of foretelling the future was widely accepted among the ancient Romans, who also believed strongly in OMENS and ORACLES. By the 100s B.C., astrological ideas influenced all levels of Roman society. Astrology even played a part in affairs of state. TIBERIUS and other Roman emperors frequently relied upon the advice of astrologers when faced with important decisions.

With the rise of CHRISTIANITY in the Roman Empire, the importance of astrology declined. Christians regarded divination as a form of pagan MAGIC and therefore unchristian. The Christian church banned divination, and Christian emperors enforced this ban. In A.D. 357, the emperor Constantius II made fortune-telling a crime punishable by death, thus ending the widespread practice of astrology. It survived as a series of superstitious beliefs and practices until its rebirth in later centuries. (*See also* **Science**.)

ATHENA

* **patron** special guardian, protector, or supporter

* **hero** in mythology, a person of great strength or ability, often descended from a god

* **trident** three-pronged spear, similar to a pitchfork

See color plate 1, vol. 2.

Athena was the Greek goddess of war, the patron* of arts and crafts, and the goddess and symbol of wisdom. Sometimes known as Pallas Athena or simply Pallas, Athena offered special protection to cities. For this reason, temples to Athena were built in cities throughout the Greek world. The Romans later adopted the goddess and called her Minerva.

The people of ancient MYCENAE were probably the first to worship Athena. According to ancient myths, she was the daughter of ZEUS and Metis. Zeus had heard a prophecy that Metis, whom he had married, would have a son who would overthrow his father. Zeus therefore turned Metis into a fly and swallowed her. Some time later, Zeus complained of a terrible headache and ordered one of the gods to split his head open with an ax. When this was done, Athena sprang from Zeus's head—fully grown and dressed in armor, ready for battle.

As the goddess of war, Athena often helped Greek warriors and intervened in their battles. However, she preferred to settle disputes peacefully through reason rather than by force. When battle did occur, Athena acted with justice and skill—in contrast to Ares, the god of war, who often flew into a fury. In the *ILIAD*, the Greek poet HOMER described how Athena helped the Greeks win victory in the Trojan War. In the *ODYSSEY*, she guides Odysseus to safety. She also came to the aid of an assortment of Greek heroes* who found themselves in difficult situations.

As a patron of the arts, Athena inspired many great works, including the construction of several important buildings. She was the patron of spinning, weaving, embroidery, and similar crafts and household activities. According to one story, the princess Arachne challenged Athena to a weaving contest after Arachne boasted of her skill in that craft. When Arachne's work turned out to be as intricate and beautiful as Athena's, the goddess flew into a rage and tore up the weaving. Arachne became so frightened that she hung herself. Athena took pity on Arachne and turned her into a spider whose descendants would endlessly weave and hang from their own thread.

Athena had a long association with the city of ATHENS. The city was named after the goddess and Athenians worshiped her as their patron. According to legend, both Athena and POSEIDON (the god of the sea), wanted to be honored as patron of the city. To settle the issue, the two gods had a contest to see who could provide the most useful gift to the city. Poseidon stuck his trident* into rocks, causing a saltwater spring to burst forth. Athena planted an olive tree. The people of Athens considered the olive tree the better gift because it provided food and oil, and they chose Athena as their patron. The Athenians built a temple on the ACROPOLIS to honor the goddess. This temple, called the PARTHENON, became the greatest shrine to Athena in the Greek world. The Athenians also held an athletic competition, the Panathenaic Games, every year in her honor.

When depicted in works of art, Athena generally appears fully clad in armor—with helmet, spear, and breastplate. She carries a round shield with an image of the monster MEDUSA, whom PERSEUS killed with Athena's help. Athena is also frequently shown with an owl, her sacred animal. (*See also* **Art, Greek; Divinities; Literature, Greek.**)

ATHENS

* **city-state** independent state consisting of a city and its surrounding territory

* **archon** in ancient Greece, the highest office of state

* **aristocracy** rule by the nobility or privileged upper class

Named after the goddess ATHENA, Athens was one of the most important city-states* of the ancient Greek world. It was located on the plain of ATTICA, about three miles from the AEGEAN SEA, and became renowned for its great achievements in art, literature, and philosophy. The city also developed an early form of democracy, which became an inspiration to people in later ages. Today, Athens is the capital and largest city of Greece, and the administrative, economic, and cultural center of the country.

EARLY HISTORY. Athens was inhabited as early as 3000 B.C. By the 1200s B.C., its inhabitants had built protective walls around the ACROPOLIS, the rocky hill in the center of the settlement. During that period, Athens flourished as a center of Mycenaean culture, which was based at the city of MYCENAE. Invasions by the DORIANS between 1100 and 950 B.C. destroyed many city-states and brought an end to the Mycenaean civilization. Athens, however, survived and developed a distinctive culture of its own.

According to tradition, sometime before the 700s B.C., the legendary hero THESEUS united Athens and the surrounding communities into a single city-state and established a monarchy. A succession of kings ruled the city-state until the 600s B.C., when a group of officials known as archons* replaced the monarchy. The Athenian aristocracy*, which

Even today, one can still appreciate the beauty of the architecture of ancient Athens. It was during the Golden Age of Pericles, in the 400s B.C., that some of the most magnificent monuments, temples, and buildings were constructed in Athens. The Temple of Athena Nike is shown here.

was part of the citizens' assembly known as the Ecclesia, elected three archons. The number of archons was later increased to nine. The aristocracy also controlled an advisory council called the Areopagus.

As the power of the Athenian aristocracy increased, the lives of the lower classes became increasingly difficult. This led to a series of social crises in the 600s B.C. In 621 B.C., hoping to restore order, the ruler DRACO established a code of laws for Athens. The Draconian Laws failed, however, because they contained extremely severe punishments for relatively minor crimes. In fact, most crimes were punishable by death. Twenty-seven years later, the chief archon, SOLON, introduced several reforms to end the unrest. Solon abolished serfdom* and modified Draco's harsh laws. He established a council of 400 representatives from the various tribal groups in the region. He also made the Ecclesia independent of the archons. By distributing power more equally among different groups of Athenian citizens, Solon laid the foundation for a democratic form of government.

In 560 B.C., the popular leader Pisistratus seized power in Athens and established himself as tyrant*. During the successive reigns of Pisistratus and his two sons, Athens became the political, economic, cultural, and religious center of the region. As Athens's power increased, the city-state began to extend its control beyond the region. Then, in 510 B.C., a new struggle for power erupted between those who favored a return to rule by archons and those who favored democracy. Those favoring democracy won. CLEISTHENES, a statesman and supporter of democracy, established ten new tribes based on political rather than social divisions. This helped decrease the power of the aristocracy. Cleisthenes also reorganized the ruling council to include citizens from all parts of Attica, the eastern region of central Greece. These reforms created the first true democracy in Athens.

RISE TO GREATNESS. The outbreak of the PERSIAN WARS in 500 B.C. led to the rise of Athens as the most powerful city-state in Greece. Athens had a significant role in the wars and won several major battles against the Persians, including a decisive army victory at MARATHON in 490 B.C. To defend itself against the Persian navy, Athens strengthened its naval force. Athens also helped organize an alliance—the Delian League—for mutual defense against Persia. The alliance, which consisted of cities on the islands in the Aegean Sea as well as on the coast of Asia Minor, eventually came under the control of Athens. The Athenians used the tribute* paid by members of the league to glorify their city.

By the end of the Persian Wars, Athens had become the strongest city-state in Greece. Moreover, it had transformed its control of the Delian League into control of an empire that consisted of more than 200 city-states. Under the leadership of Cimon and then PERICLES, Athens focused its attention on repairing the damage caused by the wars. The era of Pericles was particularly important. Pericles set a tone for excellence. He had many interests—the arts, science, philosophy, and religion—and he called Athens "the school of Hellas" (the school of the Greek world). He was able to inspire the people of Athens to strive to make their city-state the greatest in Greece, telling them that "the admiration of the present and succeeding ages will be ours."

* **serfdom** condition of servitude in which peasants owe service and loyalty to a lord

* **tyrant** absolute ruler

* **tribute** payment made to a dominant power or local government

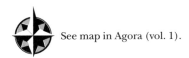

See map in Agora (vol. 1).

* **plague** highly contagious, widespread, and often fatal disease

* **oligarchy** rule by a few people

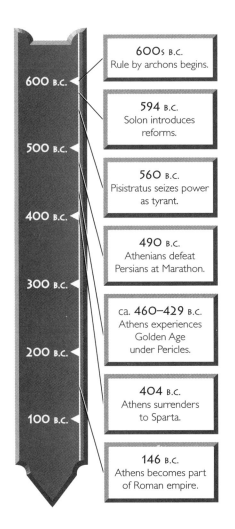

600s B.C.
Rule by archons begins.

600 B.C.

594 B.C.
Solon introduces reforms.

500 B.C.

560 B.C.
Pisistratus seizes power as tyrant.

400 B.C.

490 B.C.
Athenians defeat Persians at Marathon.

300 B.C.

ca. 460–429 B.C.
Athens experiences Golden Age under Pericles.

200 B.C.

404 B.C.
Athens surrenders to Sparta.

100 B.C.

146 B.C.
Athens becomes part of Roman empire.

Pericles' ambitious plans for Athens led to a "golden age" of Athenian civilization, a period during which democracy, art, and literature flourished and the economy of the city prospered. During this period, the Athenians constructed magnificent temples, including the PARTHENON on the Acropolis. Individuals such as the sculptor PHIDIAS and the playwrights AESCHYLUS, SOPHOCLES, EURIPIDES, and ARISTOPHANES created masterpieces of art and literature. Two great historians emerged—HERODOTUS, who traveled widely, recorded the customs of faraway lands, and related the history of the Persian Wars; and THUCYDIDES, who wrote a brilliant and detailed account of the PELOPONNESIAN WAR. The philosopher SOCRATES helped establish Athens as the intellectual center of the Greek world. Athens also prospered economically because of trade and the resources from the far-flung regions of the empire.

As Athens enjoyed this period of greatness, rivalries increased with other city-states, particularly with SPARTA in southern Greece. The Spartans distrusted Athenian democracy and resented the spread of Athenian power. The hostilities between Athens and Sparta increased, finally erupting in 431 B.C. in the Peloponnesian War. The following year a plague* spread through Athens, killing many of its inhabitants. Then, in 429 B.C., Pericles died.

The Peloponnesian War dragged on for many years with neither side gaining a conclusive advantage. However, in 413 B.C., Athens received a crushing defeat at SYRACUSE, a Greek colony on the island of Sicily. Athens lost much of its empire after this disaster, as many city-states joined the Spartan side. The war continued until 404 B.C. when Athens finally surrendered to Sparta. Utterly defeated, Athens had lost its empire as well as its supremacy in the Greek world.

YEARS OF CHANGE AND NEW THREATS. In the aftermath of the Peloponnesian War, the Spartans forced the Athenians to replace the democratic government of Athens with an oligarchy* known as the rule of the Thirty Tyrants. The Spartans also destroyed what remained of the Athenian fleet and demolished the Long Walls, a series of fortified walls that linked Athens with its seaport of Piraeus.

Despite these losses, Athens recovered quickly as conflicts between other city-states forced Sparta to focus its attention elsewhere. By 403 B.C., the Athenians had ousted the government of the Thirty Tyrants. Within ten years, they had rebuilt their navy and the Long Walls. Athens then allied itself with several city-states, thus creating a balance of power in Greece. Although Athens had revived itself, it never regained its former greatness.

During the 300s B.C., the rising power of King PHILIP II of MACEDONIA posed a serious threat to Greece. Athens resisted Philip's initial offensives into Greece. However, after the Macedonians crushed the Greeks at the Battle of Chaeronea in 338 B.C., Athens was forced to join a new alliance controlled by Macedonia. Athens regained some of its independence under Philip's son, Alexander III (the Great). However, an attempt to overthrow Macedonian rule after Alexander's death resulted in a major Greek defeat that marked the end of Athens's role as a military power.

Athens remained an important center of culture and learning in the 300s and early 200s B.C. During these years, two of Greece's greatest philosophers, PLATO and ARISTOTLE, taught in Athens, and the schools of philosophy known as Epicureanism and STOICISM arose in the city. However, as HELLENISTIC CULTURE spread throughout Alexander's empire, other cities, such as ALEXANDRIA in Egypt, surpassed Athens as cultural centers. Even so, Athens continued to command respect for its past achievements. Many people, including foreign kings, visited the city to marvel at its art and architecture, to listen to its philosophers, and to honor its glorious history.

ROMAN RULE. In 146 B.C., Rome gained control of Greece, and Athens became part of the Roman province* of Macedonia. At first, Athens retained some independence and suffered little from Roman rule. However, in 86 B.C. the Roman general SULLA sacked the city because of its support for a king from Asia Minor, Mithradates VI of Pontus, who was fighting against Rome. As a result, Athens lost all political independence, and its economy declined as well.

* **province** overseas area controlled by Rome

Despite these losses, Athens continued to be an intellectual center throughout much of the Roman period. In the A.D. 100s, Athens experienced an economic revival, but in the next century barbarian tribes sacked the city and the economy faltered once again.

Beginning in about A.D. 300, Athens began to decline as a center of Greek culture. With the adoption of Christianity as the official religion of the Roman Empire, the city's pagan* temples were converted into Christian churches, and its religious heritage faded in importance. In addition, the city of CONSTANTINOPLE became the largest and most important city in the eastern Roman world, replacing Athens as the preeminent center of culture and learning. Athens became a small provincial city, its past glory visible only in its monuments and buildings on the Acropolis. (*See also* Cities, Greek; Democracy, Greek; Golden Age of Greece; Government, Greek; Greece, History of; Polis; Tyrants, Greek.)

* **pagan** referring to a belief in more than one god; non-Christian

ATHLETICS

See *Games, Greek.*

ATTICA

Attica is a region in the eastern part of central Greece. Its ancient capital of ATHENS became an important city-state, one that dominated much of early Greek history.

Attica is a triangular peninsula about 1,000 square miles in area and cut off from the rest of Greece by mountains and the sea. Its landscape is shaped by four mountain ranges. Between the mountains lie three large plains where the cities of Athens, Eleusis, and MARATHON emerged during ancient times. The peninsula had little arable* farmland, although Attica did become famous for its olive oil. However, its most valuable resources—marble, silver, lead, and clay for pottery—came from its mountains and hills.

* **arable** suitable for plowing and producing crops

According to tradition, ancient Attica consisted of twelve independent communities that were constantly at war with one another. The legendary king THESEUS was said to have united these communities into a single state, which had its power base in Athens. In reality, this unification was probably a slow and gradual process. By 700 B.C., Attica was unified under Athenian rule. All free men in Attica were considered citizens of Athens. They had organized themselves into four phylae, or tribes, each headed by a landowning family of the aristocracy*.

In 508 B.C., the statesman CLEISTHENES decided to break the power of these strong families by reorganizing Attica's citizens on a more democratic basis. He established ten new phylae based on geography rather than on family connections. Each phyle contained a mix of people from the city (Athens), the seacoast, and the countryside. The new system gave representation to more people in each area, and was, therefore, more democratic. As the power of Athens increased, the independent status of Attica decreased. By the 400s B.C., Attica was dominated by the Athenian city-state*, and its history became a part of the history of Athens.

* **aristocracy** referring to the privileged upper class

* **city-state** independent state consisting of a city and its surrounding territory

ATTILA

See *Huns.*

AUGUR

An augur, a type of priest, had a special official function in ancient Rome. The augur's main responsibility was to observe natural phenomena and to determine whether the gods approved or disapproved of a planned public action. The Romans generally consulted augurs before taking important steps, such as founding a city, fighting a battle, building a temple, or passing a law. Augurs might even be consulted before a marriage.

Originally, Rome had three official augurs, but this number gradually increased to sixteen. They remained in office for life. After 104 B.C. the augurs were chosen by popular election. Their role in Roman society gave them a great deal of power and prestige. The Roman statesman CICERO called augurs "the highest and most responsible authorities in the state."

Augurs relied on omens, or signs from the gods. The most important omens were those deliberately looked for, perhaps by observing the behavior of animals or the condition of an animal's internal organs. For example, an augur looking for a omen before a battle might observe a group of chickens. If the chickens ate in a certain way, this was considered a favorable sign for battle. Augurs also studied the flight patterns of birds and paid attention to lightning and thunder. Omens not deliberately sought, such as a sudden storm or the appearance of animals sacred to the gods, were often considered unfavorable. If the omen was deemed significant, the Senate called in the augurs for interpretation. The augurs might interpret these incidents as signs of an impending terrible event, such as the death of a powerful individual.

Augurs usually looked for omens before every important public activity. People did not have to accept their advice, but most Romans considered it reckless to ignore signs from the gods. The term *augury,* derived from the word *augur,* is used today to mean the practice of using omens or happenings to predict the future. (*See also* **Religion, Roman.**)

AUGUSTINE, ST.

A.D. 354–430
EARLY CHRISTIAN BISHOP

* **philosophy** study of ideas, including science

* **theology** study of the nature of God and of religious truth

* **pagan** referring to a belief in more than one god; non-Christian

* **rhetoric** art of using words effectively in speaking or writing

* **heretical** characterized by a belief that is contrary to church doctrine

Although his mother was a Christian, St. Augustine did not convert to Christianity until his early 30s. In his autobiography, *Confessions,* Augustine wrote about his early life and the reasons for his conversion. The book had a tremendous influence on later Christian writers. This fresco of St. Augustine from the A.D. 600s is in the Lateran Palace in Rome.

Augustine (Aurelius Augustinus) was bishop of Hippo, a town in North Africa. Through his writings, Augustine became one of the most significant figures of the early Christian church. His works include texts on philosophy* and religious education as well as a major autobiography. His books about theology* greatly influenced other Christian writers.

Augustine was born in North Africa into a family of mixed faiths. His father was a pagan* and his mother was a Christian. As a teenager, he traveled to CARTHAGE to study rhetoric* at the university. During this period, he showed little interest in Christianity, and instead learned about various other beliefs. From CICERO, he learned about the importance of true wisdom, and began to follow Manicheanism—an eastern religion concerned with the conflict between goodness and evil in the world. He saw Manicheanism as the way to gain wisdom.

At the same time, Augustine pursued a career as a teacher of rhetoric. He taught at Carthage and Rome and, in 384, moved to Milan in northern Italy. In Milan, he heard the brilliant preaching of Bishop Ambrose, who later became St. Ambrose. Ambrose taught that evil is merely the absence of good, not a force in its own right. Augustine was impressed by Ambrose's arguments and, at the age of 31, decided to become a Christian.

The conversion to Christianity affected Augustine deeply. He returned to Africa and was ordained as a priest in A.D. 391. Four years later, he became bishop of Hippo. There he turned his skill and knowledge to writing. Unlike many thinkers of his time who wrote in Greek, Augustine wrote in Latin. Nevertheless, his works became some of the most influential in all of Western civilization.

His early works, produced before he became a priest, include *The Life of Happiness* and *On Free Will.* They take a thoughtful tone, comparing Christian ideas with those of other philosophies. Later, as a priest and then as a bishop, he focused more on issues that troubled the Christian church. Several of his books defend Christian belief against other systems that were considered heretical*, including the ideas of Manicheanism.

Augustine wrote *Confessions,* his autobiography, to provide guidance for others. His account of his own spiritual growth shows a deep understanding of himself and of human nature in general. Augustine also wrote about basic Christian beliefs in books such as *On Christian Doctrine.* Most famous, however, is a 22-volume work called *The City of God.* It contrasts life in an earthly city with life in the ideal city of heaven. The ideas he expressed about faith and politics include some of the most influential teachings of Christianity.

The City of God was written to support the Roman Church at a time of crisis. In A.D. 410, the Goths invaded the city of Rome. They brought with them their version of Christianity, known as Arianism. Augustine's passionate defense of Roman Christianity, however, helped to ensure its survival as the dominant church of western Europe. (*See also* **Christianity.**)

AUGUSTUS, CAESAR OCTAVIANUS

63 B.C.–A.D. 14
FIRST ROMAN EMPEROR

Caesar Augustus was the first emperor of Rome. A great statesman and administrator, Augustus brought order to the Roman world after a difficult period of civil war. He established an era of peace and prosperity known as the *Pax Romana,* or Roman peace, which lasted for over 200 years. During his reign, he helped to create the greatest and most powerful empire in the ancient world.

EARLY YEARS.   Born on September 23, 63 B.C., Augustus was the son of Gaius Octavius (a Roman senator) and Atia (a niece of Julius Caesar). Originally named Gaius Octavius after his father, he later took the name Gaius Julius Caesar Octavianus in honor of his great-uncle. The name Augustus came later, during his meteoric rise to power.

Caesar Octavianus Augustus had a long and distinguished career. In 44 B.C., at the age of 18, Octavian (as he was then known) was adopted by the Roman general Julius Caesar. After defeating Mark Antony at the Battle of Actium in 31 B.C., Octavian became the first emperor of the Roman Empire. He reigned for 45 years. This statue, known as the Augustus of Prima Porta, was sculpted in 19 B.C.

After his father's death in 59 B.C., his mother supervised his education and upbringing. His great-uncle, Julius Caesar, also took particular interest in the boy and, in his will, made him his heir since he had no legitimate male heir of his own. In 45 B.C., Octavius accompanied Caesar on a military campaign in SPAIN. When he returned, he was sent to Epirus in GREECE to study philosophy* and other subjects. His studies were cut short, however, by the assassination of Julius Caesar in 44 B.C. After learning that he had been named his great-uncle's heir, he changed his name to Gaius Julius Caesar Octavianus and returned to Rome to claim his inheritance. Octavian, as he became known at that time, also hoped to avenge Caesar's brutal death.

* philosophy study of ideas, including science

STRUGGLE FOR POWER.   Meanwhile, Marcus ANTONIUS (Mark Antony) had seized Caesar's property and aimed to be his political successor. Antony refused to yield to the 18-year-old Octavian and was determined to assume Caesar's power. Octavian sought help from the Roman Senate and the powerful statesman and orator CICERO. The Senate, anxious to limit Antony's power, recognized Octavian's claim and sought to use him as a weapon against Antony. Octavian and his supporters defeated Antony at the Battle of Mutina in northern Italy in 43 B.C.

Octavian became CONSUL after Antony's defeat, but the Senate, thinking the young man was now under its control, began to ignore him. Realizing that he needed strong allies to achieve his goals, he turned to the defeated Antony and to Marcus Lepidus, another friend of Julius Caesar. The three men assembled their armies and marched on Rome in late 43 B.C. They established the Second Triumvirate, a government of three leaders who shared power equally. Soon after establishing the triumvirate, they killed many of their political enemies, including Cicero. With their power in Rome secure, Octavian and Antony took their armies to Greece, where their armies defeated the troops of Cassius Longinus and Marcus BRUTUS, Caesar's assassins, at the Battle of Philippi in 42 B.C.

His great-uncle's death avenged, Octavian returned to Rome to rule Italy, while Antony went to Egypt to rule the eastern Roman provinces. In 41 B.C., Antony's brother Lucius and his wife Fulvia led a revolt in Italy against Octavian. The uprising, because it was centered around the town of Perusia (modern Perugia), became known as the Perusine War. The struggle strained relations between Octavian and Antony. The two men met in southern Italy in 40 B.C. to settle their differences and, soon after, Antony married Octavian's sister Octavia to strengthen the relationship.

In 37 B.C., Octavian, Antony, and Lepidus renewed the triumvirate and divided the empire among themselves. Octavian ruled Italy and the western provinces*; Antony ruled the eastern ones; and Lepidus ruled Africa. Octavian now focused his efforts on consolidating his power in Italy. In 36 B.C., Octavian's boyhood friend and staunchest supporter, Marcus Agrippa, defeated Sextus Pompeius, son of Gneaus Pompeius (Pompey the Great). Sextus Pompeius, a powerful naval commander, had controlled the islands of Sicily and Sardinia. His defeat eliminated a major rival for power in Italy. Because Lepidus had supported Pompeius,

* province overseas area controlled by Rome

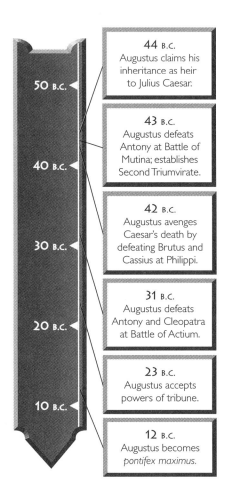

50 B.C.

44 B.C.
Augustus claims his inheritance as heir to Julius Caesar.

43 B.C.
Augustus defeats Antony at Battle of Mutina; establishes Second Triumvirate.

40 B.C.

42 B.C.
Augustus avenges Caesar's death by defeating Brutus and Cassius at Philippi.

30 B.C.

31 B.C.
Augustus defeats Antony and Cleopatra at Battle of Actium.

20 B.C.

23 B.C.
Augustus accepts powers of tribune.

10 B.C.

12 B.C.
Augustus becomes *pontifex maximus*.

Octavian stripped him of his powers in the triumvirate. As a result, the Roman empire now had only two rulers—Octavian in the west and Antony in the east.

Octavian began preparing to confront Antony. Antony had angered many Romans because of his relationship with the queen of Egypt, CLEOPATRA. Octavian took advantage of this anger to gain further support against Antony. In 31 B.C., the Roman Senate declared war against Cleopatra, and in September of that year, Octavian's forces met those of Antony and Cleopatra at Actium, in Greece. Octavian succeeded in defeating his enemy in the great sea battle that followed. Antony committed suicide the following year, and Octavian became the sole ruler, thus technically ending the period known as the Roman Republic and beginning the period known as the Roman Empire.

THE PRINCIPATE. Octavian hoped to avoid the fate of Julius Caesar, who had made enemies when he established a military dictatorship. Octavian had no intention of truly relinquishing power, but he made it seem that he would. Following the defeat of Antony, Octavian declared that the Roman Republic and its democratic government should be restored, and he offered to turn over control of his provinces to the Senate. His supporters in the Senate protested and urged to him to remain in control. Octavian agreed, and over the next few years, the Senate gave him various titles in honor of his loyalty and personal sacrifice to Rome. These titles included *imperator* (commander), from which the word *emperor* is derived; *princeps* (first citizen), from which the word *prince* is derived; and *augustus* (revered). Thereafter, Octavian became known as Caesar Augustus. The government he created was called the Principate.

Despite the restoration of the republic, Augustus was firmly in control of the empire. His control of the Roman armies, in particular, gave him much power. In 23 B.C., Augustus gave up the position of consul in order to allow more senators to hold the office and thus assure Romans that he was sharing power. In its place, he accepted the powers of a TRIBUNE, which gave him the power to convene meetings of the senate and initiate legislation. He also received the power to intervene in all provinces of the empire, even those controlled by the senate and provincial governors. In 12 B.C., Augustus became *pontifex maximus,* or high priest, of the Roman state religion. In 2 B.C., he was given the title *pater patriae* (father of his country). These positions, and the influence that accompanied them, gave Augustus enormous prestige and even greater control of the empire. In effect, the Roman Republic had ended and the imperial* period had begun. Yet, Augustus continued to maintain the illusion that he was only one of many elected officials. He did this by insisting that his various offices be renewed periodically rather than granted for life. Augustus maintained this type of leadership throughout his reign. Only in his later years did he become more tyrannical and attempt to govern as an absolute ruler.

ROME UNDER AUGUSTUS. Augustus spent the early years of his rule attempting to stabilize the empire and extend its boundaries. In 29 B.C., he reorganized and reformed the Roman armies. He reduced the number

> **Remember:** Words in small capital letters have separate entries, and the index at the end of Volume 4 will guide you to more information on many topics.

* **imperial** pertaining to an emperor or empire

AUGUSTUS, THE MAN

Augustus was a man of simple tastes. He shunned luxury and grandeur, and he preferred the joys of family above his role as emperor. A believer in strict morality and virtue, he practiced what he preached. When his daughter, Julia, committed adultery, he had her banished from Rome. He did the same with his granddaughter, also named Julia. Such personality traits earned him enormous respect among the Roman people and contributed greatly to their support for him and his policies.

* **cult** group bound together by devotion to a particular person, belief, or god

of legions from 60 to 28 and posted them far from Rome in the provinces. He supplemented these troops with forces drawn from the native inhabitants of the provinces. This policy not only helped to keep peace in the provinces and to defend Roman frontiers, it also removed a potential threat from his rivals in Rome. Augustus provided army officers with land in the provinces and encouraged them to settle there. This helped colonize the empire and ensure loyalty to Rome. Augustus also created a new army unit, the Praetorian Guard, to act as his personal bodyguards. In addition, he established a police force for the city of Rome, known as the Urban Cohorts.

Augustus and his armies had numerous successes. He brought Spain under full Roman control, strengthened Roman rule in Gaul, and advanced into the territories of the Germans beyond the Rhine and Danube rivers. German military victories, particularly one at the Battle of the Teutoburger Forest in A.D. 9, eventually halted this drive and persuaded Augustus to abandon attempts to conquer Germany. Little new territory was gained in that region, where Augustus ruled through local kings who pledged loyalty to Rome. He used these kingdoms as buffers between himself and rival powers, such as the Parthians of Persia. Augustus's policy became one of securing the empire's borders. He placed the greatest concentrations of legions away from Rome—eight on the Rhine frontier, seven on the Danube, three in Syria, three in Spain, and two in Egypt—to fix stable frontiers on the perimeter of the empire.

Augustus initiated many social and religious reforms. A strong believer in ancient Roman traditions and virtues, Augustus sponsored several laws designed to encourage people to marry, have more children, and restore and strengthen family life. He curbed abuses of power among public officials and attempted to root out corruption in government. Augustus also revived old religious traditions, filled vacancies in priesthoods, repaired old temples, and built new ones. In the Roman provinces, he encouraged the development of religious cults* that worshiped him as a god.

Culture flourished under Augustus, and his reign became a golden age of art, architecture, and literature. Augustus sponsored some of the leading artists and writers of the time, including the historian Livy, and the poets Ovid, Vergil, and Horace. Magnificent new buildings and monuments were constructed in Rome and throughout the empire. According to the Roman writer Suetonius, Augustus proclaimed that he had "found Rome a city of bricks and left it a city of marble." A vast system of roads was also built to connect the provinces and to stimulate commercial activity. After years of conflict and wars, Rome, under Augustus, was able to enjoy unprecedented peace and prosperity, and the *Pax Romana* continued long past Augustus's death.

SEARCH FOR A SUCCESSOR. Throughout his reign, Augustus was concerned with finding a suitable successor so that power struggles and civil war would not erupt after his death. He had only one child, a daughter Julia, but needed a male heir. The people he had hoped would succeed him—his nephew Marcellus, son-in-law Agrippa, and grandsons Gaius and Lucius—all died before him. Finally, but somewhat reluctantly, he

AURELIUS, MARCUS

chose his stepson TIBERIUS, the son of his second wife Livia. Although he disliked Tiberius, no one else seemed suitable. Thus he adopted Tiberius and named him successor in his will. Upon the death of Augustus in A.D. 14, Tiberius became the second emperor of Rome. Soon afterward, the Senate raised Augustus to the status of a god. (*See also* **Armies, Roman; Caesar, Gaius Julius; Civil Wars, Roman; Dictatorship, Roman; Government, Roman; Law, Roman; Rome, History of; Senate, Roman; Triumvirates, Roman.**)

AURELIUS, MARCUS

A.D. 121–180
ROMAN EMPEROR

* **philosophy** study of ideas, including science

* **imperial** pertaining to an emperor or empire

* **co-emperor** emperor who shares office with another emperor

* **plague** highly contagious, widespread, and often fatal disease

Marcus Aurelius, who became emperor of Rome in A.D. 161, had a lifelong interest in philosophy*. Two important works commemorating his life have lasted to the present. One is a triumphal column, a monument erected in Rome to celebrate his military victories. Carved scenes showing events from his campaigns cover the column. The other is his deeply personal and philosophical diary, now known as the *Meditations*. The two works present a startling contrast. The column depicts a powerful ruler who defended the empire against invasion. The diary reveals a thoughtful individual who pondered the meaning of human life.

Raised by his grandfather, who was a friend and relative of the emperor HADRIAN, Marcus Aurelius studied with some of the most celebrated teachers of his day. Early in his education, he began to show an interest in philosophy. He was fluent in both Greek and Latin, as were most educated Romans of his day. When Marcus was in his late teens, Hadrian's adopted son Antoninus Pius adopted Marcus. Antoninus Pius became emperor in A.D. 137 and in the years that followed, Marcus received official powers in the Roman government, indicating that he would be the next emperor.

THE RULER. In A.D. 161, Antoninus died, and Marcus Aurelius prepared to take his place. He decided that he would share the imperial* title and power with his adopted brother, Lucius Verus, and quickly arranged for Lucius to become co-emperor*. This was the first time that the Roman Empire had two rulers.

The brothers faced considerable unrest on the empire's frontiers—in Europe, Britain, and Asia Minor. Before long, the Roman army suppressed the British and Asian threats (although the soldiers returning from Asia brought with them an epidemic of the plague*). However, Germanic tribes of northern Europe succeeded in crossing the Alps into Italy. This, the worst crisis for Rome in more than 200 years, was also the first of the challenges that eventually would destroy the Western Roman Empire.

Lucius Verus died in A.D. 169 during the war against the northern tribes. Marcus Aurelius and his generals, however, were able to drive most of the Germans out of Italy and back across the Danube River. One strategy that Marcus used was to invite certain tribes to settle on undeveloped land in the empire. This divided some Germanic forces, making it easier to defeat the others.

91

The emperor's military troubles did not end here, though. Africans invaded Spain, and tribes from Hungary invaded Greece. One of the most powerful Roman generals joined a rebel group and had himself declared emperor. But Marcus Aurelius survived these challenges—the army fought off the invasions and the rebellion failed. He then faced the problem of choosing his successor. During the Roman Empire, the position of emperor did not pass automatically to the emperor's son. The Roman Senate had to grant power to the next ruler. Four years before his death, Marcus Aurelius made his own son Commodus co-emperor, ensuring an orderly succession*.

THE PHILOSOPHER. The surviving manuscript of Marcus's diary, written in Greek, is simply titled "Notes to Himself," although today the work is commonly known as *Meditations*. Historians believe that he wrote the diary late in his life, some of it during his celebrated German campaigns. Yet his words are humble, resigned, and accepting. He was clearly influenced by STOICISM, a philosophy that promoted acceptance of whatever life brought. The Stoics believed the spirit (or mind) was divine, while the body led to corruption. Therefore, they thought they should concern themselves only with things they could control—their own thoughts and feelings. Marcus and some of the Stoics were particularly concerned with ethics, the principles of doing what is right and just in relation to others. Acting justly was especially important because they believed all human beings belonged to one universal spirit, to which they would return after death. In his diary, Marcus takes comfort in the idea that life is short, and that death will reunite him with the rest of the universe.

In the first section of his diary, Marcus notes what he has learned from various teachers and family members. In later sections, he examines questions about life and individual responsibility. In one passage, Marcus describes how difficult he finds waking up in the morning. He reminds himself that every creature—from an ant, to a spider, to a human being—was made by the creator to do some particular work. Therefore, he should rise and do the work he is meant to do. Marcus's writings reveal the sensitive nature of a man who was one of the most powerful rulers of the ancient world. (*See also* **Barbarians; Colonies, Roman; Rome, History of.**)

* **succession** transmission of authority on the death of one ruler to the next

BACCHUS

See *Dionysus.*

BANKING

Banking enabled people in the ancient world to exchange money, obtain loans, and conduct other financial transactions. Certain individuals, such as priests and wealthy businessmen, usually provided these financial services. Gradually, both private and public banks developed throughout the Greek world and the Roman empire.

In early Greece, most banking activities occurred in the temples. Priests provided loans to individuals and held deposits for them. A

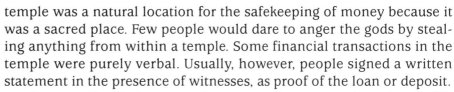

temple was a natural location for the safekeeping of money because it was a sacred place. Few people would dare to anger the gods by stealing anything from within a temple. Some financial transactions in the temple were purely verbal. Usually, however, people signed a written statement in the presence of witnesses, as proof of the loan or deposit.

As more Greek city-states began to coin money, the coinage differed from place to place. This led to the rise of professional money changers who knew the value of the various coins and could arrange for fair exchanges. Money changers set up tables at local markets in cities throughout Greece. They played an especially important role in trade, since merchants traveling through the Mediterranean world had to deal with various foreign currencies. In addition to exchanging coins, the money changers accepted deposits, transferred money between accounts, and made loans. In this way, they acted as private bankers. They usually operated as individuals but sometimes formed small associations. However, transactions occurred in the marketplaces or in private residences—not in banks, as they are today. By the 300s B.C., the money changers had taken most financial activities out of the temples.

During the Hellenistic* period, some Greek cities created public banks to conduct the financial business of the city. One of the most significant developments during this period was the creation of a large public banking system in Egypt under the Ptolemaic dynasty*. The most highly organized banking system in ancient times, it included a central bank in the city of ALEXANDRIA, a network of royal banks throughout Egypt, provincial* banks in important Egyptian cities, and branch banks in small cities and towns. This system employed thousands of people and carried out almost all the banking activities in Egypt. Its most important responsibilities included collecting tax revenues for the kingdom and supplying money for the monarchy's expenses.

The Romans adopted certain banking practices from the Greeks and developed new ones. During the first centuries B.C. and A.D., most Roman banks were small. In place of professional bankers, wealthy businessmen and merchants conducted most financial transactions. They established new methods that improved the banking system. One of the most important of these was the introduction of bills of exchange, which are written authorizations to pay a sum of money to a specific person. This is similar to the use of checks today. Instead of cash transactions, most Roman bankers conducted business through these bills of exchange. This system gradually spread throughout the Roman world.

As the Roman empire expanded, the owners of large estates handled most local banking activities. As a result, banks remained small. During the A.D. 200s, however, the Roman imperial* government took over some banking within the empire and created a more organized banking system. Over time, the government passed laws to regulate the banking system, and some of these laws influenced banking during the Middle Ages and afterward. (*See also* **Coinage; Money and Moneylending; Ptolemaic Dynasty.**)

* **Hellenistic** referring to the Greek-influenced culture of the Mediterranean world during the three centuries after Alexander the Great, who died in 323 B.C.

* **dynasty** succession of rulers from the same family or group

* **provincial** referring to a province, an overseas area controlled by Rome

* **imperial** pertaining to an emperor or empire

BANQUETS

A banquet is a formal meal or feast. Among the ancient Greeks and Romans, banquets served many public and private functions. Public banquets given by the state or by officials generally had civic, religious, or political purposes. Private banquets provided an opportunity for the upper classes to exchange ideas or display their wealth.

GREEK BANQUETS. Civic life in Athens and other Greek city-states* often included banquets sponsored by various organizations to which citizens belonged: philosophical societies, religious groups, community organizations, and clan* and family associations. All of these groups held feasts for their members from time to time to celebrate various occasions. Such banquets created a sense of unity within each organization and also reinforced the social order by reminding each citizen of his place in the larger community. Governments also occasionally sponsored feasts for their citizens.

Private dinner parties called symposia were the favorite evening pastime among wealthy and educated Greeks. (The term *symposium* is still used today. It means a conference where people meet to discuss a particular topic.) Guests at symposia reclined on couches while drinking wine and eating rich foods. Professional entertainers—mostly women—danced, sang, and played musical instruments while the guests ate, drank, and talked. Guests sometimes played games, and told jokes as well. A symposium often included lighthearted conversations

* **city-state** independent state consisting of a city and its surrounding territory

* **clan** group of people descended from a common ancestor or united by a common interest

See color plate 2, vol. 4.

In addition to the elaborate food and drinks consumed during the meals, banquets provided entertainment and social interaction for both Greeks and Romans. The Romans, unlike the Greeks, included women in the festivities. This painting of a banquet scene comes from the Roman city of Pompeii.

on various issues or more serious discussions on philosophical or literary topics. In his work *Symposium*, PLATO describes an occasion on which the guests discussed the nature of love. Over time, Greek symposia became increasingly elaborate and expensive.

ROMAN BANQUETS. During the time of the Roman Republic*, public feasts at the state's expense generally were reserved for high officials and the upper class. Often, however, wealthy individuals gave banquets for anyone who attended or participated in the funeral of a relative who had died. This practice began as a way of honoring the memory of the deceased. In time, the wealthy also used such banquets as a way of gaining favor. Generals, politicians seeking office, and others eager to win popular support also adopted the custom of giving public banquets. In 27 B.C., the emperor AUGUSTUS banned public banquets, except those given by himself. He hoped, in this way, to keep others from winning the affection and support of the Roman populace.

Private Roman banquets were often large, lavish affairs. As in ancient Greece, the guests generally reclined on couches while they ate, drank, talked, and enjoyed various entertainments. Banquet meals usually consisted of numerous courses. The Romans described such meals as including everything *ab ovo usque ad mala* (from eggs to apples), or as we might say, "from soup to nuts." First came a series of appetizers, primarily different types of seafood. Then came the actual meal, consisting of as many as seven courses, which usually included whole roasted animals, such as pigs, ducks, and rabbits. Hosts and cooks often competed to create the most elaborate and exotic dishes. The centerpiece of a banquet, for example, might be small roasted birds (such as larks) inside a roasted duck, which might be inside a large roasted bird (such as a peacock). The third part of the meal was dessert, which usually included fruits and sweets. Various wines, generally mixed with water, were served throughout the meal.

The Romans were famous for their love of fine cuisine. A cookbook written by noted gourmet Marcus Gavius Apicius was widely used for at least two centuries. Lucius Licinius Lucullus, Roman general and epicure*, became famous for holding grand banquets featuring exotic foods from throughout the Mediterranean region. The term "Lucullan feast"—an extravagant dinner given by gourmets—still bears his name. (*See also* **Festivals and Feasts, Greek; Festivals and Feasts, Roman; Food and Drink.**)

* **Roman Republic** Rome during the period from 509 B.C. to 31 B.C., when popular assemblies annually elected their governmental officials

* **epicure** person with refined taste in food and drink

A ROMAN MENU

During the 100s B.C., a Roman named Mucius Lentulus Niger gave a banquet for nearly 700 people to celebrate his advancement to a high office. Among the many delicacies he served as appetizers were oysters, roasted thrushes with asparagus, mussels, deer and boar ribs, and oyster and mussel pies. The meal itself included a boar's head, boar and fish pies, boiled ducks and hares, roasted chickens, and pastries. Such feasts were vastly different from the simple meals of grains, lentils, and vegetables eaten by most country folk and the urban poor.

BARBARIANS

The ancient Greeks and Romans both referred to foreigners as barbarians. At first, the Greeks used the word *barbaros* simply to mean any person who could not speak their language. To the Greeks, other languages had sounds that resembled "bar bar." Even foreigners who learned Greek but spoke it poorly were called barbarians. Used in this way, the term did not have a negative meaning. It could apply both to people of civilized cultures, such as the Egyptians or the Persians, and to those the Greeks considered less civilized. In time, however, the word *barbaros* took on the meaning of uncivilized or inferior, because the Greeks believed their culture superior to the cultures of all other peoples.

See map in Visigoths (vol. 4).

The ancient Romans adopted the Greeks' idea of barbarian and used the Latin word *barbarus* to refer to any foreigner. During the period of the Roman Empire, the word came to be applied to people who lived outside the empire, particularly to those hostile to Rome. This included many tribes of people to the north and east of the empire, known collectively as GERMANS. (*See also* **Migrations, Late Roman.**)

BASILICAS

See *Churches and Basilicas.*

BATHS, ROMAN

Although the Greeks had public bathhouses, the Romans made bathing into an elaborate ritual, designing the most luxurious private and public baths the world had ever seen. Only the wealthiest Roman households had private baths. Ordinary people settled for sponge baths at home or went to the public baths in their cities and paid a fee.

To the Romans, a bath had several stages. First, bathers cleaned themselves by rubbing their bodies with oil. They did not have soap. Then they soaked in a series of tubs or pools, moving from lukewarm to hot water. Often they exercised, received a massage, or spent time sitting in a steam room. Then they, or their slaves, scraped their bodies with curved metal or ivory tools called strigils that removed the oil and dirt from the skin. The final step in the bathing process was a dip in cool or even cold water.

Bathing was a social activity, and public bathhouses were important structures in the community. Most Roman men visited the baths in the afternoons. While soaking, they gossiped, met friends, or discussed politics. Men and women generally bathed separately, either at different times, in different buildings, or in separate facilities under the same roof. Sometimes men and women bathed together, although respectable Romans disapproved of this practice and several emperors banned it.

The oldest existing Roman public baths, built in the 100s B.C., are located in the city of Pompeii. Several Roman emperors built baths in and around Rome. As time passed, these imperial baths became larger and more elaborate. By the time the emperors Caracalla (A.D. 217) and Diocletian (A.D. 305) ordered the construction of the baths that bore their names, bathhouses had become enormous, high-ceilinged marble halls. Decorated with statues, wall paintings, and multicolored mosaics*, the bathing chambers contained huge swimming pools. Hundreds or even thousands of people could bathe at one time, while slaves moved through underground passages, running errands and feeding the furnaces. These impressive bath buildings were the centers of large, walled pleasure grounds that included gardens, gymnasiums, halls for lectures and poetry readings, and libraries.

The ruins of bathing chambers in private houses can be found in Rome and throughout the territories that came under Roman influence.

* **mosaic** art form in which small pieces of stone or glass are set in cement; also refers to a picture made in this manner

Some of the public baths of the ancient Romans were luxurious structures, including several different pools that contained water at various temperatures. The most extravagant baths, built during the reigns of the emperors Caracalla and Diocletian, were decorated with statues, mosaics, and wall paintings. This picture of the remains of the Baths of Caracalla shows some of the artwork that adorned the building.

Such private baths usually consisted of a small room for each stage of the bath—a cold room *(frigidarium),* a warm room *(tepidarium),* and a hot room *(calidarium).* In some houses, slaves heated water over wood or charcoal fires and carried it to the warm and hot bath rooms in basins. Other houses had more complex systems using a hypocaust, a space beneath the floor where steam or boiling water from furnaces circulated through pipes in the floors and walls to heat the warm and hot baths.

The ruins of the baths of Caracalla and Diocletian can still be seen in Rome, as well as the remains of many smaller and less splendid public baths built by the Romans throughout Europe and the Middle East. (*See also* **Social Life, Roman; Aqueducts.**)

BIRDS

See *Animals; Food and Drink; Omens.*

BOETHIUS

ca. A.D. 480–524
ROMAN PHILOSOPHER AND
STATESMAN

* **Scholasticism** medieval philosophy based on analytical thinking and the ideas of Aristotle

* **classical** relating to the civilization of ancient Greece and Rome

Anicius Manlius Severinus Boethius, the last of the great Roman philosophers, was an admirer of the ancient Greeks. He translated PLATO, ARISTOTLE, and other Greek philosophers into Latin, which helped preserve their writings. Boethius also paved the way for Scholasticism*, a way of thinking that combined classical*, Christian, and worldly knowledge into a single system of beliefs that gained popularity during the Middle Ages.

Descended from an old and prominent Roman family, Boethius entered public life at an early age. From 510 until his death in 524, he served as head minister to Theodoric, the OSTROGOTH king who had conquered Italy. However, in about 522 Theodoric accused Boethius of treason, claiming that Boethius had plotted against him with JUSTINIAN I, the emperor of the Eastern Roman Empire. Falsely accused, Boethius was imprisoned, tortured, and executed without a trial.

Boethius wrote his most famous book, *Consolation of Philosophy,* while in prison. The book is a dialogue between the writer and the spirit of philosophy; it argues that the pursuit of knowledge and the love of God are the only true sources of happiness. During the Middle Ages, it became the most widely read book after the Bible.

In his lifetime, Boethius also produced important studies on logic, grammar, music, geometry, arithmetic, and astronomy. His writings on theology, the study of the nature of God and religious truth, had a profound influence on religious thought and teaching in the Middle Ages.

BOOKS AND MANUSCRIPTS

* **scribe** person who copies manuscripts by hand

The ancient Greeks and Romans wrote and copied by hand all of their literary works, as well as any written material concerned with everyday matters—business accounts, personal letters, law codes, and public notices. The printing press was not invented until the A.D. 1400s, many centuries after the end of the Roman period. In the ancient world, the people who copied written material served an important function. These scribes* made poems, plays, histories, and other works available to readers beyond the author's relatively small circle of friends and family.

WRITING MATERIALS. Ancient writers used a variety of materials to record their words in some lasting form. One method involved using a pointed stick called a stylus to write on clay or wood tablets coated with wax. The writer could rub out the marks in the wax and reuse the tablets. Other writing materials included bark, animal skins, and papyrus, which was the most common material.

Papyrus—the source of the English word *paper*—is a plant that grows in the delta of the Nile River. By 3000 B.C., the Egyptians had learned to make flat paperlike sheets from the inner stalks of the plant. They glued these sheets together into long rolls. The Greeks probably began importing papyrus in the 500s B.C., and it became the principal writing material of the ancient world. From the Greek word for papyrus, *byblos,* came their word for book, *biblion,* which was the source of the English word *bible.*

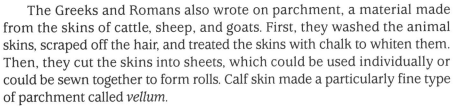

The Greeks and Romans also wrote on parchment, a material made from the skins of cattle, sheep, and goats. First, they washed the animal skins, scraped off the hair, and treated the skins with chalk to whiten them. Then, they cut the skins into sheets, which could be used individually or could be sewn together to form rolls. Calf skin made a particularly fine type of parchment called *vellum*.

Writers working on papyrus usually used an ink made of soot and vegetable gum. The ink, which dissolved in water, could be sponged clean. Another type of ink, which adhered better to parchment, was made of vegetable dye mixed with iron sulfate. Writers used pens made from dried reeds. They trimmed one end of a reed to a point, then split the point so it would hold ink. Some better and more expensive pens had metal tips.

See color plate 8, vol. 1.

USING A MANUSCRIPT ROLL.   During most of their history, the ancient Greeks and Romans wrote their books and other long documents on papyrus or parchment rolls. A famous Greek vase from around 440 B.C. shows the poet SAPPHO reading from a roll. She grips the roll with both hands, winding the portion already read with her left hand and unrolling the text about to be read with her right hand.

The Greeks and Romans wrote in capital letters and did not use spaces to separate words. Punctuation was rarely used—only occasionally to separate or join syllables, to separate clauses and sentences, to show when one speaker stopped and another started, and to mark sections in poetry.

Writers and scribes working on a manuscript roll wrote left to right in narrow columns. They preferred to use only the inside of the roll. If writing appeared on the outside, it was usually because the work was extremely long or the writer was too poor to afford another roll. In most cases, a writer or scribe who accidentally left out a word or wanted to make a change would write the new word at the top or bottom of the roll, with an arrow showing where it should go. Writing was too time-consuming and the materials too costly to start over after a mistake.

The writer or scribe might put the title of the work and the author's name next to the final column of text. The title might also be noted on a tag (*titulus* in Latin) outside the roll. People stored their rolls in boxes and buckets, on shelves, or in narrow compartments called pigeonholes.

FROM ROLL TO BOOK.   Even after the introduction of papyrus, ancient writers continued to use tablets for types of writing that would be needed for only a short period of time, such as school lessons, letters, or temporary business accounts. Wax-covered wooden tablets could be utilized again and again. The Greeks and Romans joined two such tablets together with clasps or leather thongs to form notebooks.

The Romans used a notebook made of parchment or papyrus, called a codex (plural codices). It was lighter and easier to carry than wood. Professional people, such as doctors and lawyers, found codices useful. Scribes produced inexpensive editions of noted authors in codex form. Early Christians used codices for biblical texts, which helped to spread both the teachings of Christ and the codex form. During the A.D. 300s, the codex began to replace the roll as the primary format for books. People saw that codices were easier to carry than rolls and more practical for storing and using information.

MAKING A PAPYRUS ROLL

The first step in making a papyrus roll was to cut the papyrus stalks into strips. Then two layers of strips were set out, one on top of the other, with the first layer arranged lengthwise and the second layer arranged crosswise. The person making the papyrus dampened the strips and pressed the two layers together. When dry, the layers formed a sheet. Finally, using a paste made from wheat and vinegar, the papyrus maker glued the sheets together to form a strip 35 to 50 feet long and rolled the strip around a cylinder of wood or ivory.

COPYING AND SELLING BOOKS. For many years—long after authors began writing their poems, plays, and histories on papyrus or parchment—most literary works were recited before an audience. The performer or reader used books as memory aids. Eventually, however, books came to be valued for themselves. The buying and selling of books probably began in Athens in the 400s B.C. The book business seems to have developed quickly, and soon Athens was exporting books to cities on the Black Sea.

Rome had professional booksellers by 100 B.C. These booksellers—the equivalent of today's publishers—maintained staffs of scribes (usually skilled slaves) to produce copies of books. Because there were no copyright laws to protect an author's rights to his or her work, anyone could copy a book for private use or for sale. In addition to booksellers, Rome had dealers who specialized in used books or old and rare books. (*See also* **Alphabets and Writing; Libraries; Literacy.**)

BREAD

Bread was the staple food of the ancient Greek and Roman diet. It could be made from a variety of grains, but when grain supplies ran short, famine often resulted. The importance that ancient people gave to eating bread has come down to us in the word *companion,* derived from the Latin words *com* and *panis,* meaning "one with whom one breaks bread."

The early Greeks used barley to make bread, preparing a flat cake called *maza.* Although barley produced an inferior bread, the grain produced high yields in the thin, rocky soil of Greece. Many Greeks—especially poor people and slaves—relied on barley bread. The SPARTANS fed barley bread to their army, and a popular saying of the time declared that "a barley cake is the next best thing to a loaf." By the 300s B.C., wheat bread replaced bread made from barley. Wheat bread was tastier, more nutritious, and easier to digest than barley bread.

The Romans used several different varieties of wheat to make their bread. The early wheat breads were made from a grain called emmer and were shaped into cakes. In the days of the Roman Republic* and then during the Roman Empire, a softer wheat—which made a better quality loaf—gradually replaced emmer.

The process for making bread started with milling the grain to separate the kernel from the husk. The kernels were ground and passed through sieves, refining the grain further and producing flour. The baker added water and leavening agents to the flour, which caused the dough to rise. The dough was then kneaded and allowed to rise again. Finally, the dough was placed on leaves or tiles and baked in a low hearth or a wall oven.

The color, taste, and texture of bread varied from region to region and from class to class. In Roman times, poor people ate dark, gritty bread. This rough-textured bread might contain bits of husk, or sometimes even particles of dust from the millstones used to grind the flour. The upper classes ate lighter, more refined loaves. While women generally made bread at home for their families, many Roman cities had bakeries that produced loaves for sale to the public.

* **Roman Republic** Rome during the period from 509 B.C. to 31 B.C., when popular assemblies annually elected their governmental officials

See color plate 13, vol. 1.

The failure of a wheat crop often led to famine. When wheat ran out, the ancient Greeks and Romans sometimes used chestnuts to make bread. The Greek historian XENOPHON wrote about a group of Greek soldiers who found a hoard of chestnuts in Armenia and baked them into loaves. (*See also* **Agriculture, Greek; Agriculture, Roman; Famine; Food and Drink.**)

BRIDGES

* **Hellenistic** referring to the Greek-influenced culture of the Mediterranean world during the three centuries after Alexander the Great, who died in 323 B.C.

As early as the BRONZE AGE, beginning around 4000–3500 B.C., the people of Greece built wooden bridges to cross rivers or wetlands. Bridge builders of this time also laid stone paths through shallow rivers, sometimes making arches of large, overlapping stones through which the water could flow. Stone bridges appeared around 500 B.C. During the Hellenistic* period, from 323 B.C. to 31 B.C., people in northern Greece and ASIA MINOR built bridges that spanned as much as 1,000 feet. These bridges consisted of stone piers, or supports, holding removable roadways that were made of wooden planks.

The Romans were the greatest bridge builders of the ancient world, just as they were the greatest road builders. In the city of Rome, at least 12 bridges crossed the Tiber River. Elsewhere, engineers traveled with the Roman armies to build bridges so that soldiers could cross the rivers they encountered on their way to battle. Some of these were temporary wooden bridges. Others were pontoon bridges, or floating bridges, of boats placed side by side.

* **pier** support between two arches or openings

On secondary roads, the Romans built wooden bridges, but for their major roads, they constructed sturdy stone bridges. The earliest known of these was built in 179 B.C. These stone bridges had one or more stone arches that rested on large piers*. The grandest Roman bridges were built somewhat later, at the direction of the Roman emperors. A bridge built under the emperor AUGUSTUS to cross the Nera River on the busy Flaminian Way north of Rome had an arch 62 feet high and 100 feet wide. The emperor TRAJAN commissioned the building of a bridge nearly 3,700 feet long across the Danube River. To span the largest rivers like the Danube, Roman bridge builders used a combination of stone and wood. Piers were constructed of stone and arches were made of wood.

None of the Roman wooden bridges survives today, but some of the stone bridges are still intact. One of the best preserved stone bridges in Italy is the Ponte di Augusto, completed in A.D. 20 at Rimini. In western Spain near Mérida, a bridge built by the Romans in A.D. 106 still carries traffic over the Tagus River. Its six arches rise 245 feet above the river.

BRITAIN

* **province** overseas area controlled by Rome

In Roman times, Britain—or Britannia as it was known by the Romans—was the northernmost province* of the empire. Today, this large island off the coast of northwestern Europe contains the countries of England, Scotland, and Wales.

ROMAN INVASION AND CONQUEST. Julius CAESAR led Roman forces in an invasion of Britain in 55 B.C. and again the next year. Each time, Caesar's armies faced fierce resistance from local tribes of CELTS. The Romans accomplished little by their invasions, and the Celts remained in control of their land. Over the next century, the Celts established strong kingdoms in southern Britain, which discouraged further Roman attempts to invade and conquer.

Years of internal conflict eventually weakened the power of the Celtic kingdoms. In A.D. 43, the emperor CLAUDIUS launched another campaign against Britain. This time the Romans landed unopposed. Over the next four years, they gained control of much of southern Britain and established Roman settlements, including Londinium (present-day London). The region was organized as an imperial* province of Rome.

* **imperial** pertaining to an emperor or empire

Like any typical imperial province, towns in Britannia were created and administered in Roman style. This map shows the Latin and modern names for some towns in Britain.

ROMAN BRITAIN

CALEDONIA
(SCOTLAND)

NORTH
SEA

0   250   500 Miles

Hadrian's Wall

Corstopitum
(Corbridge)

Eburacum
(York)

UPPER
BRITAIN

HIBERNIA
(IRELAND)

IRISH SEA

Lindum
(Lincoln)

Deva
(Chester)

Venta Icenorum
(Caistor-by-Norwich)

LOWER BRITAIN

Camulodunum
(Colchester)

Glevum
(Gloucester)

Verulamium
(St. Albans)

Thames River

Londinium
(London)

Aquae Solis
(Bath)

Venta Belgarum
(Winchester)

Isca Damnoniorum
(Exeter)

ENGLISH CHANNEL

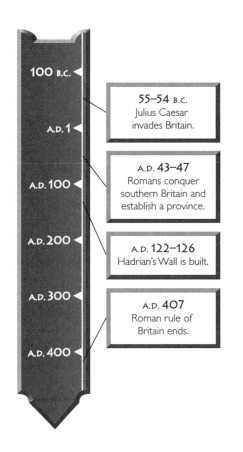

100 B.C.

A.D. 1

55–54 B.C.
Julius Caesar
invades Britain.

A.D. 100

A.D. 43–47
Romans conquer
southern Britain and
establish a province.

A.D. 200

A.D. 122–126
Hadrian's Wall is built.

A.D. 300

A.D. 407
Roman rule of
Britain ends.

A.D. 400

The Roman conquest of northern Britain continued for many years. During this time, the Romans had to put down several revolts by native peoples, including one led by Queen Boudicca, a tribal ruler. Boudicca's forces destroyed and burned several Roman settlements before the Romans brought the revolt under control. By A.D. 85, the Roman occupation of Britain extended almost to the border of present-day England and Scotland. Wild, hostile tribes to the north stopped advances beyond this frontier, and their presence threatened the security of Roman settlements in the region. The Romans erected a series of walls to protect the northern frontier from invasion. The first and most important of these was HADRIAN'S WALL, built between A.D. 122 and 126. It eventually marked the northernmost border of Roman Britain.

ROMAN BRITAIN. Like other Roman provinces, Britain was ruled by a provincial governor and organized by local units of self-government known as *civitates*. The Romans established military camps throughout the island. They also built towns that were enclosed by walls and constructed a network of roads to tie the different parts of Britain closer together.

The towns followed the Roman model in layout and architecture. Many included Roman-style AMPHITHEATERS, TEMPLES, and BATHS. The Roman town of Aquae Solis, built on the site of natural hot springs, featured a huge pool and a system of water channels that still exist in the modern-day city of Bath in southern England.

Roman Britain enjoyed a degree of prosperity, and its population may have reached around 2 million. The Romans tapped the province's mineral wealth and improved its agricultural practices, exporting surpluses to Rome. To govern more efficiently, the Romans divided the province into Upper and Lower Britain. Although Britain became very Roman in character, elements of Celtic culture remained strong, especially among people without education and those living in rural areas.

In the late A.D. 200s, the Saxons, a Germanic tribe of northern Europe, began attacking the coasts of Britain. As these assaults continued, the Romans found it increasingly difficult to defend the province. In the late A.D. 300s and early 400s, political instability in Rome led to a withdrawal of Roman troops from Britain. The weakened Roman position encouraged Saxons and other hostile tribes to increase their attacks. Finally in A.D. 407, Emperor Constantine III pulled the remaining troops out of Britain, effectively ending Roman rule in the region. With no army to defend it, the province quickly fell to Germanic invaders and Roman civilization in Britain collapsed. (*See also* **Migrations, Late Roman; Provinces, Roman; Rome, History of.**)

BRONZE AGE, GREEK

The Bronze Age refers to a period of human history during which people made most of their tools and weapons of bronze—a mixture of copper, tin, and other metals. The Bronze Age occurred at different times in different areas of the world. In the region around the AEGEAN SEA, it lasted from about 3000 B.C. to 1200 B.C. During that time, three unique civilizations emerged in the Aegean region: the Cycladic, the Minoan, and the Mycenaean civilizations.

103

These Aegean cultures laid the early foundations for the development of Greek civilization.

CYCLADIC CIVILIZATION. The CYCLADES are a group of islands located in the Aegean Sea between the Greek mainland and the coast of ASIA MINOR. Bronze Age culture began in these islands in about 2500 B.C. In addition to using bronze for their tools and weapons, the inhabitants of the Cyclades also fashioned objects from lead, silver, and marble. People of the Cycladic civilization lived in small, unfortified communities scattered among the islands. They practiced subsistence farming and traded with communities on the mainland. Religion seems to have centered around the worship of fertility goddesses. The Cycladic civilization disappeared around 1900 B.C., but its influence was felt on the Greek mainland, along the coast of Asia Minor, and on the large island of CRETE to the south.

MINOAN CIVILIZATION. Another Bronze Age culture had developed on Crete as early as 3000 B.C. but did not reach its height until after 2200 B.C. This culture was called the Minoan civilization, named after King Minos, a legendary ruler of the island. Early Minoan civilization was similar to that of the Cyclades in several important ways—the use of bronze, a focus on agriculture and trade, and the worship of goddesses. During the high point of Minoan civilization, between about 2200 and 1500 B.C., the Minoans established carefully planned towns and cities on Crete and built networks of roads to connect them. They also extended their trading networks throughout the Mediterranean region.

Minoan rulers built great multiroom palaces, decorating the walls with lively frescoes* of dolphins, athletic young men and women, and other subjects. The Minoans also developed a form of writing based on pictographs*, which modern archaeologists call Linear A. Around 1450 B.C., this was replaced by Linear B, an early form of the Greek language. At about the same time, the Minoan civilization mysteriously faded into obscurity. Archaeologists believe that a large volcanic eruption on the Aegean island of Thera destroyed many Cretan cities, ruined agriculture, and caused the civilization's decline. It is also probable that people from mainland Greece invaded Crete in the aftermath of this disaster, met little resistance from the peace-loving Minoans, and destroyed much of their culture.

MYCENAEAN CIVILIZATION. After the decline of Minoan civilization, the Greek mainland became the focus of Aegean culture. Around 2000 B.C., a group of people known as the Mycenaeans invaded Greece from the north and developed a Bronze Age culture centered in the Peloponnese, the large peninsula that forms the southernmost part of Greece. By 1600 B.C., Mycenaean civilization had spread throughout Greece and into the coastal regions of Asia Minor.

Mycenaean civilization was notable for its massive stone architecture and heavily fortified cities with walls of huge stones. Unlike the Minoans, the Mycenaeans had a warlike culture, and they controlled

* **fresco** method of painting in which color is applied to moist plaster and becomes chemically bonded to the plaster as it dries; also refers to a painting done in this manner

* **pictograph** picture used to represent a sign or symbol, as in ancient writing

territory and extended their power through military might. Mycenaean warrior kings built great palaces and royal tombs, and they collected taxes and crops from their subjects. Between 1600 B.C. and 1400 B.C., the Mycenaeans competed with the Minoans for trade dominance in the Mediterranean. This contact with Minoan culture helped inspire Mycenaean civilization. The Mycenaeans, for example, decorated their graves with the beautiful craftwork of Minoan artists. After the Mycenaeans invaded Crete in the 1400s, however, the Mycenaean culture largely overtook the Minoan culture and contributed to its decline.

Around 1200 B.C., Mycenaean domination of the Aegean region was disrupted by invasions from the north and by internal strife. Thereafter, Mycenaean civilization declined and Greek civilization began to take shape. This period is known as the Dark Age because so little is known about Greece during this era of its history. It was during this period that the Mycenaean king AGAMEMNON and other legendary heroes* destroyed the city of TROY in Asia Minor, an event celebrated in the epics of the Greek poet HOMER. (*See also* **Archaeology of Ancient Sites; Architecture, Greek; Greece, History of: Early Greeks; Mycenae; Trade, Greek.**)

See color plate 3, vol. 2.

* **hero** in mythology, a person of great strength or ability, often descended from a god

BRUTUS, MARCUS

85–42 B.C.
ROMAN POLITICAL LEADER AND ASSASSIN

* **tyrant** absolute ruler

* **Roman Republic** Rome during the period from 509 B.C. to 31 B.C., when popular assemblies annually elected their governmental officials

Marcus Brutus is best known for his role in the assassination of Roman ruler Julius CAESAR. The Romans and some historians differed in their opinions of Brutus. Some saw him as a traitor to Caesar, who had been his friend and ruler. Others considered Brutus a patriot who helped bring down a tyrant* in the hope of preserving the Roman Republic*.

Born into a distinguished Roman family, Brutus had a distant ancestor who was said to have liberated Rome from the tyrant Tarquin the Proud, the last of the seven kings of Rome, before the founding of the republic. Brutus became involved in a similar struggle in 49 B.C., when civil war erupted between Caesar and POMPEY the Great. Fearing Caesar's growing power, Brutus supported Pompey the Great and the republican side. Caesar defeated Pompey the Great, but he pardoned Brutus for his opposition and asked him to serve as governor of GAUL.

In 44 B.C., Brutus again turned against Caesar. This time, he was drawn into a conspiracy with Cassius, one of Caesar's enemies. Because Brutus was respected as a thoughtful and honorable man, dozens of prominent citizens joined him in the plot to assassinate Caesar on the Ides (the fifteenth day) of March. After the assassination, Brutus and Cassius had to fight Caesar's supporters, led by Mark Antony (Marcus ANTONIUS) and Octavian (later the emperor AUGUSTUS). Antony defeated the forces of Brutus and Cassius at Philippi in Greece in 42 B.C., leading Brutus to commit suicide.

Apart from his notoriety as one of Caesar's assassins, Brutus had a reputation as a man of letters. A follower of the philosophy of STOICISM, Brutus wrote books on history and ethics, and was a distinguished letter writer. In one letter to a friend, Brutus wrote, "Our ancestors thought that we ought not to endure a tyrant even if he were our own father." (*See also* **Rome, History of.**)

BUILDING	See *Construction Materials and Techniques.*

BYZANTIUM

* **strait** narrow channel that connects two bodies of water

* **city-state** independent state consisting of a city and its surrounding territory

Byzantium was a Greek city located on the western side of the Bosporus, one of the straits* that separates Europe from ASIA MINOR. The city had great strategic importance because it was situated on a hilly, triangular-shaped peninsula and had natural protection against attack. Its large, well-protected natural harbor, known as the Golden Horn, provided a secure location for ships. Its location at the crossroads of Europe and Asia made the city an important center of trade. In late Roman times, Byzantium became the capital of the Eastern Roman Empire (later known as the Byzantine Empire) and the name of the city was changed to CONSTANTINOPLE.

Byzantium was founded in the 600s B.C. by Greeks from the city of Megara. According to tradition, it was named after its legendary founder, Byzas. Before setting sail from Megara, Byzas asked an ORACLE where he should establish a new colony. The oracle replied, "Opposite the blind." When Byzas reached the Bosporus, he found another Greek city already in place on the opposite side of the strait. It was called Chalcedon (which means "city of the blind" in Greek) because its founders had failed to take advantage of the better location on the western side of the strait, the site chosen by Byzas.

Soon after its founding, Byzantium flourished as a center of trade. Its principal products included fish, grain, furs, honey, gold, and wax, much of which came from areas around the Black Sea. In 512 B.C., the Persian king, Darius I, conquered Byzantium. It remained part of the PERSIAN EMPIRE until 478 B.C., when the Greeks, under the leadership of PAUSANIAS of Sparta, liberated the city. The next year, Athenians forced out the Spartans, and Byzantium became a member of the Delian League, an alliance of city-states* headed by ATHENS. The Athenians and Spartans competed for control of the city for almost 150 years.

In the mid-300s B.C., the people of Byzantium successfully resisted an attempt by PHILIP II of MACEDONIA to seize control of the city. However, they were unable to resist Philip's son, ALEXANDER THE GREAT. When Alexander asserted his control over Greece in 335 B.C., Byzantium acknowledged Macedonian rule. Even so, the city continued to enjoy considerable freedom.

Byzantium formed an alliance with the Romans in 146 B.C. and gradually lost its independence in the years that followed. The emperor SEPTIMIUS SEVERUS destroyed the city in A.D. 196 because its inhabitants had supported his rival during a period of civil war. He later rebuilt the city because of its strategic importance and renamed it Augusta Antonina. In A.D. 330, the emperor CONSTANTINE I chose Byzantium as the new capital of the empire and changed its name to Nova Roma, or "New Rome." Soon, however, the city became known as Constantinople, and it remained the most important city of the Eastern Roman Empire. (*See also* **Rome, History of; Greece, History of.**)

CAESAR, GAIUS JULIUS

100–44 B.C.
ROMAN GENERAL, STATESMAN, AND DICTATOR

* **republic** government in which the citizens elect officials to represent them and govern according to law

* **patrician** member of the upper class who traced his ancestry to a senatorial family in the earliest days of the Roman Republic

* **oratory** art of public speaking

* **crucify** to put to death by binding or nailing a person's hands and feet to a cross

* **military tribune** junior member of the officer corps of the Roman army

CAESAR'S WRITINGS

In addition to his military and political fame, Julius Caesar is also known for his literary achievements, most notably his *Gallic War* and *Civil War.* These personal commentaries, written in a clear and simple style, describe his military campaigns. They are the only surviving detailed accounts of ancient battles by a military commander, and they provide a firsthand look at ancient warfare. The commentaries, which present Caesar in a most favorable light, served as useful propaganda during his rise to power. They are still studied for their historic insights, and teachers often assign these works to beginning Latin students because of the simplicity and clarity of the language.

Julius Caesar was one of the most famous leaders of ancient Rome. A brilliant general and statesman, he overcame his political rivals to become dictator of Rome. His DICTATORSHIP played a pivotal role in Rome's transition from a republic*, governed by the Senate, to an empire, ruled by an emperor.

EARLY YEARS. Born on July 12 or 13, 100 B.C., Caesar came from one of the patrician* families in Rome—the Julii. Despite its antiquity, the family had little political success or wealth. In 84 B.C., Caesar married Cornelia, the daughter of a prominent citizen who had opposed the ruthless dictator Lucius Cornelius SULLA. Sulla ordered Caesar to divorce Cornelia, but he refused. Although Sulla spared Caesar's life because of his social class, Caesar wisely decided to leave Italy for military service in Asia.

Following Sulla's death in 78 B.C., Caesar returned to Rome and began his political career. Soon after, he went to the island of RHODES to study oratory*. On the way to Rhodes, he was captured by pirates and held for ransom. After his release, he raised a private naval force, captured the pirates, and had them crucified*. While in Rhodes, Caesar raised a private army to fight Mithradates VI, the king of Pontus, a kingdom in ASIA MINOR that had renewed its war with Rome. His victories over Mithradates and the pirates helped establish his reputation as a military leader.

RISE TO POWER. Caesar returned to Rome in 73 B.C. and was elected military tribune*. He then began working with the great Roman general POMPEY (Gnaeus Pompeius Magnus) to reverse some of the governmental changes made during Sulla's dictatorship. Caesar allied himself with those who represented the interests of the Roman people and who sought to regain power from the conservative nobles who controlled the Roman Senate.

In 69 B.C., Caesar was elected QUAESTOR, the first important rung on the Roman political ladder. That same year, his wife Cornelia and his aunt Julia, a prominent patrician, died. Caesar attracted public attention by giving grand orations at their funerals, and his political career gained momentum thereafter. Elected AEDILE in 65 B.C., he gained enormous popularity by spending large sums of money on lavish Roman games. He became *pontifex maximus,* or "high priest," of the Roman state religion in 63 B.C., and then became PRAETOR the following year. In 61 B.C., Caesar became governor of SPAIN, where the spoils of war from his military successes helped restore his dwindling finances.

Caesar returned to Rome in 60 B.C. to seek the office of CONSUL and to be honored by a triumph, a formal procession for a victorious general. According to Roman law, however, a general could not enter the city of Rome until the day of his triumph. A candidate for consul, on the other hand, had to be in Rome to announce his candidacy. Caesar thus faced a dilemma, and he asked the Roman Senate to grant an exception so he could receive his triumph and also run for consul. Fearful of his growing popularity and power, the Senate refused. Caesar decided to give up his triumph. He entered Rome and won the consulship with support from Pompey and Marcus Licinius CRASSUS, one of the richest and most powerful men in Rome.

As consul, Caesar negotiated with Pompey and Crassus to try to pass the legislation they supported, including the distribution of public lands to their soldiers. Faced with increased opposition from conservatives in the Senate, the three men formed a powerful political alliance—the First Triumvirate—to accomplish their goals. As a result of this alliance, Caesar received the governorship of three provinces: Illyricum (present-day Croatia, Slovenia, Bosnia, and Serbia), Transalpine Gaul (present-day southern France), and Cisalpine Gaul (present-day northern Italy). These provinces gave Caesar an important source of wealth and power.

During his meteoric rise to power, Caesar experienced several changes in his personal life. After the death of his wife Cornelia, Caesar married Pompeia, a granddaughter of Sulla and distant relative of Pompey. He divorced her because of her infidelity and married Calpurnia, the daughter of a Roman consul. These three marriages helped Caesar politically, but they produced only one child—a daughter, Julia, who married his friend Pompey. Caesar chose his great-nephew Gaius Octavius to be his successor, an action that later had a significant effect on the history of Rome.

CAESAR AT WAR. Between 59 and 50 B.C., Caesar focused his attention on conquering all of GAUL. During the GALLIC WARS, he achieved many brilliant victories and launched two preliminary invasions of BRITAIN. In the process, he gathered fiercely loyal troops and built powerful armies. Caesar's tremendous military strength and victories thrilled the Roman people and brought him enormous prestige. The Senate, meanwhile, became increasingly concerned with his growing political power.

While Caesar was in Gaul, strained relations developed between Pompey and Crassus in Rome. Caesar intervened to renew their alliance, but the triumvirate continued to disintegrate. In 54 B.C., Caesar's daughter and Pompey's wife, Julia, died, thus destroying a personal bond between the two men. Crassus was killed a year later while fighting the Parthians, Rome's greatest rivals in Asia. Thus Pompey and Caesar were left to share power. Meanwhile, conservative groups in the Senate persuaded Pompey to join them and defend Rome against any threat Caesar and his armies might pose.

In 49 B.C., the Senate ordered Caesar to disband his armies and return to Rome. Otherwise, they would declare him an enemy of the republic. In response, Caesar moved his armies to the Rubicon, a river that marked the border between Italy and his province of Cisalpine Gaul. He tried to negotiate a compromise that would allow him to retain his authority, but his enemies in the Senate rejected his offers to reach a settlement. On January 11, Caesar marched his armies across the Rubicon into Italy, remarking, "The die is cast." A civil war had begun. (The expression "crossing the Rubicon" has come to mean choosing a course of action from which there is no turning back.)

Caesar's troops quickly overran Italy and Rome, forcing Pompey and his armies to retreat to Greece. Before following them, Caesar went to Spain, where he defeated other armies that were loyal to Pompey. He then turned his attention to Greece, eventually defeating Pompey's troops at

See color plate 1, vol. 3.

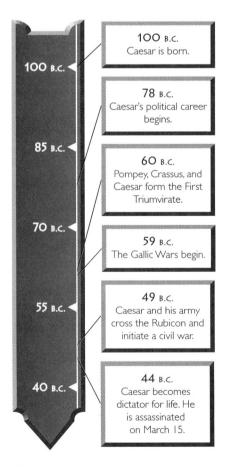

100 B.C.
Caesar is born.

78 B.C.
Caesar's political career begins.

60 B.C.
Pompey, Crassus, and Caesar form the First Triumvirate.

59 B.C.
The Gallic Wars begin.

49 B.C.
Caesar and his army cross the Rubicon and initiate a civil war.

44 B.C.
Caesar becomes dictator for life. He is assassinated on March 15.

Although justly famous for his military and political exploits, Julius Caesar made substantial changes to the social life of Romans as well. During the short duration of his rule in Rome, Caesar increased the number of senators and magisrates, founded many colonies for veterans, and instituted administrative reforms. He also introduced the Julian calendar, which remained in use in western Europe until the 1500s.

* **province** overseas area controlled by Rome

* **tyrant** absolute ruler

the Battle of Pharsalus in August of 48 B.C. Pompey fled to Egypt and was killed by the Egyptians. Caesar, who had followed Pompey to Egypt, found that country embroiled in a civil war. He joined the side of CLEOPATRA VII and helped her gain the Egyptian throne. While in Egypt, Caesar had a romance with Cleopatra, and she later bore him a son named Caesarion.

From Egypt, Caesar went to Asia Minor and put down a rebellion against Roman rule. It was this quick victory that gave rise to his famous boast, *"Veni, vidi, vici"* (I came, I saw, I conquered). He returned to Rome in 47 B.C. but soon took troops to North Africa, where he defeated other allies of Pompey. The next year, he went back to Spain and destroyed the last of the Pompeian forces at the Battle of Munda. That victory marked the end of the end of the civil war. His opposition defeated, he was now the most powerful man in Rome.

THE DICTATORSHIP. Caesar had served as temporary dictator four times during periods of crisis between 49 and 45 B.C. In 44 B.C., he became dictator for life. During his dictatorships, Caesar used his power to reform Roman government and society. He increased membership in the Senate in an attempt to reduce the power of the more conservative nobles. He also increased the number of governmental officials, which enabled more people to improve their rank in Roman society. Caesar founded new colonies and encouraged soldiers to settle there. He extended Roman citizenship to more people in the provinces* and revised the provincial tax systems. Caesar even revised the Roman CALENDAR, introducing one (the Julian calendar) that is the basis for the calendar used today.

Caesar's dictatorship differed dramatically from that of Sulla, in which opponents were ruthlessly killed and violence was used to achieve goals. Caesar pardoned his opponents and even found high positions in government for many of them. He also sought to improve the lives of ordinary Romans. Caesar's reforms made him immensely popular with the Roman people, who revered him almost as a god. A month, July, was named after him, and he received many honors from those who admired him. Caesar's opponents in the Senate, however, considered him a tyrant*. They believed that he had destroyed the republic and intended to make himself king. Their fears seemed confirmed when Caesar's friend, Marcus ANTONIUS (Marc Antony), suggested that he take the crown of a monarch. Caesar refused, and tried to assure his enemies that he did not pose a threat to them.

Caesar was unsuccessful in pacifying his opposition. A group of opponents, including many he had pardoned and given positions in government, began planning his assassination. On March 15, 44 B.C., a day known as the Ides of March, a group of about 60 conspirators led by Marcus BRUTUS and Gaius Cassius Longinus murdered Caesar in the Senate. When the assassins struck, Caesar cried out *"Et tu, Brute"* (Even you, Brutus?), shocked at being stabbed by a person whom he had pardoned and trusted.

With Caesar's death, his assassins thought they were restoring the republic. Instead, his death led to a period of civil war in which his friend Mark Antony and great-nephew Gaius Octavius competed for power. The war resulted in the collapse of the republic and the beginning of the Roman Empire under the control of powerful emperors. Caesar's nephew became Rome's first emperor and later was known as Caesar Octavianus AUGUSTUS. (*See also* **Cato the Younger; Civil Wars, Roman; Government, Roman; Patricians, Roman; Rome, History of.**)

CALENDARS

A calendar is a system for keeping track of days, months, and years. Since ancient times, people have used calendars to record and plan events, such as the planting of crops and the celebration of religious festivals and other special occasions. The term *calendar* comes from the Latin word *kalendae,* which refers to the first day of each month in Roman times.

The earliest system for keeping track of time was based on the phases of the moon. In this type of calendar, the lunar calendar, each month corresponds to the time it takes the moon to make one complete cycle through its phases. A year based on lunar months has roughly 354 days. However, a solar year, which is based on the position of the sun from day to day, has 365 days.

Roman officials used calendars to keep track of their numerous holidays and festivals. This is a fragment of a Roman calendar. It includes only the last six months of the year. The names of the months are listed across the top, and the days of the month are indicated by the letters *A* through *H* in the column under the month. Next to this letter, another letter specified what kind of day it was. The letter *F* marked an ordinary working day, the letter *C* indicated a day on which the assembly could meet, and on days marked *N* certain public activities were banned.

DAILY LIFE

PLATE 1
A fisherman displays the fresh rewards of a hard day's work at sea in this fresco from the National Archaeological Museum in Athens, Greece. Fish was an important part of the diet of the ancient Greeks and Romans.

PLATE 2

This Roman relief sculpture captures the intimate details of four servants attending to the grooming and dressing of their mistress. Although Roman women had more freedom than their Greek counterparts, a Roman woman was expected to behave in ways that would enhance her husband's reputation.

PLATE 3

This relief sculpture from an elaborate stone coffin called a sarcophagus shows a butcher in his shop. Sarcophagi were decorated in several different ways. Some carvings featured subjects from Greek myths; others depicted Roman battles. Sometimes images of the deceased person were carved on the lid.

PLATE 4
Young friends amuse themselves in this Greek relief from the base of a *kouros*,
which is a large statue of a standing or striding young man.

PLATE 5
This Greek vase painting depicts a domestic scene between two women, one spinning, the other holding a hand loom. Upper-class Greek wives were generally confined to their houses where they looked after their children and tended to the business of housekeeping.

PLATE 6

This Attic Greek pottery shows a group of women carrying water jugs called *hydriai*. These vessels had two handles at the sides for lifting and one handle at the back for pouring.

PLATE 7

This detail from a Roman marble relief sculpture captures the intensity of sailing the sometimes turbulent Mediterranean Sea. Here shipmates attempt to rescue a man who has fallen overboard.

PLATE 8

This relief sculpture on a Roman stela—a stone slab that serves as a monument or marker—shows a private session between a teacher and his students. The education of Roman children was mainly private and, therefore, limited to those who could afford it.

PLATE 9

An elaborate ceiling mosaic shows servants harvesting and treading grapes for wine. Grapes were plentiful in the warm, sunny climate of the Mediterranean, and wine was a favorite drink for all classes of Greek and Roman society.

PLATE 10

In this Roman market scene, merchants display their wares as other customers wait to be served.

PLATE 11

In this colorful pavement mosaic, Roman soldiers gather to prepare for battle.

PLATE 12
A collection of large, ornately decorated vats made up this storage area in Knossos, Crete.

PLATE 13
In this mural from Pompeii, a baker is shown selling fresh breads and cakes from his stall in the town's marketplace. The marketplace was a bustling center for trading and socializing.

PLATE 14

This relief sculpture appears on a stone slab called a stela. Such monuments were used to commemorate a person's life—like that of the tavern keeper shown here tapping wine from a barrel.

PLATE 15

The ancient Greeks and Romans hunted for several reasons: to protect their herds from wild animals, for food, and for sport. This hunting scene is from a Roman mosaic.

ROMAN MONTHS

The early Romans named several months according to their position in the year. The months of September, October, November, and December originally were the seventh, eighth, ninth, and tenth months. The names of these months came from the Latin words for these numbers— *septem, octo, novem,* and *decem.* Later reforms changed the position of these months in the year, but the names stayed the same. The Romans renamed the fifth *(quintilis)* and sixth *(sextilis)* months July and August, after Julius Caesar and Augustus Caesar—the rulers who helped perfect the calendar. The remaining months were named after gods and festivals.

Over a period of time, the difference between the length of the lunar year and the length of the solar year creates problems. For example, it is possible for a spring month on the lunar calendar to fall in the middle of summer on the solar calendar. This problem troubled ancient peoples because many of their festivals were related to the seasons and had to be celebrated at a particular time. They believed that they risked angering the gods if they celebrated at the wrong time. The Greeks and Romans found ways to resolve this problem.

GREEK CALENDARS. The early Greeks used a lunar calendar with 12 months, some with 29 days and some with 30. Each city-state had its own names for the months and the days of the month, as well as its own sequence of months. The Greeks organized the days into groups of ten called decades, but the last decade of 29-day months had only nine days. (The English word *decade* refers to a period of ten years rather than ten days.) The Greeks often kept track of years by naming them, usually after important people (such as rulers or priestesses) or events.

At first, the Greeks made no adjustments to resolve the difference between the lunar and solar year. When they did make changes, by adding extra days or a month every few years, each city followed its own system. As a result, no standard calendar existed in ancient Greece. During the 500s and 400s B.C., Greek astronomers devised more precise ways of adjusting the lunar year to match the solar year. They created various cycles in which a set number of days would be added over a certain period of years. Over time, these "astronomical cycles" became more precise and helped bring greater accuracy to calendars.

ROMAN CALENDARS. The early Romans also used a lunar calendar with months that ranged from 29 to 31 days. Unlike the Greek calendars, however, the early Roman calendars consisted of only ten months and contained 295 days. Martius (March) was the first month of the year. In about 700 B.C., the Romans added two more months to their calendar, bringing it more into line with the solar year.

The months of the Roman calendar were organized into groups, and certain days had special names. In addition to the kalends *(kalendae),* the first day of the month, the Romans had the nones *(nonae),* the 5th or 7th day of the month, and the ides *(idus),* the 13th or 15th day. The Ides of March (March 15) became famous as the day Julius Caesar was assassinated. Like the Greeks, the Romans also kept track of years by naming them after people or events.

For centuries, the Romans tried to make adjustments to their calendar to resolve the difference between the lunar and solar year. By 46 B.C. their calendar no longer corresponded to the seasons. For this reason, Julius Caesar launched a series of calendar reforms in an attempt to resolve the problem and standardize the calendar. First, he lengthened the year 46 B.C. to 445 days to bring the calendar in line with the seasons. Then, he fixed the length of a year at 365 days, with one extra day added in February every four years. He also revised the sequence of months so that the year started with Januarius (January) and established a pattern for months with 29, 30, and 31 days. This new Julian calendar, named in honor of Caesar, was far more accurate than the earlier ones.

Unfortunately, Roman officials did not fully understand the rules about adding days to the Julian calendar. Instead of adding an extra day every four years, they added one every three years. As a result, the calendar once again fell out of sync with the seasons. The emperor AUGUSTUS corrected this problem during his reign and established the proper cycle.

As Roman civilization spread, other cultures adopted the Julian calendar, and it became the standard throughout the Roman Empire. Further adjustments were made in the A.D. 300s. The Gregorian calendar, the one in use today, was adopted in the A.D.1500s. It differs only slightly from the Julian calendar.

CALIGULA

A.D. 12–41
ROMAN EMPEROR

Gaius Caesar Germanicus, known as Caligula, was the third emperor of the Roman Empire. His short reign, from A.D. 37 to 41, was marked by cruelty and bizarre behavior. The Roman biographer Suetonius called him a monster. The son of Germanicus, a popular military leader, Caligula received his nickname—which means "baby boots"—because his mother dressed him in full military uniform, including boots, when he was a small child. Caligula became emperor at the age of 25 after the death of his great-uncle, the emperor Tiberius, who had made Caligula his grandson by adoption so that he might succeed him to the throne.

Much was expected of the new emperor. He was young and the son of a great military leader. At first, Caligula seemed to meet these expectations, restoring some power to popular assemblies and spending money freely on games for the public to enjoy. But early in his reign, an illness struck that, according to some writers, left Caligula mentally disturbed, possibly insane. It was said that the emperor wanted to appoint his horse, Incitatus, to be a Roman consul. He tortured and executed his enemies and treated his friends brutally. Once, at a dinner with some high officials, Caligula burst out laughing. When asked what struck him as so funny, he replied that he had just realized he could have all his guests' throats cut right at the dinner table.

Caligula had an extreme affection for his sister, Drusilla. After her death, he took steps to have her worshiped as a goddess. Caligula thought he should be treated like a god as well. When a circus crowd once cheered for a team he did not like, Caligula announced that he wished the people of Rome had a single neck—so that he could choke them all in one stroke. Caligula's cruel, twisted rule came to an end when he was assassinated by a member of the Praetorian Guard, a special brigade assigned to protect the Roman emperor. (*See also* **Rome, History of: Roman Empire.**)

CALLIMACHUS

ca. 305–240 B.C.
GREEK POET AND SCHOLAR

Callimachus was one of the most prolific poets of the Hellenistic* period. A scholar as well as a poet, he is said to have produced 800 volumes of verse. In so doing, Callimachus helped develop a new literary style that combined elegance, wit, and scholarship. Callimachus's style greatly influenced the work of the Roman poets CATULLUS, OVID, and PROPERTIUS.

* Hellenistic referring to the Greek-influenced culture of the Mediterranean world during the three centuries after Alexander the Great, who died in 323 B.C.

* epigram short poem dealing pointedly, and sometimes satirically, with a single thought

* lyric poem expressing personal feelings, often similar in form to a song

* elegiac sad and mournful poem

Callimachus (originally called Battiades) was born in North Africa. He traveled to the city of ALEXANDRIA, Egypt, during the reign of Ptolemy II (ruled 285-246 B.C.) and was commissioned by the king to catalog the famous collection in the Alexandria library. The completed catalog comprised 120 volumes. While at the library, Callimachus began to write prose works on such diverse subjects as the wonders of the world, foreign customs, rivers, birds, and poetry. The prose works did not survive, but 6 hymns and 64 epigrams* remain. The hymns—often dealing with gods or mythological figures—were meant to be recited or read by an educated audience.

It was as a writer of epigrams that Callimachus was best known, however. These short, personal poems usually dealt with an emotional topic, such as the troubles of a lover or the death of a friend. They evolved from the brief verse inscriptions carved on grave stones. Callimachus transformed them into literature. In his epigram on the death of Heraclitus ("They told me, Heraclitus, they told me you were dead"), Callimachus addresses the dead man in a touching personal style that is both direct and eloquent.

The remainder of Callimachus's poetry exists in fragments and consists of lyric* and elegiac* poems. The most famous of the elegiac poems is the 7,000-line *Aetia (Origins)*. In it, Callimachus described a dream in which the Muses instructed him in the origins of the history of Greek myths, customs, and religious rites. Often criticized for not writing an epic poem, Callimachus defended his short poems as more attractive than epic poems. In his words, "a big book was a big evil." (*See also* **Epigrams; Poetry, Greek and Hellenistic.**)

 See map in Rome, History of (vol. 4).

* annexation addition of a territory to an existing state

* oligarchy rule by a few people

Carthage was a city in North Africa in what is now Tunisia. Its excellent harbor and location on a peninsula in the MEDITERRANEAN SEA gave the city several important advantages for defense and trade. For most of its history, the city thrived on commerce and its people engaged in a brisk trade throughout the Mediterranean region. Carthaginian sailors also explored the Atlantic coasts of SPAIN and northern Africa in search of new trading opportunities.

At the height of its power in the mid-200s B.C., Carthage controlled a vast commercial empire that spanned the Mediterranean coast from LIBYA to Morocco, and also included southwestern Spain and the islands of Sardinia and SICILY. Conflict with Rome over control of the Mediterranean Sea eventually led to the defeat and destruction of Carthage and its annexation* by the Roman empire.

EARLY HISTORY. Carthage was founded in 814 B.C. by PHOENICIANS from the city of Tyre in the eastern Mediterranean. It remained a Phoenician colony until the 600s B.C., when it gained its independence. In its early years, Carthage was ruled by a colonial governor and then by its own kings. By the 500s B.C., the city had an oligarchy*, with two ruling officials elected annually, a powerful senate whose members held office for life, and a group of elected judges who monitored the actions of other officials. The

* **mercenary** soldier, usually a foreigner, who fights for payment rather than out of loyalty to a nation

citizens of Carthage had only limited power. A large army of mercenaries* helped to defend the city and its territories.

Following its independence, Carthage gradually brought other Phoenician settlements in North Africa under its control and conquered the native peoples of the region. As its power spread, Carthage came into conflict with the Greeks, who also had extensive trading interests in the Mediterranean. In about 535 B.C., the Carthaginians allied themselves with the ETRUSCANS of Italy to defeat a Greek fleet near the island of Corsica. Thereafter, the Carthaginians extended their control into Sardinia and Spain. Their struggles with the Greeks for control of Sicily continued for centuries. By 265 B.C., Carthage was the major military power in the western Mediterranean, ruling over all the islands and trading settlements of that region.

WARS WITH ROME. As Rome grew in both strength and size, it became Carthage's major rival in the Mediterranean. Between 509 B.C. and 275 B.C., Carthage signed three treaties with Rome protecting its trading empire in exchange for promises not to interfere in Italy. Carthage even provided a fleet to help the Romans in 280 B.C. during Rome's PYRRHIC WAR against the Greeks. Eventually, however, the rivalry between the two states erupted in war.

Carthage and Rome fought a series of three wars—known as the PUNIC WARS—between 264 B.C. and 146 B.C. In the first two wars, Carthage suffered embarrassing defeats and had to relinquish territory to Rome. It was during the Second Punic War that Carthage's greatest general, HANNIBAL, became famous for leading his troops and elephants across the Alps in a daring invasion of Italy. The city of Carthage itself survived the first two Punic wars and remained strong. By the end of the Third Punic War, however, Carthage had lost its entire empire. Moreover, to ensure that the Carthaginians no longer posed a threat, the Romans plundered* Carthage, burned it to the ground, and forbade anyone to resettle there. They took control of the remaining Carthaginian territory and formed the Roman province of Africa from its north African possessions. This marked the end of the Carthaginian empire.

* **plunder** to steal property by force, usually after a conquest

UNDER ROMAN RULE. During the reign of the emperor AUGUSTUS, the Romans rebuilt and colonized the city of Carthage and made it the capital of their province of Africa. The Romans constructed large public buildings, including an AMPHITHEATER, a FORUM with a large hall called a basilica*, and lavish BATHS modeled after those in Rome. An 82-mile-long AQUEDUCT, the longest in the Roman empire, carried water from the mountains south of Carthage to the baths.

* **basilica** in Roman times, a large rectangular building used as a court of law or public meeting place

The new Roman city of Carthage grew rapidly, reaching a population of more than 300,000 by the A.D. 100s. By then, the city had become a leading cultural center, second in importance in the western Mediterranean only to Rome. Carthage also regained its commercial importance, with African grain among its major exports.

During the first centuries A.D., Roman Carthage became an important center of CHRISTIANITY. The Christian writer and thinker TERTULLIAN was born there, and the city's church leaders played a significant role in spreading the religion. In the A.D. 300s and 400s, Carthage became a center of religious controversy when Christian heresy* took root there.

* **heresy** belief that is contrary to church doctrine

In A.D. 439, the VANDALS seized Carthage and made it the capital of the kingdom they had established in North Africa. Recaptured by the Romans in A.D. 533 during the reign of emperor JUSTINIAN I, Carthage remained a part of the Eastern Roman Empire, later called the Byzantine Empire, until it was conquered by the Arabs in the A.D. 600s. (*See also* **Augustine, St.; Byzantium; Churches and Basilicas; Colonies, Greek; Naval Power, Roman; Provinces, Roman; Rome, History of.**)

CATACOMBS

* **martyr** person who suffers or is put to death in defense of a religious belief

* **fresco** method of painting in which color is applied to moist plaster and becomes chemically bonded to the plaster as it dries; also refers to a painting done in this manner

Catacombs are underground passages or rooms in which the dead were buried. Ancient catacombs have been found in many cities in Italy, including Milan and Naples, as well as throughout the Mediterranean region. The most famous catacombs are in Rome.

The Roman catacombs date from about the first century A.D. Since the Romans forbade the burying of bodies within city limits, the catacombs were located outside the city gates. Narrow passages—about three feet wide—were dug, and recesses were made in the walls for the bodies. Graves were easily dug in the soft rock, called tufa. When more space was needed, the passages were extended or new ones were dug beneath the existing ones. Some passages contained separate chambers called galleria, which were used as family vaults, or for the remains of a martyr*. These halls were sometimes adorned with frescoes*, some of which represent the earliest surviving Christian art.

The 40 catacombs surrounding the city of Rome eventually consisted of 350 miles of passages that lay 20 to 65 feet below the ground and covered 600 acres. Christians used the catacombs as hiding places during times of Roman persecution. After Christianity became the established religion of the Roman empire in the 300s A.D., the catacombs lost their usefulness, and by 400 A.D. they were largely abandoned. (*See also* **Death and Burial.**)

CATO THE ELDER

234–149 B.C.
ROMAN HISTORIAN AND ORATOR

* **Roman Republic** Rome during the period from 509 B.C. to 31 B.C., when popular assemblies annually elected their governmental officials

* **patrician** member of the upper class who traced his ancestry to a senatorial family in the earliest days of the Roman Republic

* **plebeian** member of the general body of Roman citizens, as distinct from the upper class

Cato the Elder, who has often been called the father of Latin prose literature, is famous for his speeches and for his written history of Rome. He also gained prominence in politics, using his skills in public speaking to influence the policies of the Roman Republic*.

Marcus Porcius Cato was born into a landowning family of the equestrian order, the second rank of Roman society. As a young man, he won praise for his actions during the Second Punic War. A patrician* friend and neighbor, Lucius Valerius Flaccus, recognized his talents and helped him gain public notice. Cato entered politics, serving in several government positions. As a plebeian*, he viewed the Roman people as the source of the republic's power and tended to oppose the interests of the nobility. He and Flaccus took office together as CONSULS—chief magistrates—in 195 B.C., and as CENSORS in 184 B.C.. The censors supervised public morality and public lands, and kept the official list of Rome's citizens.

As censor, Cato became known for his harsh, abrasive personality and for speaking his mind to the point of rudeness. He opposed the popularity

* **Hellenistic** referring to the Greek-influenced culture of the Mediterranean world during the three centuries after Alexander the Great, who died in 323 B.C.

of Hellenistic* culture in Rome. For a time, he made speeches against Sci-pio Africanus, a Roman leader who had adopted Greek ways. He encouraged Romans to return to the traditional values of the previous century, such as discipline and modesty. He imposed high taxes on luxuries and had senators discharged for misconduct. Cato also remained active in military activities as a leader and as a politician. As consul he led a military campaign in Spain, where he followed his own strict code of discipline and shared many of the hardships of his soldiers. In later life, he also served as Roman ambassador to the African city of CARTHAGE, Rome's archrival in the Mediterranean.

Despite his outspokenness against Greek culture in Rome, Cato's historical writing continued a tradition begun by Greek authors. Greek had been the language of historians since the 400s B.C., when HERODOTUS and THUCY-DIDES developed a new approach to exploring and interpreting events. These writers presented background information on local customs and geography, included important speeches, and discussed long-term policy trends. Cato was the first historian to follow this approach in Latin.

Cato's history, called *Origins,* began with the founding of Rome in the 700s B.C. and continued to 149 B.C., the last year of his life. Though only quotations from this work survive, it is known that there were seven books. The first three covered the beginnings of Rome and other towns in Italy; the remaining four focused on historical events, with particular attention to the issues of Cato's own time. In writing about his era, Cato included several of his own speeches. Cato also wrote books on other topics, including volumes on law, morality, and military affairs. The only work that still exists in full is *On Agriculture,* a manual on the economics of farming that contains practical information on farm equipment and management.

In addition to his histories, Cato was well known for his speeches, both in the Senate and in the law courts. Cato's speeches owed much to the style of classical Greek rhetoric*. A century later, the Roman statesman and orator CICERO wrote that more than 150 of Cato's speeches were still studied for their style and eloquence. Deeply concerned about the threat to Rome from the powerful city of Carthage, Cato often ended his speeches with the phrase *Carthago delenda est,* meaning "Carthage must be destroyed." (*See also* **Punic Wars.**)

* **rhetoric** art of using words effectively in speaking or writing

CATO THE YOUNGER

95–46 B.C.
ROMAN POLITICAL LEADER

* **Roman Republic** Rome during the period from 509 B.C. to 31 B.C., when popular assemblies annually elected their governmental officials

* **quaestor** Roman financial officer who assisted a higher official such as a consul or praetor

Marcus Porcius Cato, also called Cato the Younger, was a steadfast supporter of the Roman Republic* during its final years. He unsuccessfully tried to block Julius Caesar's rise to power. Cato's stand against Caesar made him a hero to those who glorified the Roman Republic and its ideals, especially after his death. The later historian LIVY called Cato "the conscience of Rome," and he was greatly admired by the Roman poet LUCAN.

Cato entered political life as a quaestor* in 64 B.C. and soon became tribune*. Like his great-grandfather, Cato the Elder, the younger man was a conservative who believed strongly in Roman tradition. His views were also shaped by his belief in STOICISM, a philosophy that emphasized control over one's thoughts and emotions. As a politician, Cato was uncompromising in his principles and stubbornly resisted change. He blocked several attempts by Pompey and Julius Caesar, two popular generals, to gain favors for their armies and increase their power. However, his inflexibility eventually backfired. Cato's rigid opposition led Pompey, Caesar, and Marcus Crassus to form the First Triumvirate* in 60 B.C. and seize the Senate's power. Cato's enemies soon sent him on a lengthy mission to annex* the island of CYPRUS.

In 54 B.C., Cato won election as praetor*, but he failed in any further attempts to unseat the triumvirate. Two years later, in an attempt to overthrow Caesar, Cato reversed his stand. He threw his support behind Pompey, who had become Caesar's bitter rival. When this rivalry erupted into civil war, Cato fought in Pompey's forces. After Pompey's defeat, Cato joined a group of republican supporters in the North African city of Utica. In April of 46 B.C., facing certain defeat by Caesar's army, Cato committed suicide rather than surrender to Caesar. (*See also* **Caesar, Gaius Julius; Cato the Elder; Cicero, Marcus Tullius; Civil Wars, Roman; Crassus, Marcus Licinius; Pompey; Rome, History of; Triumvirates, Roman.**)

CATULLUS, GAIUS VALERIUS

84–54 B.C.
ROMAN POET

Born into an important family in the northern Italian city of Verona, Gaius Valerius Catullus became one of Rome's greatest poets. Known for his lyric* poetry, Catullus's literary style broke with that of earlier Roman tradition. He derived many of his ideas from the Hellenistic* writers, especially CALLIMACHUS. His work influenced the later Roman poets VERGIL and OVID.

Before Catullus, Roman poetry was expected to serve some public purpose. Most poems were epics* that celebrated Rome, or dramas that were performed at religious festivals. Catullus, however, mocked the Roman ideal of public service, writing mostly short poems about his private emotions. His single book of 116 poems covers a wide range of subjects.

Behind the variety and intensity of the writing, Catullus's poems display the workings of a clever and committed mind. The opening poem in his book describes the work as "thoroughly smoothed with dry pumice*." Smoothing with pumice was how the pages of books were prepared in those days. But the opening poem also refers to the care the poet took in polishing his ideas and words.

Some of his poems written to friends and to public figures, like CAESAR and CICERO, were warm with praise, while others were verbal attacks disguised in irony*. For instance, he called the orator Cicero "the best advocate of all, by as much as Catullus is the worst poet of all." This appears to be praise, but may in fact be criticism, since Catullus probably believed himself far from the worst poet.

A subject that dominates Catullus's poems is love and anguish. In 24 love poems, his subject is a married woman called Lesbia, modeled after a real woman named Clodia. Some of his most gentle poems concern Lesbia and her small pet sparrow. In one poem, Catullus expresses his envy for the way in which Lesbia teases the sparrow to peck at her. The poem is worded like a prayer to a god. Another poem mourns the sparrow's death and expresses anger that the sparrow made Lesbia cry. Although it seems to express sorrow, the poem pictures the little bird hopping merrily through the underworld.

Both poems are parodies*, a literary device that the poet used to show that love could be powerful and ridiculous at the same time.

Catullus also wrote deeply emotional tributes to his dead brother, who had been buried in the region of Troy in Asia Minor. Troy was the setting of the Greek epic the ILIAD. The poet addresses the city as "Troy, the bitter ash of all men and virtues, which brought wretched death even to my brother."

Catullus's masterpiece and longest poem (Poem 64) echoes the bitterness the poet associated with Troy. Written in the form of a short Greek epic, "The Wedding of Peleus and Thetis" is about the parents of ACHILLES, the Greek epic hero* of the Trojan War. Catullus broke with the epic tradition by telling the story not as a narrative but rather as a description of emotions—love, doubt, fear, and anger.

The core of Catullus's work is sadness, best expressed in a short poem that begins *Odi et amo,* which means "I hate as well as love." He viewed love as an illusion that never quite lived up to its promise. He held a similar opinion regarding the epic heros praised by the Romans of his own day. Unlike Roman conservatives such as Cicero, Catullus thought Rome's glory was largely an ideal—very appealing, but something that probably never actually existed. (*See also* **Literature, Greek; Literature, Roman; Pindar; Poetry, Greek and Hellenistic; Poetry, Roman; Sappho.**)

CELTS

The Celts were a group of tribes from central Europe that spread over much of Europe between 500 and 200 B.C. They were known as skilled warriors, and they showed little interest in forming a state of their own. Eventually, they were absorbed into the Roman empire.

The Celtic homeland was central Europe, the region that today is Austria, southern Germany, Switzerland, and France. The Celts had inhabited this region from about 700 B.C., but they did not remain there. The Celts living in what is now modern France were known as Gauls, and by 400 B.C., they had invaded northern Italy and ousted the ETRUSCANS from the region north of the Apennines. In 387 B.C., a band of Celts sacked* Rome, and a century later, they raided Delphi in Greece. By 250 B.C., the Celts had spread from the British Isles to Spain and Asia Minor (the peninsula that is now the nation of Turkey). Through a combination of trading and raiding, the Celts accumulated great wealth and power.

See map in Peoples of Ancient Greece and Rome (vol. 3).

Although the Celts migrated far from their original homeland, they continued to speak their ancestral language. Celtic tribes living in different regions shared the same customs, art forms, and religious beliefs, including the idea that people possessed immortal souls. Celtic religious leaders called Druids—some of whom may have been women—occupied an important place in society.

The Romans were impressed by the physical appearance of the Celts, whom they described as tall and pale-skinned, with blond or red hair that was sometimes bleached and treated with a special soap to make it stand out straight. The men wore gold collars, called torques, around their necks and dressed in fitted pants and hooded woolen capes. Romans began wearing these practical garments, and the words *bracae* (breeches), *mantellum* (mantle), and *cappa* (cape) entered the Latin language.

Despite their exceptional fighting skills, the Celts failed to unite into a strong state. Finally, they were either overcome by other Germanic peoples or conquered by Rome. Their culture survived, however, in Scotland, Ireland, and the Brittany region of western France. Languages based on the original Celtic tongue are still spoken in these regions.

CENSOR AND CENSORSHIP, ROMAN

* **patrician** member of the upper class who traced his ancestry to a senatorial family in the earliest days of the Roman Republic

* **plebeian** member of the general body of Roman citizens, as distinct from the upper class

* **consul** one of two chief governmental officials of Rome, chosen annually and serving for a year

* **Roman Republic** Rome during the period from 509 B.C. to 31 B.C., when popular assemblies annually elected their governmental officials

A censor was the official responsible for conducting the Roman census (the official count of people and property). The position, created in about 443 B.C., also included such responsibilities as awarding state contracts for building roads and public buildings, collecting taxes, and supervising public morality. Censors had enormous power, which extended even to the Roman Senate. They could remove any member of the Senate for violating Roman laws or for exhibiting questionable moral conduct.

Rome had two censors who were elected, usually every five years, for an 18-month term. At first, all censors came from the patrician* class. Then, a law passed in 339 B.C. required that at least one censor be from the plebeian* class. The office evolved into one of the most highly respected positions in Rome, and it often went to former consuls*. The position of censor began to decline in importance under the dictatorship of SULLA around 80 B.C., and it lost its remaining significance in the first century A.D. when the emperor DOMITIAN declared himself censor for life.

The word *censorship* derived from the office of censor. Our modern idea of censorship—banning or prohibiting objectionable speech, writing, or art—comes from the censor's role as a guardian of public morality and his ability to punish those who failed to conform to certain moral standards. There was little official censorship, in the modern sense, in the period of the Roman Republic*. Romans at that time considered freedom of expression to be an important privilege of Roman citizenship. This changed, however, in the early years of the Roman Empire, when freedom of expression was challenged and then curbed. During that time, officials frequently banned or burned objectionable books, and they punished, exiled, or killed individuals who wrote anything critical of the emperors or the government. Such censorship decreased in the A.D. 100s. (*See also* **Census, Roman; Law, Roman; Ostracism; Patricians, Roman; Plebeians, Roman; Senate, Roman; Tacitus.**)

CENSUS, ROMAN

* **consul** one of two chief governmental officials of Rome, chosen annually and serving for a year

* **censor** Roman official who conducted the census, assigned state contracts for public projects (such as building roads), and supervised public morality

A census is an official count of population and property. Since ancient times, governments have used census information to determine people's liability for taxation and military service. The Roman census is thought to have originated in the 500s B.C. during the reign of King Servius Tullius. In the city of Rome itself, kings and consuls* conducted the census until about 443 B.C. It then became the responsibility of officials called censors*. Local magistrates or officials, as representatives of the censors, conducted the census in other Italian cities and in Roman provinces.

In a census, adult male citizens had to report such information as their age, occupation, and residence; the estimated value of their property and wealth; and the names and ages of the wives and children in their families. This information was recorded in an official declaration called a *professio,* and the individual had to swear an oath that the information was correct. Penalties for failing to make a *professio* included seizure of property, public beatings, and enslavement. The information from the census determined an individual's rank in society, and this became the basis for imposing taxes and determining military obligations.

The first censuses applied only to Roman citizens living in Rome and Italy. However, as the empire expanded, the Roman government extended the census to the provinces as well. In the early years of the Roman Republic, the census in Italy normally was held every four or five years. After 80 B.C., it became more infrequent and irregular as the tax burden shifted to the provinces. The last census in Italy was taken sometime between A.D. 69 and 79 during the reign of the emperor VESPASIAN. In other parts of the empire, censuses continued to be taken for hundreds of years. (*See also* **Censor and Censorship, Roman; Class Structure, Roman; Government, Roman; Taxation.**)

CENTAURS

Centaurs were creatures in Greek mythology that were half-human and half-horse. Although most centaurs were believed to be wild, brutal beasts, some were considered to be intelligent and caring, such as Achilles' tutor, Chiron. This statuette from the 500s B.C. shows a centaur galloping.

---

* **Homeric** referring to the Greek poet Homer, the time in which he lived, or his works

* **Peloponnese** peninsula forming the southern part of the mainland of Greece

In Greek mythology, centaurs were wild, half-human, half-horse creatures. Depicted in art as having the body and legs of a horse and the chest, head, and arms of a man, the centaurs were said to be the children of Ixion and the nymph Nephele. They made their home in the forests and wooded mountains of Thessaly, in northern Greece. Centaurs were violent and lustful, and they loved to drink wine. For the ancient Greeks, centaurs represented their own primitive desires and behavior. In the Greek mind, centaurs existed to remind humans of the distinction between instincts and control.

Mentions of centaurs date from Homeric* times. Many legends about them include tales of their conflict with human society. The earliest of these describes how the centaurs upset the wedding festivities of their neighbor, the Lapith king, Pirithous. Invited to the wedding, the centaurs drank too much wine and assaulted the female guests. They even tried to carry off Pirithous's bride. For their outrageous behavior, the centaurs were driven from Thessaly into the Peloponnese* by the Lapiths. In art, centaurs are often depicted fighting against the Greeks with boulders and uprooted trees.

Not all centaurs were brutal savages, however. In Greek myth, the centaur Chiron was wise and kind. Chiron had received instruction in medicine, music, hunting, and the art of prophecy from APOLLO and ARTEMIS. He himself taught many Greek heroes including ASCLEPIUS, Jason, and ACHILLES. Centaurs appear on many Greek objects of art, such as vases, and in the architectural elements of Greek buildings. One of the most famous depictions of centaurs is on the PARTHENON in ATHENS. (*See also* **Amazons; Myths, Greek; Satyrs; Wine.**)

CENTURION

See *Armies, Roman.*

CHARIOTS

A chariot is a two-wheeled, horse-drawn vehicle. Invented in the Near East around 2000 B.C., the chariot was used throughout the ancient world in warfare and in sport. Both the Greeks and the Romans used military chariots, and chariot races were a popular form of entertainment in Greece and Rome.

The early chariot consisted of a lightweight wooden frame with wooden wheels, a low front, and sides made of wicker or leather straps. A military chariot might be armored with metal plates, painted, or decorated with ivory, bronze, or silver. Two or four horses were yoked to a long pole that was fastened to the front of the frame. The driver controlled the horses with reins and a whip.

The chief military use of chariots was for rapid transport. Chariots carried warriors to the battle site, where they leaped from the chariots to fight on foot. Sometimes, however, specially trained warriors fought with spears or bows from moving chariots. In the 700s B.C. in Greece, warriors mounted on horseback (cavalry) replaced military chariots, although generals continued to travel by chariot.

Chariot racing was part of the funeral games that were held to honor Greek heroes who died in battle. Such races later became a major event at the public games. According to the Greek writer PAUSANIAS, four-horse chariot races were added to the Olympic Games in 680 B.C. The race began with a signal call. At that moment, attendants ceremoniously raised a bronze eagle and lowered a bronze dolphin. The race was 12 laps, or about 6 miles. The owner of the winning chariot and horses—not the charioteer—was considered the winner of the race.

The Romans continued the Greek tradition of chariot racing during the Republic. Races were held in the CIRCUS MAXIMUS, a Roman landmark that was originally a grassy oval between slopes where spectators sat. By Emperor TRAJAN's reign in the early A.D. 100s, the Circus Maximus had become an arena that held 170,000 people. By that time, Rome's chariot teams had become business operations, similar in some ways to modern professional sports franchises. Four main professional organizations, or factions, controlled the teams. They identified their chariots and horses with the colors white, red, blue, and green. Each faction had its own stables and its own charioteers. Almost everyone who attended the races, including the emperors, supported a particular color.

The Roman public followed the chariot races with great enthusiasm, learning the names of the horses and placing bets on the colors of the factions they backed. A good charioteer could earn a considerable amount of money from the faction that employed him. Such charioteers became the celebrities of ancient Rome. One of the most famous charioteers of the A.D. 100s was Gaius Apuleius Diocles, who was born in Spain. He raced for about 24 years, winning 1,462 of the 4,257 races he entered. (*See also* **Games, Greek; Games, Roman; Olympic Games.**)

Chariot racing was a popular spectator sport in ancient Rome. The Circus Maximus, the arena in Rome where races took place, held up to 170,000 fans. This Roman relief from the A.D. 100s depicts a quadriga, or four-horse chariot.

CHILDREN

See *Family, Greek; Family, Roman.*

CHRISTIAN ERA

See *Rome, History of.*

CHRISTIANITY

The Christian religion had its origins in the life and teachings of Jesus of Nazareth, who lived in the region of JUDAEA in Palestine during the early years of the Roman Empire. Originally the belief of a small group of devout Jews in JERUSALEM, Christianity gradually evolved during the course of the A.D. 300s into the official religion of the Roman Empire. It later spread beyond the Roman world, becoming the dominant faith in Europe during the Middle Ages.

EARLY CHRISTIANS. After the death of Jesus around A.D. 30, his followers gathered in Jerusalem to prepare for his return to create the kingdom of God, which they believed was foretold in the Jewish scriptures, or sacred texts. At first, followers of Jesus preached his teachings only to their fellow Jews. However, some Christians, especially St. Paul, began converting Gentiles, or non-Jewish people, to the new faith. Thereafter, Christianity came to be viewed as a universal religion, open to men and women of any nation who were willing to follow the teachings of Jesus.

Early Christians formed *ecclesiai* (Greek word meaning "assemblies"), or churches, in various cities in the Near East. Missionaries traveled throughout the Roman empire spreading the faith in Greece, North Africa, and Rome itself. They were particularly successful in converting middle-class people in the cities. In addition to establishing churches, the early Christians developed a hierarchy of leadership and authority to help ensure the survival of the faith. Leaders of the church were called bishops. Believed to be the spiritual successors of Jesus's apostles*, bishops were responsible for spreading and protecting Christian belief. The bishops of the leading religious centers—Rome, Jerusalem, ALEXANDRIA in Egypt, ANTIOCH in Syria, and, after about A.D. 325, CONSTANTINOPLE—possessed more authority than other bishops. The bishop of Rome was considered to be the successor of St. Peter, the leading apostle of Jesus.

* **apostles** early followers of Jesus who traveled and spread his teachings

Early Christians wrote numerous accounts of Christ's life and teachings, and apostles, such as Paul, wrote letters that circulated among the early Christian communities. Between the late A.D. 100s and 500s, church leaders compiled some of these writings as Christian scriptures to be used along with Jewish sacred writings. Later known as the New Testament, these writings served as the basis of the church's missionary activities and liturgy*. The New Testament was later combined with the Jewish scriptures, or Old Testament, to form the Christian Bible.

* **liturgy** form of a religious service, including spoken words, songs, and actions

DIFFERENCES IN BELIEF. As Christianity spread, disagreements developed among Christians regarding the basic beliefs of the religion. Early Jewish Christians opposed St. Paul's conversion of Gentiles. GNOSTICISM, a movement that arose in the A.D. 100s, emphasized the distinction between the physical and spiritual worlds and rejected attempts to build a religious community. Still other movements challenged the role of church leaders as the only guides to salvation*.

* **salvation** deliverance from the effects of sin, such as eternal punishment

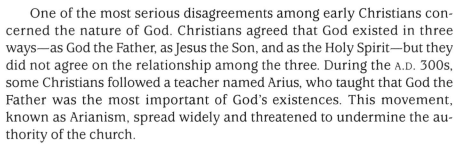

One of the most serious disagreements among early Christians concerned the nature of God. Christians agreed that God existed in three ways—as God the Father, as Jesus the Son, and as the Holy Spirit—but they did not agree on the relationship among the three. During the A.D. 300s, some Christians followed a teacher named Arius, who taught that God the Father was the most important of God's existences. This movement, known as Arianism, spread widely and threatened to undermine the authority of the church.

Councils of church leaders attempted to resolve the issue of God's nature and relationship to Jesus Christ. The Council of Nicaea in A.D. 325 succeeded in adopting a statement of belief which became known as the Nicene Creed, an important part of official Christian doctrine*. The first Council of Constantinople in A.D. 381 ended the long controversy about the relationship of the Trinity—the union of the Father, Son, and Holy Spirit. The bishops decided that the Father, Son, and Holy Spirit were three equal existences of one God and that God and Christ were of one essence.

The decisions of these councils did not satisfy all Christians, however, and they resulted in divisions in the church. The Christians who lived in Egypt, known as the Copts, emphasized the unity of the human and divine qualities of Jesus Christ. When the Council of Chalcedon in A.D. 451 declared that Christ had two separate natures—God and man—and condemned the ruling division of the Coptic Church, most Copts formed an independent church and clergy.

Besides the councils, Christian beliefs were also defined by theological* works of Christian writers such as Origen, TERTULLIAN, and St. AUGUSTINE. These theologians* provided a strong intellectual foundation for the development of Christian thought. However, beliefs that differed from those accepted by the leaders of the church were considered heresies*, and bishops often excommunicated* people who believed in these ideas.

CHRISTIANITY AND THE ROMAN EMPIRE. During the early years of Christianity, Roman authorities viewed Christians with suspicion, concerned about their potential to create social unrest. Although some early Christians were killed for their beliefs, widespread persecutions occurred infrequently. This situation changed during the early and mid-A.D. 200s, when the emperors Decius and Valerian persecuted Christians for their refusal to worship the pagan* Roman gods. Then in A.D. 303, the emperors DIOCLETIAN and Galerius issued a series of edicts* that began a period known as the Great Persecution. These edicts ordered the destruction of churches and the burning of sacred books. All clergymen who did not cooperate were arrested, and all Christians were removed from public service and from the army. A final edict ordered all Christians to make sacrifices to the pagan gods or face execution—an order that was enforced in all the eastern provinces* and in Africa, although not elsewhere in the western empire.

This oppression ended in A.D. 313, when the emperor CONSTANTINE I issued an edict promising toleration for all religions, including Christianity. He later granted Christians various privileges and strengthened the authority of church leaders. His actions marked the first steps in making Christianity the official religion of the Roman Empire. Constantine also

* **doctrine** principle, theory, or belief presented for acceptance

* **theological** pertaining to the nature of God, the study of religion, and religious belief

* **theologian** person who studies religious faith and practice

* **heresy** belief that is contrary to church doctrine

* **excommunicate** to exclude from the rites of the church

* **pagan** referring to a belief in more than one god; non-Christian

* **edict** proclamation or order that has the force of a law

* **province** overseas area controlled by Rome

founded the city of Constantinople in A.D. 324 and made it the new capital of his empire. In contrast to Rome, with its numerous pagan temples, Constantinople was planned as a great Christian city.

When Julian became emperor in A.D. 361, he attempted to reestablish pagan religion in the Roman Empire. (Julian became known as JULIAN THE APOSTATE—the unfaithful one.) Christians lost their privileges, and pagan temples and institutions were revived. By that time, however, Christianity had become so widely accepted and the church had become so strong that these measures failed to extinguish the church. After Julian's death in A.D. 363, the Christian church immediately regained its authority. In A.D. 391, the emperor THEODOSIUS I banned all pagan religions, closed all pagan temples, and made Christianity the official religion of the empire.

In the A.D. 400s, the Roman Empire split into eastern and western parts and the Christian church became divided as well. The patriarch, or bishop of Constantinople, became the leading bishop of the Greek-speaking Eastern Church, while the bishop of Rome, called the pope, led the Western Church. By the final years of the Western Roman Empire, the Christian faith had spread beyond the empire to other peoples of Europe. However, it took centuries in the West until Christianity could establish itself in central and western Europe under the leadership of Rome. Christianity continued to play a major role in the development of Western civilization during the Middle Ages. (*See also* **Churches and Basilicas; Religion, Roman; Rome, History of: Christian Era.**)

PAUL OF TARSUS

Paul, who was both a Jew and a Roman citizen, became one of the most important leaders of the early Christian church. Once a persecutor of Christians, Paul was converted to Christianity while traveling on the road from Jerusalem to Damascus, where he reportedly saw the risen Christ. In the A.D. 40s and 50s, Paul made three long journeys through Greece and Asia Minor, bringing Christianity to those areas. His letters to his followers in Corinth, Galatia, Philippi, and Ephesus became the earliest books of the New Testament.

CHURCHES AND BASILICAS

A church is a place where Christians gather to worship. Churches can also serve as schools, where Christians learn the principles of their faith, and as centers of charity. During the early history of CHRISTIANITY, changes in the form and size of churches reflected the changing role of Christianity in the Roman Empire. After the Emperor CONSTANTINE officially tolerated Christian activities in A.D. 313, cities throughout the empire built large new churches, using elements of Roman architecture in their designs. In the centuries that followed, churches helped keep these architectural styles alive in Christian lands and also carried them to non-Christian cultures.

THE FIRST CHRISTIAN CHURCHES. Within a few years of the death of Jesus, perhaps as early as A.D. 35, Christians in various cities had begun to assemble in groups to worship together. These early assemblies did not have buildings. They met in the private homes of believers. These early Christians sometimes remodeled the interiors of their houses to create rooms that were large enough for group worship. Some of these early church-houses have been excavated* by modern archaeologists*.

By the A.D. 200s, Christians had begun to create new, specifically Christian structures, such as small shrines* in special places. In Rome, for example, Christians constructed a shrine over the tomb thought to hold the remains of St. Peter. Public churches did not yet exist, however, because Christianity did not have official status. Most Christians had to hide their religion from the pagan* Roman authorities.

* **excavate** to uncover by digging

* **archaeologist** scientist who studies past human cultures, usually by excavating ruins

* **shrine** place that is considered sacred because of its history or the relics it contains

* **pagan** referring to a belief in more than one god; non-Christian

THE IMPERIAL CHURCHES. The emperor Constantine's adoption of Christianity as an official state religion brought new power, wealth, and status to the Christian religion and ushered in the age of official Christian buildings across the empire, beginning with the great churches of Rome. The builders of these churches adapted Roman architectural techniques to the needs of Christian worshipers.

Christians did not want their churches to look like the pagan temples that the Greeks and Romans had been building for centuries. Furthermore, churches functioned very differently than the temples had. Pagan temples were houses for the gods, who were often represented by statues. Rituals inside the temples generally involved only a few priests or priestesses. Ceremonies with large numbers of worshipers, if they occurred at all, took place outside the temples. In contrast, churches had to be large, enclosed spaces in which many people could worship at the same time. To create such spaces, church builders returned to the basilica form.

The basilica, introduced in Rome in the 100s B.C., had become a basic element of Roman civic architecture, an all-purpose hall used as a marketplace, courtroom, or public meeting room. Basilicas were large, rectangular structures with high, vaulted roofs of timber beams supported by columns. One end wall of a basilica often featured an apse—a semicircular recess or niche that appeared on the outside of the building as a projection. When the basilica form was used for churches, the altar* was placed within the apse.

Constantine allocated large sums of money for the construction of churches. He sponsored the huge Church of St. John Lateran in Rome, as well as the churches of St. Peter, St. Agnese (Agnes), St. Lorenzo (Lawrence),

* **altar** raised structure in the most sacred part of a church or temple

First appearing in Rome in the 100s B.C., a basilica served as an all-purpose meeting place, courtroom, and marketplace. The large Roman basilicas served as excellent models for the architecture of Christian churches. The basilica pictured here was begun by the emperor Maxentius in A.D. 306 and completed by his successor, Constantine, in A.D. 313.

* province overseas area controlled by Rome

and others outside the walls of Rome. Other structures followed as Christianity gained converts and influence throughout the empire. By the middle of the A.D. 400s most Roman communities, even in the provinces*, had churches.

THE LEGACY OF ROME.   The basilica was not the only Roman contribution to church architecture. Roman builders had also achieved great success with domed structures. Domes with their large, open interiors made good churches. Several churches used the dome, rather than the basilica, as their basic structure. St. Lorenzo in Milan, built in the A.D. 300s, is one example. The most famous domed church was Hagia Sophia, Church of the Holy Wisdom, which the emperor JUSTINIAN I built in CONSTANTINOPLE in the A.D. 500s. Centuries later, after Constantinople fell to the Islamic Turks in 1453, Hagia Sophia became a mosque, an Islamic place of worship. The dome, which had passed from Roman pagan and Christian architecture into Islamic architecture, became the traditional shape of the mosque in Islamic lands.

The Roman churches created another legacy that influenced styles in decoration for many centuries—the emphasis on richly ornamented interiors. Pagan temples in general had fairly plain interiors. If these temples were decorated at all, those decorations tended to be on the outside, where people could see them as they passed the structure. Churches, on the other hand, were decorated on the inside, where the ritual took place. The vaulted or domed ceilings of churches created large interior spaces that architects filled with light and color. Roman builders perfected techniques of decorating walls and floors with slabs of colored marble, mosaics*, and paintings.

* mosaic art form in which small pieces of stone or glass are set in cement; also refers to a picture made in this manner

Even churches that were fairly plain on the outside—such as St. Vitale in Ravenna, Italy, built in the A.D. 500s—were elaborately decorated on the inside with marble panels, mosaics on the floor and walls, objects of silver and gold, and hangings made of costly fabrics, such as silk and velvet. The richness of a church's decorations was thought to honor God, in whose name the church had been built. Rich decorations also reflected the growing wealth and power of Christianity. (*See also* **Architecture, Greek; Architecture, Roman; Religion, Greek; Religion, Roman.**)

CICERO, MARCUS TULLIUS

106–43 B.C.
ROMAN ORATOR AND POLITICIAN

* orator public speaker of great skill
* Roman Republic Rome during the period from 509 B.C. to 31 B.C., when popular assemblies annually elected their governmental officials

Cicero, the greatest of the Roman orators*, was a man of action who made an art of using words as weapons. Cicero believed passionately in the principles of the Roman Republic* and struggled to oppose Julius Caesar and all those who would destroy its noble achievements. A versatile and practical man, Cicero exemplified the best of the Greek intellectual heritage that he so greatly admired and the Roman genius for law and politics.

CAREER.   Born into a wealthy family in an Italian country town, Marcus Tullius Cicero was educated in Rome, Greece, and Rhodes. He studied Latin and Greek literature as well as rhetoric* and philosophy* with Greek masters. An ambitious young man, Cicero began his political career by defending cases in the law courts. Under the Roman system, legal advocates

* **rhetoric** art of using words effectively in speaking or writing

* **philosophy** study of ideas, including science

* **sovereignty** ultimate authority or rule

* **praetor** Roman official, just below the consul in rank, in charge of judicial proceedings and of governing overseas provinces

* **consul** one of two chief governmental officials of Rome, chosen annually and serving for a year

* **oration** formal speech or address

* **triumvirate** ruling body of three

* **triumvir** one member of a ruling body of three

* **augur** Roman religious official who read omens and foretold events

* **proconsul** governor of a Roman province

* **province** overseas area controlled by Rome

* **republican** favoring or relating to a government in which citizens elect officials to represent them in a citizen assembly

* **oratory** the art of public speaking

* **proscribe** to declare someone an outlaw

were paid not with money but with favors, and Cicero accumulated a large number of favors owed to him. His growing reputation received an enormous boost in 70 B.C. when he prosecuted Verres, the corrupt governor of Sicily. This case enabled Cicero to give expression to his belief in the essential sovereignty* of the Roman people. It also enhanced his own reputation, furthered his career, and exposed the problems of the Roman Republican government.

Following his successful case against Verres, Cicero's political star rose quickly. In 66 B.C. he was elected praetor* and delivered his first speech to the people. In it, he supported giving an important military command to the general he would admire for most of his life—POMPEY. Two years later, his careful political maneuvering and accumulation of powerful friends paid off. He was elected consul*, the highest office in the republic, at the earliest age allowed by law.

Cicero gained even more renown when he delivered a series of orations* unmasking a conspiracy by a rival politician, Catiline, to seize the government. Although hailed as a national hero, Cicero's political fortune soon changed. His ally Pompey decided to join Julius Caesar and Marcus Crassus to form the First Triumvirate*, which took power in 60 B.C. The trio invited Cicero to join them, but he refused. He distrusted Caesar and despised Crassus. As a result of his refusal, the trio failed to protect Cicero from one of his greatest enemies, Publius Clodius. In 58 B.C., Clodius succeeded in having Cicero exiled on the charge that he had put the Catiline conspirators to death without public trials. Cicero's enemies destroyed his house in Rome, and he was forced to leave Italy for Macedonia.

Recalled to Rome in 57 B.C., Cicero tried to drive a political wedge between Pompey and Caesar but failed to do so. He was forced to swallow his pride and spent several years defending friends of the triumvirs*, a humiliating task that he detested. He was elected augur*, and in 51 B.C. he was sent as proconsul* to govern Cilicia, a province* in Asia Minor. When he returned the following year, Caesar and Pompey had finally broken their alliance and had plunged Rome into civil war.

Cicero had always supported Pompey, and though he had less faith in Pompey as a true republican* at that time, he decided to enlist with the general and his followers in Greece. After the Battle of Pharsalus in 48 B.C., at which Caesar defeated Pompey, Cicero received Caesar's pardon and returned to Italy. He retreated from public life and devoted his energies to writing on oratory* and philosophy.

Although Cicero had not participated in the assassination of Caesar in 44 B.C., he rejoiced because it meant an end to Caesar's dictatorship and hope for the failing republic. Regarded by many Romans as an elder statesman and representative of the republican spirit, Cicero returned to politics and tried to prevent Mark Antony from replacing Caesar. In a series of orations called the *Philippics* (named for a famous series of speeches of the Greek orator DEMOSTHENES against Philip of Macedonia), Cicero attacked Antony, trying to characterize him as a would-be Eastern king. However, Antony joined forces with Octavian and Lepidus to seize power in a second triumvirate, and the three men proscribed* hundreds of their opponents, including Cicero. The great orator tried to escape from the country he loved so dearly, but he was captured and killed.

* **invective** violent verbal attack

* **treatise** long, detailed essay

* **monarchy** nation ruled by a king or queen

* **oligarchy** rule by a few people

ORATIONS. In Cicero's time, public eloquence was a highly prized art form, the rules of rhetoric were laid down in detail, and a great speaker could powerfully sway public opinion. An orator was expected to excel in invention (finding arguments), organization, style, memory, and delivery. Like an actor, Cicero animated his speeches through gestures and varied vocal tones. He aimed at appealing to both the intellect and the emotions, and he changed his style to fit his subject and his audience.

Cicero delivered many speeches in the courts of law. Roman courts were held in the open air before a jury that might number 50 or 75 men, or before a panel of more than 100 judges, as well as a large crowd of cheering (or jeering) bystanders. In most cases, Cicero wrote out only the *prooemium,* or introduction, in advance. He then improvised most of the main body of the speech from his notes. The texts of many of Cicero's speeches were written down by listeners and published later, so that the versions people read today can only approximate the fiery live performances. Cicero was especially renowned for the rousing *perorations,* or conclusions of his speeches. He was masterful at appeals for mercy. He once delivered a peroration while holding a baby in his arms.

Cicero's most famous orations are those against Catiline in the *Catilinarian Orations,* all of which use a wide array of rhetorical devices to achieve their purposes. In them, Cicero used brilliant character sketches, fierce invective*, pointed examples drawn from Roman history, repetition, and memorable figures of speech. In the first speech against Catiline, for example, he opens with a string of repeated questions directly addressed to Catiline and designed to humiliate him and render him powerless:

> How far, then, Catiline, will you go on abusing our patience? How long, you madman, will you mock at our vengeance? . . . Do you not see that all your plans are discovered? Do you not realize that your conspirators are bound hand and foot by the knowledge that every man here has of you? Which of us do you think is not aware of what you did last night, or the night before, where you were, whom you summoned, what plans you made? What times we live in, what scandals we permit! The Senate knows these things, the consul sees them; yet this man lives.

OTHER WORKS. In addition to speeches, Cicero wrote dialogues in imitation of PLATO, treatises* on rhetoric, philosophical essays, poetry, and many letters. The dialogue *De Oratore* sets forth many of his fundamental beliefs about the role of rhetoric in society and his vision of the orator as statesman—a highly cultured person who combines technical skill, strength of character, and wide knowledge of philosophy and literature. *De Republica* is a dialogue that sets out to demonstrate that Rome is history's finest example of the best kind of government—a mixture of monarchy*, oligarchy*, and democracy. In the *Tusculan Disputations,* set in Cicero's villa at Tusculum, he explores the beliefs and attitudes of STOICISM, to which he was deeply drawn. Cicero was an eclectic philosopher— one who drew on ideas from various schools of philosophy and explored how these ideas could apply to the real world of law and public life.

Perhaps the best way to become acquainted with Cicero the individual is to read some of his letters. In particular, the letters collected in *Ad familiares (Letters to friends)* and the letters to his best friend, Atticus, provide a vivid portrait of Roman political and social life. They range from sharp observations on major political events to casual comments on the matters of everyday life. The letters reveal a proud and emotional man who could also be vain, a well-known orator who admitted being nervous before his speeches, and a devoted citizen whose words played a major part in the development of Roman civilization. (*See also* **Antonius, Marcus; Class Structure, Roman; Education and Rhetoric, Greek; Education and Rhetoric, Roman; Government, Roman; Law, Roman; Oratory; Philosophy, Greek and Hellenistic; Philosophy, Roman; Rome, History of.**)

CIRCUS MAXIMUS

* **tier** one of a series of rows arranged one above the other, as in a stadium

In Roman times, the arena for chariot racing was called a *circus,* a Latin word meaning "circle" or "ring." The oldest and most famous circus was the Circus Maximus in Rome. Originally built in the ETRUSCAN period, but rebuilt and expanded several times, by the A.D. 300s the Circus Maximus could seat nearly 250,000 people. Up to 12 chariots, each drawn by four horses, could race at a single time.

The Circus Maximus was an elongated U-shaped structure with raised tiers* of seats on three sides and a series of 12 starting gates called *carceres* along the open end. The sand-covered race track was about 700 yards long and 135 yards wide. A low barrier wall called the *spina* divided the length of the race track. Decorated with statues, monuments, and shrines, the *spina* also had tall posts at each end to mark the turning points of the course. An arcade of shops lined the outer walls of the Circus Maximus.

In a typical race, chariots lined up in the starting gates awaiting the signal to begin. At the starting signal—the dropping of a white cloth—the starting gates flew open and the horses began racing counterclockwise around the arena. The race continued for seven laps around the track, a distance of about five and one-half miles. Laps were counted by markers at either end of the spina that could be lowered or turned—egg-shaped markers at one end and dolphin-shaped markers at the other. (Eggs and dolphins were considered objects sacred to the gods—eggs to Castor and Polydeuces, and dolphins to Neptune.) Officials announced the winner at the completion of the race.

The races in the Circus Maximus were controlled by professional racing organizations called *factiones.* These groups operated horse farms, trained horses and charioteers, and attended to all maintenance and services at the races. The *factiones,* each represented by a different color, sponsored various teams of chariots. The spectators generally supported a particular color, and they closely followed the careers of different charioteers and horses. The chariot races at the Circus Maximus were great public events, held as many as 64 days a year, with at least 24 races each day. (*See also* **Amphitheater, Roman; Chariots; Games, Roman.**)

CIRCUS, ROMAN

See *Games, Roman.*

CITIES, GREEK

* **city-state** independent state consisting of a city and its surrounding territory

Urban life in ancient Greece developed after 800 B.C. with the rise of political units called city-states*. Although each city-state, or POLIS, included villages and farmland, its cultural, economic, and political center was the Greek city. Compared to modern cities, most Greek cities were small, containing 5,000 or fewer people. Even Athens, the most populous Greek city, never held more than 250,000 to 300,000 inhabitants during ancient times. However, despite their small size, Greek cities played a major role in shaping Greek culture.

ORIGINS OF THE GREEK CITY. The city was not a Greek invention. Earlier civilizations of the Near East had established large cities thousands of years before Greek civilization arose. Like these earlier cities, Greek cities usually sprang up in river valleys and along the seacoast. Such locations offered good land for farming and access to transportation routes, which made contact and trade with other cultures easier. Historians are unsure exactly when the first Greek cities appeared, but by the 700s B.C., the basic pattern of city life in Greece had begun to take shape.

At the same time, several Greek cities began to establish colonies in Sicily, Italy, Africa, and the Black Sea region. The city that sent out colonists was referred to as the metropolis (mother city). Greek colonies in Asia Minor soon came into contact with civilizations of the Near East, such as Assyria and Babylonia. Trade with these civilizations brought the Greeks knowledge of new arts and sciences and helped advance Greek culture. It is quite likely that contact with these civilizations also influenced the design and layout of Greek cities.

CITY DESIGN AND PLANNING. Defense was a main concern of the ancient Greeks who collected in the towns and cities. The earliest communities formed around a fortified hilltop, called an ACROPOLIS, where the residents could take shelter if they were attacked. The acropolis contained shrines to the city's chief gods and other important buildings. Over time, as the cities grew, the Greeks often built protective walls around the larger settlement areas, but the residents could still retreat to the acropolis as a second line of defense.

While the oldest cities, such as Athens, grew haphazardly into a tangled maze of streets, the Greeks eventually adopted careful city planning. Like the peoples of the Near East, they began laying out their cities in a gridlike pattern in which the streets ran at right angles to each other. One advantage of this simple pattern, which the Romans would later use, was the ability to plan and build new cities quickly. This was especially important for colonists preparing to organize, house, and defend their new communities against any unfriendly neighbors.

The planned Greek city was typically laid out in blocks that were divided by wide avenues as well as by narrower streets. The original plan might feature three or four avenues running in a north-south direction, intersected by three or four more running in an east-west direction. Several smaller streets ran between the avenues. Each block contained two rows of houses, set back-to-back, often separated by a narrow alley. This formed the core of the city's grid pattern.

HOUSING AND LIVING CONDITIONS. Most of what remains today of ancient Greek cities are magnificent halls and temples made of gleaming MARBLE. While many public buildings were indeed beautifully designed and constructed, the typical Greek home was simple. Houses were made of mud bricks and were small, measuring about 30 to 35 feet on each side. Built to be more useful than impressive, they probably were not even whitewashed to make them more attractive. Some houses were pleasant or even luxurious inside, but even these would have looked plain on the outside.

By modern standards, the residential areas of most Greek cities were crowded and dirty. There was no running water, garbage pickup, or sewage system. The water supply usually remained uncovered and frequently became contaminated. By contrast, later Roman cities were much more sanitary, since the Romans took great care to provide clean water and dispose of their sewage. Greek streets were narrow, with rows of identical, mud-brown houses. There were few parks or open squares except for one large central commons, the AGORA.

THE AGORA. The heart of the Greek city was the agora, which means "gathering place." Citizens gathered in this large public area to conduct their daily business and to socialize. The agora served as the marketplace as well as the hub of political activity and government. The most important temples and religious shrines were usually located there as well. The agora was so vital to Greek city life that the Greek historian PAUSANIUS questioned whether a city without an agora could be considered a true city.

In early times, the agora was simply a large open area. As cities developed, the Greeks refined the space with their most splendid architecture. They designed grand stoas, which were long colonnaded* porches that ran along one or more sides of the open plaza. Around the agora stood elegant temples, government buildings, fountains, statues, baths, and monuments. In a later era, the Romans invested similar grandeur and importance in the public area called the forum, their version of the agora.

PUBLIC LIFE IN GREEK CITIES. The contrast between the magnificence of the agora and the dreariness of the residential areas reflects the importance of public life over private life in ancient Greece. Because slaves did most of the heavy work in Greek cities, most of the citizens enjoyed much leisure time. Intellectual, cultural, and social activities were very important to most city dwellers and usually occupied their spare time. Theaters, gymnasiums, stadiums, and other facilities that emphasized large group activities were all considered essential to a city.

Of course, not all public life was fun and entertainment. Along with the privileges of living in the city came certain obligations. Citizens were usually required to participate in city government, and the armies of most cities consisted of citizens as well. It was the involvement of

MANY INHABITANTS, FEW CITIZENS

Very few of the residents of most Greek cities were actually citizens with full rights under the law. In Athens, for example, only adult males whose parents were both Athenians were eligible for citizenship. Before 451 B.C., no woman could be a citizen, regardless of her birth. Citizenship was occasionally granted for outstanding service to the city, but this was rare. Of the 250,000 or so residents of Athens in 431 B.C., only about 45,000 were counted as citizens. Slaves made up a large portion of the population of every Greek city. Some historians estimate that at least half of the residents of Athens were slaves.

* colonnade series of regularly spaced columns, usually supporting a roof

the citizens in public affairs that accounted for much of the strength and vitality of the Greek city. (*See also* **Archaeology of Ancient Sites; Architecture, Greek; Cities, Roman; Colonies, Greek; Forum; Household Furnishings; Houses; Markets; Slavery; Social Life, Greek; Trade, Greek; Waterworks.**)

CITIES, ROMAN

* **archaeologist** scientist who studies past human cultures, usually by excavating ruins

* **aqueduct** channel, often including bridges and tunnels, that brings water from a distant source to where it is needed

Ancient Rome was one of the world's greatest cities. According to legend, Rome was founded in 753 B.C. by ROMULUS AND REMUS, the twin sons of the god Mars. Archaeologists*, however, believe it actually formed when a cluster of villages on the hills near the TIBER RIVER merged to make one town. By 600 B.C., Rome was a major city that dominated the surrounding area. At its height, during the empire, Rome had a population of more than a million people.

Throughout the lands they conquered, the Romans energetically founded new cities and improved existing ones. They took great pride in their cities and provided inhabitants with many services, such as water from aqueducts* and entertainment at THEATERS.

PLANNING AND BUILDING ROMAN CITIES. Rome and other early Italian towns arose without plans. Towns developed around forts, mines and QUARRIES, religious sites, river crossings, and road junctions. In contrast, many of the Greek colonies in southern Italy were carefully designed. Roman rulers used these Greek cities as models as they constructed new areas of Rome or rebuilt areas that had been destroyed by fire. When founding new cities in conquered territories, the Romans planned these settlements on the Greek models, but incorporated characteristics of the city of Rome as well. These new cities often began as military settlements to provide security in hostile areas. By 338 B.C., more than a dozen colonies had been founded in Italy to protect Rome from unfriendly peoples. Later, the Romans established colonies in western Europe and in North Africa.

Numerous Roman officials and professionals worked on establishing a new city or town. Military surveyors worked on town planning. An augur* performed religious rites to determine the best site for the town. Retired soldiers were often the first settlers in a new town. The typical Roman town was planned as a rectangle. A plowed furrow marked the lines where the city walls would be built. Two main streets crossed the rectangle in the center at right angles. Other streets ran parallel to the main ones, forming a grid pattern, insofar as the features of the land permitted. The forum* and public buildings were constructed in the center.

* **augur** Roman religious official who read omens and foretold events

* **forum** in ancient Rome, the public square or marketplace, often used for public assemblies and judicial proceedings

The governments of new colonies were based on that of Rome. The Romans also took over cities that already existed. These cities, called *municipia,* received a charter that set forth how they were to be governed. Cities often petitioned the emperor for a charter, which was conferred as a mark of favor. The charter was inscribed on bronze and posted in the city center where everyone could see it. Rulers and other wealthy Romans would construct grand public buildings in cities that they favored.

* **colonnade** series of regularly spaced columns, usually supporting a roof

* **basilica** in Roman times, a large rectangular building used as a court of law or public meeting place

* **curia** in Rome, the meeting place of the Senate; in other urban areas, the meeting place of the town council

* **Roman Republic** Rome during the period from 509 B.C. to 31 B.C., when popular assemblies annually elected their governmental officials

* **gladiatorial** refers to the public entertainments in ancient Rome in which slaves or captives fought

GREAT CITIES PAST AND PRESENT

Many Roman cities still flourish today. Some still have names similar to their Roman ones, while others have quite different names. Here are a few Roman cities with their modern names:

Tingis	Tangier, Morocco
Aquincum	Budapest, Hungary
Lutetia	Paris, France
Lugdunam	Lyons, France
Londinium	London, England
Eburacum	York, England
Aquae Solis	Bath, England
Toletum Augusta	Toledo, Spain
Trevirorum Colonia	Trier, Germany
Agrippensis	Cologne (Köln), Germany

LIFE IN THE CITY. The forum was the center of Roman city life. A public square and marketplace, the forum was surrounded by public buildings and often had a continuous colonnade* that included shops and offices. A forum typically featured an important temple at one end. In the city of Rome, the original forum was located between hills in an area that had once been a marsh. As the city grew, the forum repeatedly had to be expanded.

The public buildings that lined the sides of a forum included the basilica*, the curia*, TEMPLES, and the market. The basilica and curia housed the government. Adjoining the curia was an open space for public assemblies, called the comitium. Temples, dedicated to the gods and goddesses, served as places for religious ceremonies. The market, or *macella,* was originally a meat market, but the term became used for a market building with various shops. The market in Rome built by the emperor TRAJAN contained over 150 individual shops. Romans honored outstanding citizens with statues, COLUMNS, and other monuments in the forum.

Prosperous cities and towns had sidewalks and streets paved with stone. Raised stone walkways over streets helped people cross streets without getting dirty. The walkways had gaps between the stones so vehicles with wheels could pass through them. Reflecting its basically unplanned nature, the city of Rome had many crooked, narrow streets. In the last years of the Roman Republic*, the city became so crowded that a law prohibited most wheeled vehicles from passing through it during the daytime. Until the A.D. 300s, most streets had no lighting and were often unsafe at night. Many streets had no names, and houses had no numbers.

Rome and other major cities provided many public services. The government cleaned the streets and built sewer systems. There was no garbage collection, however, and people sometimes threw their trash out windows, although that was illegal. The emperor Augustus established fire and police forces. He also organized the supply and distribution of grain, which was stored in large warehouses. Grain was sold to bakers or distributed free directly to the people.

Aqueducts delivered water for drinking, bathing, and cooking. Aqueducts brought water to Rome from as far away as 60 miles. Although wealthy people had running water in their homes, most others did not, so cities provided public fountains and lavatories. Rome had 600 public fountains. Cities also built public baths. The baths were the cities' social centers. The largest, such as those built by the emperors Caracalla and DIOCLETIAN in Rome, occupied many acres.

People in the cities loved spectacles of all kinds, such as plays, chariot races, and gladiatorial* contests. Roman cities had public theaters for dramatic and musical performances. The Roman senator Pompey built the first permanent theater in Rome in 55 B.C., although other cities may have had theaters earlier. Several different kinds of structures were built for athletic games and competitions. Most of these were basically open-air structures, although the area where the audience sat might have awnings, and theater stages were covered with roofs. Every year, many days were proclaimed as holidays and devoted to public entertainment.

While the emperors lived in luxurious palaces, most people in cities lived in town houses or apartments. The town house, or *domus,* was a single-family house. The domus was built in several styles, the most common consisting of several rooms arranged around a courtyard, or atrium. Only a door and a few windows opened on the street to ensure security and quiet. Some town houses had more than one story.

As the population of Rome and other large cities grew, apartment houses were built. Eventually, by the end of the republic, a majority of Rome's inhabitants lived in apartments rented from landlords who owned the buildings. Apartment buildings, like town houses, were built around courtyards and had several stories, although Augustus issued a regulation limiting them to five stories. They often had shops in front facing the street. The buildings were generally poorly constructed, and apartments on the upper floors lacked running water and heating facilities. Apartment buildings in Rome's port of Ostia can still be seen today.

CITIES OF THE EMPIRE. In addition to Rome, many cities flourished in the Roman empire. Alexandria, on the delta of the Nile River in Egypt, was the second largest city, with perhaps 500,000 people. Although renowned as a cultural and religious center, it was also notorious for its high crime rate. Unfortunately, since the modern city has been built over it, little of ancient Alexandria survives today.

Other cities include the North African city of Carthage, destroyed by Rome in 146 B.C. at the end of the Punic Wars. Augustus, however, founded a new city on the site in 29 B.C., and later emperors built a great aqueduct and huge public baths there. Ephesus, a port in Asia Minor, was the leading city of the region and the capital of Rome's province of Asia. Its public library held about 12,000 books. Augustus founded Trier, the most important city in northeastern Gaul, on the Mosel River in what is now Germany. It became the home of several later emperors.

Pompeii, in Italy, was not a large city, but it has great importance for our knowledge of Roman life. Vesuvius, a nearby volcano, erupted in A.D. 79, killing virtually all the inhabitants of the city. The tons of lava and ash from the volcano, however, preserved the town's streets and buildings in astonishingly good condition. (*See also* **Aqueducts; Archaeology of Ancient Sites; Architecture, Roman; Baths, Roman; Colonies, Greek; Colonies, Roman; Forum; Houses; Rome, City of.**)

CITIZENSHIP

Ancient Greek and Roman societies granted their citizens rights and responsibilities that slaves, foreigners, and other people who were considered subordinate did not possess. Citizenship rights changed over time. While the Greeks tended to limit citizenship to children born to citizens, the Romans were more willing to extend citizenship to include others who had previously been excluded, such as freed slaves.

CITIZENSHIP IN ANCIENT GREECE. In Greece, citizenship meant sharing in the duties and privileges of membership in the polis, or city-state*. Citizens were required to fight in defense of the polis and expected to participate in the political life of the city by voting. In return, they were the only ones allowed to own land and to hold political office. Because citizens

* **city-state** independent state consisting of a city and its surrounding territory

THE SONS OF PERICLES

The Athenian statesman Pericles proposed the law granting citizenship only to those whose parents were both citizens. He thought his own family was safe with regard to this law. After all, he had two sons, Xanthippus and Paralus, with his Athenian wife, and, though he and his wife divorced, both sons were considered citizens. But during the plague that devastated much of Athens in 430 B.C., both Xanthippus and Paralus died. Pericles had another son, also named Pericles, but his mother was not a citizen. Needing an heir, the elder Pericles asked the Athenian assembly to make an exception to his own law. Out of compassion for Pericles's loss of his two other sons, the Athenians awarded citizenship to his surviving son.

* **Hellenistic** referring to the Greek-influenced culture of the Mediterranean world during the three centuries after Alexander the Great, who died in 323 B.C.

* **oligarchy** rule by a few people

controlled the wealth and power of the polis, the Greeks carefully regulated who could obtain citizenship. In general, only those free residents who could trace their ancestry to a famous founder of the city were considered citizens. Only on rare occasions would a polis grant citizenship to outsiders, usually only to those who possessed great wealth or valuable skills.

Much of our knowledge of Greek citizenship comes from ATHENS. The statesman CLEISTHENES reformed Athenian political life in the late 500s B.C. by assigning all citizens to a deme, or village. Each deme recorded and maintained a list of its citizens. As a result, the deme's name became part of the official name of every Athenian citizen. A citizen might therefore be known as "Megacles, son of Hippocrates, of the deme of Alopeke." Cleisthenes' reforms allowed many more people to be counted as citizens, including, for the first time, poor Athenians.

Athenians jealously guarded their citizenship. Only after two years of military service were young men included on the citizenship lists. In 451 B.C., the Athenians passed a law limiting citizenship to those whose mother and father were both citizens. By the middle of the 300s B.C., it even became illegal for an Athenian citizen to marry a noncitizen. Only during the Hellenistic* period did Athenian citizenship become easier to obtain, and it was sometimes even purchased by wealthy people.

Most people in Athens did not have full citizenship rights. Although they might be citizens, women could not participate in most activities of the polis. While men held public positions, women were restricted to their households and their role limited to that of wife or daughter. The Greeks owned many slaves, who had no rights at all. Many resident aliens, called *metics*, lived in Athens, but they could not own land or vote, and they were required to pay special taxes.

Other Greek city-states limited citizenship rights even more than Athens did. In Greek oligarchies*, not all citizens were equal—only the wealthy or members of ruling families had full rights. In Sparta, citizenship was limited to members of the warrior class. An adult Spartan male had to serve in the military and keep himself trained and fit, or else lose his citizenship. Spartan citizens were freed from all work not directly related to the military. A large class of HELOTS, conquered native people owned by the Spartan state, produced all the food the citizens required.

CITIZENSHIP IN ANCIENT ROME. The Romans shared the Greek belief that citizenship involved certain responsibilities and privileges. Citizens in ancient Rome had the right to vote, the right to make legally binding contracts, and the right to enter into a marriage recognized as legal by the state (which established the legitimacy of children and the right to inherit). In return, Roman citizens were required to fulfill specific duties, including paying special taxes and serving in the military. Citizenship in ancient Rome was not the same for everyone. For example, certain inhabitants of Italy held partial citizenship, called *sine suffragio*, granting them all rights except the right to vote and hold office. Some noncitizens possessed limited rights, including the right to marry. Wealthy Romans also had more privileges by law than poorer citizens.

A person could become a Roman citizen in several ways, most commonly through a citizen father who was legally married. Unlike the Greeks,

the Romans were generous with the granting of citizenship to non-Romans, and this policy helped secure Rome's empire. Certain peoples of ITALY could become Roman citizens simply by moving to Rome. Slaves automatically became citizens when they were freed by their masters. Rome rewarded foreigners for their service to the state with citizenship. During the Roman Empire, citizenship was extended to favored individuals, cities, and sometimes entire provinces*. In A.D. 212, the emperor Caracalla granted citizenship to all free inhabitants of the empire. By that time, however, the right to vote had disappeared, and the most important rights of citizenship were held only by the nobility. (*See also* **Class Structure, Greek; Class Structure, Roman; Democracy, Greek; Government, Greek; Government, Roman; Land: Ownership, Reform, and Use; Oligarchy.**)

* **province** overseas area controlled by Rome

CITY OF GOD

See *Augustine, St.*

CITY-STATE

See *Polis.*

CIVIL WARS, ROMAN

* **Roman Republic** Rome during the period from 509 B.C. to 31 B.C., when popular assemblies annually elected their governmental officials

* **consul** one of two chief governmental officials of Rome, chosen annually and serving for a year

* **triumvirate** ruling body of three

A civil war (*bellum civile* in Latin) is a war between citizens of the same country. During the years of the Roman Republic*, Romans fought several civil wars that were caused by rivalries between powerful generals. During the period of the Roman Empire, disputes about who would be emperor also led to civil wars.

The first civil war took place from 88 to 83 B.C. The generals Gaius Marius and Lucius Cornelius SULLA were the principal rivals. Marius had gained great popularity by persuading the Senate to grant land to the poor citizens in his army. Sulla was serving as consul* and had been appointed army commander for Rome's possessions in the East, although he and his army were in Italy.

In 88 B.C., Mithriadates, king of Pontus in Asia Minor, invaded Rome's eastern territories. The general who led the war against Mithridates would be in a position to acquire great wealth. Marius wanted the command and, supported by large crowds in Rome, succeeded in seizing it from Sulla. In retaliation, Sulla and his army marched on Rome, regained the command, and forced Marius to flee. While Sulla was in the East fighting Mithriadates, Marius returned to Rome and captured the city in a bloody battle. He died soon after. Sulla and his army returned to Rome in 83 B.C. and defeated Marius's followers. Sulla executed many of his opponents and gave their land to his soldiers. He retired after ruling as dictator for several years.

The second civil war resulted in the end of the Roman Republic. The generals Pompey and Caesar and the wealthy Crassus had formed the First Triumvirate* in 60 B.C. and dominated Rome. Crassus died several years later at the Battle of Carrhae, a humiliating defeat for Rome. While Pompey ruled in Italy, Caesar conquered Gaul and invaded Britain. Soon, however, Pompey and Caesar became enemies. The wealthy classes in Rome, who controlled the Senate, tended to support Pompey. Caesar made himself the favorite of the poorer citizens.

In 49 B.C., Caesar defied the Senate by taking his army into Italy and defeated Pompey in a series of battles. The decisive one was at Pharsalus in Greece in 48 B.C. Although Caesar had the smaller army, he routed Pompey, who fled to Egypt where he was killed by the Egyptian government dominated by Rome. After defeating Pompey's allies, Caesar returned to Rome and established a dictatorship. Caesar's dictatorship, however, was short-lived.

A group led by Brutus and Cassius, wishing to restore the republic, assassinated Caesar on the Ides of March (March 15) in 44 B.C. War then resumed between Caesar's supporters and opponents. Two of Caesar's followers, Marcus ANTONIUS (Mark Antony) and Lepidus, joined with Octavian, Caesar's adopted son, to form the Second Triumvirate. They defeated Brutus and Cassius, both of whom committed suicide, and divided the empire among themselves. The triumvirate collapsed after several years. Lepidus joined a rebellion against Octavian and was defeated. Antony had fallen in love with Cleopatra and had made an alliance with her, which resulted in his loss of support in Rome.

Octavian waged war against Antony and Cleopatra. A decisive sea battle occurred at Actium in northwest Greece in 31 B.C., which was won by Octavian's great general Marcus Agrippa. Both Antony and Cleopatra fled to Egypt and committed suicide the following year. Octavian then had no rivals to oppose his authority, and in 27 B.C., he began his reign as Emperor Augustus.

During the Roman Empire, many civil wars occurred over succession* to the imperial* throne. Over the years, various armies would each proclaim their general as emperor, and civil war generally followed. This occurred, for example, in A.D. 69, the so-called "Year of the Four Emperors." In that year, three generals—Galba, Otho, and Vitellius—each in turn attempted to rule as emperor after the suicide of Nero, until Vespasian finally secured the throne and restored some stability to the empire.

Another civil war occurred after the death of the emperor Pertinax in A.D. 193. The Praetorian Guard, the imperial bodyguard, made Didius Julianus emperor. General Septimius Severus, however, marched on Rome and had the new emperor murdered. Defeating two rival generals, Severus ruled for nearly twenty years and established the Severan dynasty*, which lasted until A.D. 235. Several more civil wars occurred throughout the remaining years of the empire. (*See also* **Rome, History of.**)

* **succession** transmission of authority on the death of one ruler to the next

* **imperial** pertaining to an emperor or empire

* **dynasty** succession of rulers from the same family or group

CLASS STRUCTURE, GREEK

Like most human societies, the ancient Greeks were divided into several social classes, based primarily on heredity, wealth, or citizenship status. Although Greek class structure evolved over time, Greek society generally was split between a large group of people who owned little or no land and a small group of wealthy landowners who possessed most of the political power.

CLASS STRUCTURE IN EARLY GREECE.

As described in the poems of HOMER and HESIOD, membership in the Greek community in the 800s B.C. meant belonging to an *oikos,* or household. An *oikos* consisted of an adult male and his relatives and slaves. Each *oikos* was expected to be a self-sufficient unit—able to take care of all of its own needs—and was largely devoted to farming and herding. Nonagricultural activities, such as trade and craftmaking, were performed by outsiders or *thetes,* the lowest members of the community. *Thetes* owned little or no land and survived by attaching themselves to larger households or by working in return for food and shelter. At the top of Greek society was a small, elite class of warriors called *basileis,* or chieftains. These warriors ruled one or more villages and measured their wealth by the size of their landholdings, herds, and flocks. Movement from a lower class to a higher one was extremely limited.

CLASS STRUCTURE IN THE ARCHAIC PERIOD.

The Archaic period (750–500 B.C.) was an age of great social change and conflict. The Greek population increased rapidly, and the society as a whole grew wealthier. Those who inherited their aristocratic* status became more powerful, ruling over the new city-states* that arose during the period. Although some non-noble Greeks also became rich through such activities as slave trading and fighting as mercenaries*, they were denied political power. The increased population made it difficult for most Greeks to own enough land to make a living by farming, and many fell into debt. Some became craftsmen, making pottery or working on the temples that were funded by rich citizens. Others emigrated to one of the new Greek colonies in ITALY or ASIA MINOR, where they could own more land and accumulate wealth. In general, however, tensions remained high between the aristocrats, the wealthy non-nobles, and poorer citizens. The Greeks resolved these crises in a variety of ways, including the formation of tyrannies* in some city-states.

Like other Greek city-states in the early Archaic period, Athens was ruled by an aristocracy that held all political power. The rest of society was divided into farmers and *demiourgoi,* who were craftsmen and other nonagricultural workers. The aristocracy owned most of the land and charged high rents, forcing many of the farmers into debt. By the late 600s B.C., many Athenians were close to rebelling against the aristocracy. In 594 B.C., the statesman SOLON was appointed sole archon* to resolve the crisis. He reorganized Athenian society into four new groups based on wealth instead of birth. Solon's reforms helped some people who were not aristocrats gain some political power. Athenian society remained unequal, however. The right to hold office was limited to the two wealthier groups.

The Spartans solved the conflict between rich and poor by conquest. Faced with a lack of farmland and a growing population, the Spartans conquered Laconia, in the southeastern part of the Peloponnese*, and Messenia, the region to the west. The conquered territories were divided among Spartan warriors, and the native inhabitants were enslaved by the state. By the late 600s B.C., the Spartans developed a stable social structure. The conquered peoples of Laconia and Messenia, called

* **aristocratic** referring to people of the highest social class

* **city-state** independent state consisting of a city and its surrounding territory

* **mercenary** soldier, usually a foreigner, who fights for payment rather than out of loyalty to a nation

* **tyranny** rule by one person, usually obtained through unlawful means

* **archon** in ancient Greece, the highest office of state

* **Peloponnese** peninsula forming the southern part of the mainland of Greece

FOREIGNERS

Free foreign workers, called *metoikoi* or *metics,* were important members of Athenian society. Although most metics came from the Greek city-states in Asia Minor, some were Syrian, Egyptian, or Phoenician. *Metics* did not have the rights of Athenian citizens. Unable to own land in Athens, they turned to commerce, manufacturing, banking, and skilled crafts. Some educated *metics* became writers. Herodotus, the great historian of the Persian Wars, was a *metic* from Halicarnassus in Asia Minor.

* **classical** in Greek history, refers to the period of great political and cultural achievement from about 500 B.C. to 323 B.C.

* **Hellenistic** referring to the Greek-influenced culture of the Mediterranean world during the three centuries after Alexander the Great, who died in 323 B.C.

* **oligarchy** rule by a few people

HELOTS, were required to supply the Spartans with food. A class of free people, called *perioikoi,* handled trade, crafts, and other economic functions. Freed from economic concerns, the Spartans devoted themselves solely to military and civil affairs. Although there was still a Spartan aristocracy, all citizens were considered equals. This structure remained in place for 300 years and helped Sparta maintain internal stability and military power.

CLASS STRUCTURE IN THE CLASSICAL PERIOD. During much of the classical* period, the city of Athens experienced a high level of peace and economic growth. Due to the reforms that began with Solon and CLEISTHENES in the 500s B.C., all male citizens participated in the city government for the first time. However, the leaders of Athens still came from the aristocracy. The great wealth of the city, collected from its empire, made possible extensive construction projects requiring large numbers of artisans and laborers. Many Athenians continued to take advantage of overseas colonies. Foreign workers in Athens, called *metics,* were prohibited from owning land, but they could still earn money in trade and commerce. Much of the hard labor was performed by the many thousands of slaves owned by Athenians.

Since other city-states did not have the financial resources of Athens, poor Greeks did not have as many financial opportunities, and relations between classes remained tense. Even in Sparta, which had the same social structure for centuries, the gap between rich and poor increased, especially after the Helots of Messenia were freed in 369 B.C.

CLASS STRUCTURE IN THE HELLENISTIC PERIOD. After the reign of the Macedonian king ALEXANDER THE GREAT, who conquered much of the world known to the Greeks in the late 300s B.C., new opportunities for advancement arose for Greeks outside of Greece. The ruling elite in Egypt and Asia consisted entirely of Greek citizens, many of whom emigrated to cities where they became the leaders of economic and political life. On the other hand, the native populations in these areas were treated as serfs. During the Hellenistic* period, the native people frequently rebelled against the Greek leaders as they attempted to restore their own governments, while conflict among the Greeks themselves was much rarer.

In Greece itself, the gap between the rich and poor grew during the Hellenistic period and created ever greater tension between classes. Most city-states were ruled by oligarchies*. As the rich grew richer, the poor became poorer, inspiring proposals to redivide land among the poor and to cancel debts. The Spartan situation was especially desperate: of the 700 remaining Spartan citizens, only 100 owned land, and most of them were in debt. During the 200s B.C., the Spartan kings Agis IV, Kleomenes III, and Nabis canceled all debts, gave land to the landless, and extended citizenship to some of the lowest classes. Reforms such as these served only to outrage Greek aristocrats, who were interested in preserving their privileges and wealth. (*See also* **Agriculture, Greek; Citizenship; Democracy, Greek; Government, Greek; Greece, History of; Land: Ownership, Reform, and Use; Slavery.**)

CLASS STRUCTURE, ROMAN

Ancient Romans classified themselves according to their wealth and heredity. At the top of society were wealthy landowners from prominent families, whose privileged place was recognized by the state and marked by special clothing. At the bottom were peasants, tenant farmers, the urban poor, and slaves.

Roman society operated under a patron-client system. In public, privileged Romans expected open displays of deference from their clients, such as supporting the patron in his private and political life, and especially by coming to the patron's home in the early morning to greet him. Though the terms of respect varied from period to period, the subordination of the lower classes was found in every Roman age.

Roman literature reveals that there was little support for the idea of equality, and no one gave serious thought to changing the class system. In his work *De Republica,* the Roman orator* CICERO criticized the idea that people were equal. He believed that the basic flaw of democracy was that it gave its citizens equal rights. "Equality itself is unfair," he wrote. "It makes no distinctions in accordance with social rank." This same attitude was expressed by other Roman writers.

CLASS STRUCTURE IN THE ROMAN REPUBLIC. Early Roman society was divided into two orders, the PATRICIANS (members of the upper class) and the PLEBEIANS (ordinary Roman citizens). These orders were formally defined by the state as determined in the CENSUS. During the census, each citizen's personal wealth, including his property holdings, was evaluated in order to determine his rank in the political community.

In the early republic, the patrician class dominated Roman society. A closed circle of privileged families, they held a monopoly on Roman high political offices and priesthoods. According to Roman tradition, the patricians were descendants of the 100 men who had been in the first Roman Senate. Membership in the patrician class was inherited.

All Roman citizens excluded from the patrician class—from peasants and artisans* to landowners—belonged to the large class of plebeians. The patricians attempted to separate themselves further from the plebeians by banning intermarriage between the two classes. The law code established in 451–450 B.C., called the Twelve Tables, included this ban, but the ban was repealed five years later. The plebeians challenged the patrician monopoly on privileges.

Eventually, plebeians gained access to nearly all the important political offices and priesthoods formerly held by the patricians. The greatest success for the plebeians came with the passage of the Licinian-Sextian laws in 367–366 B.C. Plebeians gained the right to become CONSULS, the highest officials during the Roman Republic*. The wealthiest plebeians thus joined the patricians in forming a small and exclusive group that dominated Roman politics thereafter: the "patricio-plebeian nobility." Also, a limit was placed on the amount of land any single Roman could own, although before 133 B.C., wealthy people generally ignored this law.

As Rome conquered additional territories during the mid and late republic, slave labor gained popularity. Slaves worked on the estates of wealthy landowners, forcing many peasants to sell or abandon their

* **orator** public speaker of great skill

See color plate 2, vol. 1.

* **artisan** skilled craftsperson

* **Roman Republic** Rome during the period from 509 B.C. to 31 B.C., when popular assemblies annually elected their governmental officials

small plots of land. The growing discontent caused by the increasing numbers of desperately poor people finally erupted into violence and class conflict.

In 133 B.C., Tiberius Gracchus took up the cause of poor plebeians. He proposed a reform program to provide landless citizens with acreage from public lands. However, the Roman Senate blocked the plan, sending assassins to kill Tiberius and his followers. Ten years later, Tiberius's younger brother Gaius introduced an even more ambitious reform plan. His reforms provided subsidized grain for the urban poor.

Gaius's reforms were not restricted to the poor. By Gaius's time, two groups of wealthy citizens together made up the highest census classification—the senators first, and just below them, the equestrians. The equestrians, or knights, were those individuals who by reason of their wealth had been granted a horse in order to fulfill their civic military duty or had sufficient wealth to qualify them to have a public horse. (By a law passed in 129 B.C., senators and their families were excluded from the ranks of the equestrian order, making the remaining nonsenatorial wealthy members a clearly distinct second order just below the senators.) Gaius's reforms offered benefits to the equestrians by transferring the privilege of jury service from senators to themselves. The most prominent members of the equestrian order were *publicani,* or public contractors. Gaius favored the *publicani* with a law giving them the profitable job of collecting taxes in the recently gained provinces* in Asia. Gaius wanted to establish Roman colonies in the provinces and grant CITIZENSHIP to all Italians as well.

Violence erupted once again, leading to the assassination of Gaius and many of his supporters. The assassinations of the Gracchi brothers marked the beginning of a century of political violence and civil war that ended only with the creation of the empire under AUGUSTUS.

CLASS STRUCTURE IN THE ROMAN EMPIRE. When Augustus became emperor, he took steps to deal with the social unrest. He distributed land to retired soldiers and resettled many of the urban poor in colonies in the provinces. To curb violence in the city of Rome, he established a permanent police force. Augustus restored the Senate to its former elite social standing in order to compensate for its loss of political power. He also helped the equestrian order by appointing more knights to government positions. These efforts by Augustus succeeded in establishing a stability in Roman society that lasted for two centuries.

During the empire, the top three social orders were senators, knights, and local notables, called *curiae.* The senatorial order included about 600 senators and their families. This tiny group of privileged Romans possessed tremendous wealth and power. Although the Senate lost most of its political power to the emperors, individual senators continued to hold the highest administrative offices and major military commands. To fill vacancies in the Senate, new senators were recruited from the local aristocracies* in Italy and the provinces. Members of the equestrian order were only slightly less privileged than the senatorial class. Like senators, knights were primarily men of landed wealth and high birth. They wore golden rings to indicate their class.

Remember: Consult the index at the end of volume 4 to find more information on many topics.

* **province** overseas area controlled by Rome

* **aristocracy** referring to the privileged upper class

The third highest class, the *curiae*, was the backbone of the government. They were the local MAGISTRATES and senators. People in this class were set off from the majority of people by their wealth and high birth. Men of low status, including freed slaves and undertakers, were excluded from the curial order. Because local magistrates were not paid but were expected to pay for public buildings and food distributions, they had to be wealthy.

The great majority of Romans were working freemen. Most worked the land, either as independent farmers or as tenant farmers who worked for others. These rural tenants were the principal source of labor on the estates of the wealthy. Free workers in the city lived in cramped quarters, enduring poor sanitation, food shortages, and frequent fires. While some were relatively well-off, most poor citizens barely made ends meet. They survived by begging, working occasional odd jobs, or attaching themselves as clients to wealthy patrons. When poor Romans died, their corpses were dumped into unmarked mass graves.

A large percentage of city workers were former slaves, some of whom became prosperous artisans. Some ex-slaves continued to work for their former masters, while others worked for themselves. Although freed slaves were barred from membership in the three aristocratic orders, some managed to become wealthy and powerful by serving the emperor. Senators and knights, who were sometimes left in the position of having to court an emperor's freedman for favors, resented the influence these former slaves had with the emperor.

Slaves were at the bottom of the social order. Most rural slaves received only enough food and clothing to keep them alive and working. Some were kept in chains. In the cities, many slave artisans were free to engage in business, as long as they gave their owners the profit. Although slaves were not permitted to own property, a few managed to amass small fortunes with the permission of their masters, and some even owned slaves of their own. (*See also* **Government, Roman; Gracchus, Tiberius and Gaius; Law, Roman; Rome, History of; Senate, Roman; Slavery.**)

SLAVE REVOLT

Tensions between rich and poor led to several uprisings during the late Roman Republic. One of the most dramatic began in 73 B.C., when Spartacus, a gladiator from Thrace, escaped from a gladiator's school in the southwest Italian city of Capua. He fled to Mt. Vesuvius, where 90,000 slaves, outlaws, and poor peasants joined him. The rebels defeated several Roman forces sent against them, and then plundered the Italian countryside. Spartacus was finally killed in battle in 71 B.C. To serve as a warning to other potential revolutionaries, the Romans crucified 6,000 of the captured slaves along the Appian Way.

CLASSICAL STUDIES

* **Renaissance** period of the rebirth of interest in classical art, literature, and learning that occurred in Europe from the late 1300s through the 1500s

* **Hellenistic** referring to the Greek-influenced culture of the Mediterranean world during the three centuries after Alexander the Great, who died in 323 B.C.

Classical studies refers to the collection, translation, and analysis of the work of ancient Greek and Roman philosophers, historians, poets, and other writers. Renaissance* scholars were the first to group Greek and Roman literature together in this way, believing that the writings of these two ancient cultures far surpassed any that had been produced since. In fact, our word for this literature—"classics"—is derived from the Latin word *classicus,* the ancient Roman term for the highest tax bracket and a popular Roman expression that meant "of the highest class."

The study of classical literature began with the ancient Greeks and Romans themselves. As early as the 500s B.C., the Greeks were analyzing passages of HOMER's poetry. During the Hellenistic* age, scholars at the great LIBRARIES at ALEXANDRIA (in Egypt) and PERGAMUM (in Asia Minor) collected and edited the manuscripts of Greek poets and philosophers. Early Roman writers translated these works into their language, Latin, while at the same time producing their own literature in imitation of the Greeks. The Roman

* **epic** long poem about legendary or historical heroes, written in a grand style

* **pagan** referring to a belief in more than one god; non-Christian

* **vernacular** language or dialect native to a region; everyday, informal speech

* **Roman Republic** Rome during the period from 509 B.C. to 31 B.C., when popular assemblies annually elected their governmental officials

poet VERGIL, for instance, wrote his masterpiece, the AENEID, in the epic* style of Homer. Later, Roman scholars adapted the skills acquired from their study of Greek texts to the analysis of Latin writings.

By the end of the Roman Empire, the quality of scholarship had declined. Nevertheless, both Christians and pagans* wrote epitomes, or summaries, of Greek and Roman writings, which helped preserve the thought of the ancients until the Middle Ages. Around A.D. 400, St. AUGUSTINE, the early church leader, attempted to summarize classical knowledge from a Christian point of view. BOETHIUS, who worked in the early A.D. 500s, set about to translate all the works of ARISTOTLE and PLATO into Latin. His contemporary, Cassiodorus, compiled his *Introduction to Divine and Human Readings* for the instruction of the monks in the monastery he had founded. Also important for the survival of classical literature after the fall of the Roman Empire was the continued use of the Greek and Latin languages. In the Byzantine Empire, affairs of state and religion were carried out in classical Greek, while in the West, Latin remained the official language of the western Catholic Church. Latin was promoted at the court of Charlemagne in the late A.D. 700s, where scholars collected and copied ancient Roman manuscripts. At the same time, monks in Ireland and Italy painstakingly preserved in Latin the works of both Christian and pagan authors.

After a period of some decline, a renewed interest in ancient literature in the A.D. 1100s spurred the study of Latin writers, as well as the translation of some ancient Greek literature. This interest reached its peak during the Renaissance in western Europe with the Italian poet Petrarch, who argued that the study of the classics provided the best possible education. Petrarch and his followers collected and analyzed numerous ancient Greek and Latin writings, many of which had been thought lost. He and other scholars interested in reviving ancient learning modeled their own writings on the Latin of the Romans, especially that of CICERO. By 1600, most surviving classical writings had been printed, many in the vernacular*, and European scholars now had at their disposal much of the written material produced by the ancients.

For much of the next 200 years, classical studies dominated European education and became part of "the education of a gentleman." Students in England, for instance, were expected to translate a passage from their own language into Latin or Greek. This education stressed patience, hard work, and accuracy—qualities that were admired during the Industrial Revolution as indicators of a person's success later in professional life.

The ideals expressed by the classical writers of ancient Greece and the Roman Republic* inspired many statesmen of the 1700s and 1800s, including the leaders of the American and French revolutions. At the same time, there was a surge in interest in the life of ancient Greece, as many people studied and copied Greek art, fashion, and literature (particularly the works of Homer).

By the early 1900s, education in the classics decreased in importance relative to natural science and modern languages. However, the notion of "scholarship" has generally included a knowledge of the works of the ancient Greeks and Romans. In addition, the classical writers have continued to inspire 20th-century artists. Eugene O'Neill *(Mourning Becomes Electra)*, Jean Giraudoux *(Tiger at the Gates)*, and Jean-Paul Sartre *(The Flies)*, are only a few of many modern playwrights who have incorporated the stories or themes of ancient writers into their works. *(See also* **Education and Rhetoric, Greek; Education and Rhetoric, Roman; Philosophy, Greek and Hellenistic; Philosophy, Roman.)**

CLAUDIUS

10 B.C.–A.D. 54
EMPEROR OF ROME

* **imperial** pertaining to an emperor or empire

* **province** overseas area controlled by Rome

* **Praetorian Guard** elite and politically influential corps that served as the emperor's bodyguard

Because of a speech impediment and a limp, Claudius was considered simpleminded by his family. He had little involvement in the palace intrigues of his time, until his nephew's assassination resulted in his being named emperor. In the end, Claudius was an intelligent and effective ruler—especially when compared to his successor, Nero.

Claudius was a most unlikely Roman emperor. Hindered by severe physical disabilities, and viewed with disdain by members of his large imperial* family, he held no position of responsibility in his youth or early adulthood. Yet his appearance belied his intelligence and political sharpness. He completed the conquest of BRITAIN begun by Julius CAESAR almost a century before and made Britain an imperial province*. At home, he actively dispensed justice. Claudius was a moderate ruler, especially when compared to the cruel and vain NERO, who succeeded him.

Tiberius Claudius Nero Germanicus was born in GAUL, in the area that is now the French city of Lyons. He was the youngest child of the military hero Drusus and Antonia, the daughter of Marcus ANTONIUS. His grandfather was the emperor AUGUSTUS and his uncle was TIBERIUS. Claudius's physical symptoms—a speech defect, a limp, and a tremor—might have been the result of cerebral palsy. In his own time, however, Claudius was regarded as simpleminded and was, therefore, kept out of the public eye. He led a quiet, scholarly life, writing accounts of Augustus's reign as well as histories of Etruria and CARTHAGE. When the emperor CALIGULA was murdered in A.D. 41, he left no direct heirs. The only surviving adult male of the family was Caligula's uncle, Claudius. The Praetorian Guard* quickly declared the reluctant Claudius emperor even as the Senate was discussing the restoration of the republic.

As emperor, Claudius surprised many people. Despite his lack of experience, he personally took part in the invasion of Britain in A.D. 43 and thus strengthened an already solid bond with the military. Living conditions and chances for promotion improved for the soldiers in Claudius's army. At home, he upgraded the harbors and drained the marshes. He urged senators to pay greater attention to their duties, but made little attempt to rule with their advice. He instituted new laws and made efforts to carry out existing laws. He was concerned about inheritance and property rights, sedition (treason), and the rights of slaves, women, and minors. He also spoke out for the admission of Gauls to the Senate and the extension of citizenship to conquered peoples. The civil service was improved through Claudius's establishment of departments for the handling of government business, and freedmen were put in charge of the administration of the government.

Claudius was married four times. Two of his later wives, Messalina and Agrippina, were politically powerful and schemed for more power within the imperial household. Claudius's death in A.D. 54 may have been the result of poisoning by Agrippina. Her son (and Claudius's stepson), Nero, inherited the throne. *(See also* **Armies, Roman; Government, Roman; Rome, History of.)**

CLEISTHENES

DIED ca. 500S B.C.
ATHENIAN STATESMAN

* **classical** in Greek history, refers to the period of great political and cultural achievement from about 500 B.C. to 323 B.C.

* **archon** in ancient Greece, the highest office of state

* **tyrant** absolute ruler

* **clan** group of people descended from a common ancestor or united by a common interest

* **aristocrat** person of the highest social class

* **ostracism** banishment or temporary exclusion from one's community

Cleisthenes was one of the founders of Athenian democracy and an important political reformer. His reforms of 508–507 B.C. remained the basis of Athenian local government throughout the classical* period. He was the son of Megacles and the heir of the Alcmaeonid family, which played a leading role in the politics of Athens. Cleisthenes became archon* under the tyrant* Hippias in 525 B.C. He was later exiled for his opposition to Hippias. Cleisthenes returned to Athens in the early 500s B.C., and sought the archonship once again. Although defeated by Isagoras, Cleisthenes appealed to the public by presenting a program of reform. After a brief political skirmish with his political opponent, Cleisthenes prevailed and his reforms went into effect. He gave citizenship to all free adult males of ATTICA and reorganized the citizens of Athens from the original four clans* of the landowning aristocrats* into ten new ones. The new clans comprised citizens from the cities, the coast, and the countryside and were more representative of the citizenry. Prior to the reorganization, aristocrats could limit membership in the Athenian assembly by restricting citizenship to those they favored. Through his reforms, Cleisthenes ensured that whole clans would never automatically be on the same side, and in this way he weakened their power and influence.

Cleisthenes is also credited with the concept of ostracism*. His intention was to help Athenians reach a peaceful solution to factional strife by giving them the opportunity to exile one citizen a year on the grounds that Athens would be better off without him. The exile would last for ten years but would not result in the loss of the person's property or status. At least 6,000 votes were needed to ostracize someone. The votes for exile were written on pieces of broken pottery called *ostraka* and the process was called *ostrakismos*. (*See also* **Citizenship; Democracy, Greek; Government, Greek; Polis.**)

CLEOPATRA

69–30 B.C.
QUEEN OF EGYPT

* **Roman Republic** Rome during the period from 509 B.C. to 31 B.C., when popular assemblies annually elected their governmental officials

Cleopatra was the legendary, last, and best-known ruler of the PTOLEMAIC DYNASTY of Egypt. She was a fearless ruler and a skilled diplomat whose career coincided with the end of the Roman Republic*. During her reign, she increased Egypt's territory and kept it free from direct rule by Rome. She accomplished this through the use of her charm, intelligence, and alliances with powerful men—first with Julius CAESAR and later with Marcus ANTONIUS (Marc Antony).

The daughter of Ptolemy XII Auletes, Cleopatra inherited the throne following her father's death in 51 B.C. At first, she ruled Egypt alone, but later she shared the throne with her two younger brothers, Ptolemy XIII and Ptolemy XIV. (Ptolemy XIII later drowned fleeing Caesar's forces, and Cleopatra had Ptolemy XIV killed after Caesar's death.)

Driven from the throne in 48 B.C., she was restored to it by Julius Caesar who was in Egypt in pursuit of his enemy POMPEY. In 46 B.C., Cleopatra followed Caesar to Rome but returned to Egypt after his assassination in 44 B.C. Cleopatra sided with Marc Antony during the struggle for power that followed Caesar's death. She remained Antony's ally and provided money and supplies when he was fighting for Caesar's heir, OCTAVIAN. Later, when Octavian declared war on her and Antony as enemies of the

Roman state, she supplied ships to engage the Roman fleet at Actium. When Octavian's general Marcus Agrippa won the sea battle of 31 B.C., Cleopatra asked for peace terms, but Octavian refused. With the prospect of being led as a captive in a triumph for Octavian in Rome, Cleopatra committed suicide by allowing herself to be bitten by an asp, a poisonous snake. Her story is told by PLUTARCH in his *Life of Antony*. (*See also* **Egypt; Rome, History of.**)

CLIMATE, MEDITERRANEAN

See map in Geography and Geology, Mediterranean (vol. 2).

The climate—the long-term regional weather patterns—of the lands surrounding the Mediterranean Sea had a significant influence on the lives of the ancient Greeks and Romans. Climate affected their diet by determining the foods they could grow each season. It affected the economy of ancient communities, which relied heavily on farming. It also affected architecture and the types of shelters that were built to protect the people from various weather conditions.

To learn about climate conditions of the past, scholars study ancient texts that describe the weather and the seasons. Physical evidence, such as tree rings, reveals climate patterns and changes over time. Although some climate changes have occurred in the Mediterranean region over the centuries, the region between 300 B.C. and A.D. 400 had much the same climate that it has today.

TEMPERATURES AND RAINFALL. The Mediterranean region has two main seasons: cool, wet winters and hot, dry summers. Winter lasts roughly from October to May—a little longer in the northern and western areas and shorter in the southern and eastern areas. Although these months are considered the wet season, it does not rain all the time. Much of the precipitation occurs in sudden, heavy rainstorms, and many winter days are sunny and clear.

Rainfall varies from place to place within the Mediterranean region. Most rain comes from the west. This means that the western Mediterranean and the western slopes of hills and mountain ranges are wetter than the eastern Mediterranean and eastern slopes. Rome and Gibraltar, in the western part of the Mediterranean basin, each receive an average of 36 inches of rain annually. The cities of Athens and Alexandria, in the eastern Mediterranean basin, are drier. Athens receives an average of 16 inches of rain each year, and Alexandria receives about 8. However, rainfall can vary dramatically from year to year—some years much wetter than average and others much drier.

Winter temperatures are generally mild. In many Mediterranean cities, the coolest months average 25° (Fahrenheit) colder than the hottest months. Temperatures rarely fall to freezing levels except in the mountains. Snow is rare, falling perhaps once or twice each year in Athens and melting within a few hours. Yet, winter weather in the Mediterranean is not always pleasant. Storms often sweep across the sea and raise waves to dangerous heights. The ancient Greeks and Romans avoided sailing during this season.

Hilly and mountainous regions have considerably colder winters than the lowlands. Most of the higher mountains receive winter coatings of snow, but very few of them keep the snow through the summer. Snow from these peaks was prized by ancient Greeks and Romans who could afford to have it carried down from the mountains to cool their summer drinks.

The hot, dry summer season lasts from May to October. In most of the Mediterranean basin, the months between June and September are almost rainless. In ancient times, these were the months for sea voyages and military campaigns. Summer can be uncomfortably hot in some parts of the Mediterranean. For example, summer temperatures in Libya on the North African coast rise above 120°F. In most parts of the Mediterranean, however, occasional thundershowers break the summer heat and drought.

WINDS AND WEATHER.   The Mediterranean is a windy region. Some of the major winds around the Mediterranean Sea are so prevalent they have their own names. One of these is the mistral—a cold, dry winter wind from the north that sweeps through southern France. The mistral can be violent and destructive, uprooting trees and carrying vehicles off the roads. Other cold winds from the north are the bora, which blows along the eastern coast of the Adriatic Sea, and the gregale, which sweeps off the Balkan Peninsula across the Ionian Sea.

Hot, dusty winds sometimes blow across the Mediterranean in the other direction, sweeping north from the Sahara desert. In Italian, this wind is known as the sirocco. Passing through North Africa, the sirocco is intensely dry and hot and causes terrible sandstorms that coat every surface with dust. As the sirocco crosses the Mediterranean, it picks up moisture. Clouds form in the sirocco, and the rain that results is red from the dust carried in the wind. Siroccos are most common in spring.

Not all winds are destructive. During the summer, steady breezes from the north make sailing easy—at least in a southerly direction. These steady winds also help carry cooler northern air to Alexandria in Egypt, and allow sailing vessels to travel several hundreds of miles upstream on the Nile River.

CLIMATE AND CULTURE.   Climate greatly influenced agriculture in ancient Greece and Rome. Olives were a popular food, and olive oil was an important trade product because the olive tree flourished in the region's mild winters and dry summers.

Most of the Mediterranean region receives enough rainfall for farmers to grow grains, such as barley and winter wheat. These grains were staples of the Greek and Roman diet. However, because rainfall can vary widely from year to year, there were many years in which crops failed. The threat of grain shortages or FAMINE was always present. It was the responsibility of the Roman government to store grain and distribute it to the people during food shortages.

Climate shaped ancient customs and habits, too. The mild temperatures and limited rainfall of the Mediterranean climate encourage outdoor activities. Ancient athletes, clad only in loincloths, competed in the sunny, open air, and students assembled outdoors for their classes. Open marketplaces and theaters, temples with outdoor altars, and houses with

CLIMATE AND HISTORY

To study the climate of the ancient world, some scientists use the growth rings in trees. Each ring represents a year in the tree's life. The width of each ring shows whether that particular year was warm or cold. Using samples from the oldest known trees, scientists have constructed a history of the Mediterranean for the past several thousand years. Tree rings for 218 B.C., for example, show that it was an unusually warm year. In that year, Hannibal of Carthage stunned Rome by bringing an army—and some elephants—across the high, snowy Alps. If the weather had been a few degrees colder, his bold venture might have failed.

courtyards open to the sky all reflect the love the Greeks and Romans had for the outdoors. (*See also* **Agriculture, Greek; Agriculture, Roman; Games, Greek; Games, Roman; Vegetation, Mediterranean.**)

CLOCKS AND TIME TELLING

The Greeks and Romans needed a way to divide each day into segments of time. They also needed tools to help them measure the passage of time. To meet these needs, they adopted practices that the Babylonians and Egyptians had developed much earlier.

Each day began at sunrise and lasted for 24 hours—12 daylight hours and 12 darkness hours. The length of an hour, however, changed over the course of the year. In summer, when the days were longer and the nights were shorter, day and night still had 12 hours each, but the daytime hours were longer and the nighttime hours shorter. The opposite was true in winter, when days were shorter and nights were longer. This system of flexible hours remained in use for everyday purposes throughout the Greek and Roman eras. Only astronomers making precise studies of the stars bothered to measure hours of fixed length.

People told time—at least roughly—by observing the position of the sun during the day and of the moon and stars at night. An early method of telling time was a crude shadow table, using the measured length of a man's own shadow. Shadows were longest in the early morning and late evening, while at noon they almost disappeared.

Another method of time telling involved the use of a sundial and shadows. According to the Greek historian HERODOTUS, the Greeks adopted the sundial from the Babylonians. By the 200s B.C., it was widely used in the Mediterranean region. The sundial consisted of a pointer that cast a shadow onto a round disk that was divided into 12 sections like the pieces of a pie.

Shadow tables and sundials were useless at night or in cloudy weather. At these times, the Greeks and Romans used a *klepsydra,* or water clock. The *klepsydra* was a vessel from which water dripped at a steady rate, measuring fixed intervals of time. If a clock held just enough water to empty itself in the 12 hours between sunset and sunrise, the user knew that 4 hours had passed when a third of the water had dripped out. The Greeks used the *klepsydra* to time how long a person could speak in a court of law.

The Greeks and Romans made many ingenious machines. Certainly they could have produced accurate mechanical clocks measuring fixed periods of time. It seems that they felt no need for such timepieces but were satisfied with practical, centuries-old methods of measuring time. (*See also* **Calendars.**)

CLOTHING

The ancient Greeks and Romans, like all peoples, developed their own distinctive styles of clothing. Styles were determined by the materials available, the activity for which the clothing was worn, tradition, and fashions adopted from other cultures. Styles changed much more slowly in the ancient world than they do today. Although fashions in color and decoration varied, the basic designs of Greek and

Roman clothes remained unchanged for a thousand years. Near the end of the Roman Empire (in the late A.D. 400s), however, classical robes gave way to new types of clothing, including the forerunner of modern shirts and trousers.

Knowledge about ancient clothing comes from three sources: the remains of garments, literary works that mention clothing, and images of clothing in sculpture and painting. No garments have survived whole from ancient times, but scraps of fabric found in tombs show how the Greeks and Romans made their TEXTILES. Ancient literary and historical writings give the names of garments and also contain clues about the significance of particular garments. For example, an author might mention the social class of the person who wore a certain style of cloak. Unfortunately, most written references give little information about what the garment actually looked like.

The best source of information about ancient clothing is ancient art. Many Greek and Roman carvings, statues, decorated vases, and paintings show clothed figures. The problem with these images is that the artist may have shown how he wanted the people to look, not what they really looked like. Some artworks almost certainly show people wearing costumes, such as theatrical or old-fashioned clothes, rather than real everyday clothing. Still, classical art and literature give us a good idea of how the Greeks and Romans dressed.

GREEK CLOTHING

Ancient Greek garments were fundamentally different from modern European and American clothes in several significant ways. The most significant difference is that modern garments are made of pieces of cloth cut and sewn together to fit around the torso, arms, and legs, often quite snugly. Greek garments, on the other hand, consisted of a single piece of cloth draped loosely on the body. The garment was held in place by a belt, pins, buttons, or stitching, but it was never fitted to the body.

Remember: *Consult the index at the end of volume 4 to find more information on many topics.*

BASIC GARMENTS. Most of the time, the Greeks wore one or more of four basic garments. Greek men and women wore an undergarment called a *perizoma,* a loincloth that passed between their legs and around their waist or hips. Sometimes, athletes and soldiers wore only the *perizoma.*

The chiton was a large rectangle of material folded once and sewn together along the edge opposite the fold to form a tube. A man's chiton was stitched across the top, with holes for the head and arms. A woman's chiton, which was longer and wider than a man's, could be sewn at the shoulders or fastened with pins rather than stitches. Over the chiton a woman might wear a peplos. The peplos was a larger rectangle draped around the body under the arms, loosely enough that it could be pulled up to fasten, like the chiton, with pins at the shoulders. A belt held the peplos in place. Often the fabric at the top of the peplos was turned out and down to form a loose outer fold over a woman's upper body. Unlike the chiton, the peplos was not stitched. It was open along the woman's right side.

Men wore a loose robe or cloak called a himation, alone or over a chiton. The himation was a large rectangle of cloth draped over one shoulder and then wrapped loosely around the hips. Younger men, especially horsemen and travelers, wore a shorter cloak called a chlamys, which was pinned on one shoulder. A woman could wear a himation outdoors, perhaps pulling it around her head to form a hood. Married women also wore veils in public.

Because the basic Greek garments were so simple in design, they often served more than one purpose. A peplos could be turned into a himation, and both garments could be used as a blanket.

MATERIALS AND COLORS.　The women of each Greek household manufactured the fabrics for the clothing of the family members. For warm clothing, the Greeks used wool. Women took pride in their ability to turn sheep's wool into fine yarn, which they knitted into cloth or wove on a loom. For lighter clothing, they used linen, which they weaved from the stems of the flax plant. The Greeks probably learned to make flaxen cloth after Phoenician traders brought Egyptian linen to Greece in the 700s B.C. Garments could also be made from silk, which was being imported to Greece from East Asia by the mid-300s B.C. or perhaps earlier.

Linen was difficult to color, but wool could easily be colored with dyes from animal and vegetable sources. Women liked to color their own garments with bright yellow dye from the saffron plant, while men's cloaks were often dark red. The most costly dye was a deep purple made from sea snails found in Syria and Phoenicia. Women used colored wool to create patterned fabrics. Some patterns were shapes, such as squares or spirals, and others were figures of animals or people.

This Roman relief, from the Ara Pacis in Rome, shows a procession of relatives of the emperor Augustus. The woman at the far left is wearing the garment called a palla, and the man she is looking at is wearing a short tunic under a cloak. The children are wearing the traditional toga usually worn by male Roman citizens.

* **aristocratic** referring to people of the highest
  social class

CHANGES IN FASHION. By the 500s B.C., Greek fashions had become luxurious and elaborate. Women's linen chitons had many fine, crinkly folds. Robes and cloaks were long and full and trailed on the ground. But around 480 B.C., the Greeks tired of complicated draperies and aristocratic* styles. Clothing became simpler and more democratic. Men wore shorter chitons. Women turned from the billowing robe back to the straight peplos.

In democratic Greece, people generally wore whatever they wanted, but they did follow certain customs. Elderly men and women wore longer chitons than young men. Philosophers wore dark-colored, shabby cloaks as a sign that they were not concerned with status and wealth. Farmers, craftspeople, slaves, and poor people wore narrow chitons, generally fastened only on the left shoulder so that the right arm was bare.

After the 300s B.C., Greek fashion once again became elaborate. Richly patterned and embroidered fabrics, some imported from Asia, gained popularity. The basic forms of the garments, however, did not change.

ROMAN CLOTHING

The Romans inherited their clothing styles from the ETRUSCANS, people who ruled central Italy before Rome came to power. The Etruscans had borrowed Greek fashions, so early Roman dress was very similar to Greek dress.

Roman clothing differed from Greek clothing in two significant ways. First, Roman garments were more complicated than Greek garments. Every piece of Greek clothing was woven as a single rectangle, uncut and with minimal stitching. Roman garments, in contrast, used rounded and cross-shaped pieces of material, as well as rectangles. Some garments consisted of several pieces of fabric sewn together.

Second, Greek dress expressed the choices of the individual. A person could wear party clothes or a traveling outfit, for example, whenever he or she wanted. Roman dress was specialized. People wore certain clothes according to their social class, their age, and the occasion. The rules of proper dress were enforced not only by custom, but sometimes by law as well.

BASIC GARMENTS. Roman men and women wore the *subligaculum,* a linen undergarment similar to the Greek *perizoma.* Women might also wear a *strophium,* or brassiere. Made of linen or leather, the *strophium* was a band that supported and wrapped the breasts.

The basic Roman garment was the tunic. It consisted of two pieces of material, usually wool, stitched together at the sides with holes for the arms. Sometimes the tunic had short sleeves. The wearer slipped the tunic on over his or her head and fastened it with a belt, often pulling it up to hang in a loose fold over the belt. A man's tunic reached to his calves, but a woman's was generally longer and looser.

The most traditional and important outer garment was the toga. During most of Roman history, a male Roman citizen who did not wear a toga ran the risk of being mistaken for a workman or a slave. The toga was so much a part of the Roman identity that the poet VERGIL called Romans the *gens togata,* meaning "toga-wearing people."

FASHIONS IN REBELLION

In the A.D. 500s, some Romans showed their opposition to the emperor Justinian's rule through fashion. To set themselves apart from other Romans, they copied the hairstyle of the barbarian Huns. They let their beards and mustaches grow, shaved the fronts of their heads, and let their hair grow long at the back. They wore tunics with outrageously wide, long sleeves tightly fastened at the wrists. When these men clapped or waved their arms at public shows such as the circus, their puffy sleeves flapped and billowed. These showy barbarian fashions were a way of rebelling against imperial rule.

The toga was descended from the Greek himation. Like the himation, the toga was made from a single piece of cloth. It was not a rectangle, however, but had one rounded or curved side. The toga was worn like the himation, draped over one shoulder and loosely fastened at the waist or hip. The curved side was worn at the bottom.

Ordinary citizens usually wore plain, white togas. Some Romans wore togas that had a decorated border, the width and color of which were determined by the wearer's age and social class. Certain colors and patterns were reserved for the highest-ranking officials. For example, from the time of Augustus only the emperor could wear a purple toga. This is why becoming emperor is sometimes referred to as "taking the purple."

Children of both sexes wore togas, but among adults, the toga was a man's garment. Any woman who wore one was assumed to be a prostitute. Instead of the toga, women wore a square himation called the palla. Married women were expected to cover their heads in public. One Roman aristocrat divorced his wife because she went to the theater bareheaded.

GROWTH OF CLOTHING INDUSTRIES. During Rome's early centuries, women made textiles and clothing in the home. By the 100s B.C., however, they could buy cloth in marketplaces. Home production no longer filled the needs of the growing population and the large armies, and a textile industry came into being. The Romans developed new and more efficient types of looms and set up cloth-making factories in conquered Asian and European lands.

The Romans also began to manufacture clothing. Rome and other large cities of the empire had workshops and factories that produced cloaks and other garments. Although mass production of fabric and clothing was a Roman innovation, other crafts and businesses related to clothing had also existed among the Greeks. These included the making of hats, sandals, and jewelry. Both the Greeks and the Romans had professional fullers, whose business was the cleaning of woolen clothes.

THE TRIUMPH OF "BARBARIAN" FASHIONS

Both the Greeks and the Romans regarded their clothing as one of the things that set them apart from other, barbarian* peoples. Among these barbarians were the people of the PERSIAN EMPIRE, who wore leather pants and sleeved jackets, and the CELTS, who wore fitted pants and tight shirts. Yet with the passage of time, both the Greeks and the Romans adopted some foreign fashion elements. By the 400s B.C., a few Greek women and children were wearing Persian-style jackets, and a century later, ALEXANDER THE GREAT shocked the Greeks at home by encouraging his troops in Asia to wear "barbarian" dress.

Roman fashions changed considerably during the later years of the Roman Empire, from A.D. 250 to 600. The gap widened between everyday dress and special costumes for religious or ritual occasions. The clothing of royal and noble Romans became even more splendid than it had been. Garments of silk were ornamented with fringe and

* **barbarian** referring to people from outside the cultures of Greece and Rome, who were viewed as uncivilized

embroidered with gold thread. Meanwhile, the toga gradually fell out of fashion. The emperor, senators, and aristocrats still wore togas, but middle-class Romans replaced the toga with a round hooded cape. Roman Christians replaced the toga with the pallium, a man's version of the square-edged palla.

During these centuries the long-sleeved tunic and the long trousers of the barbarians also came into common use. In the early A.D. 400s, several Roman emperors passed laws forbidding such barbarian fashions as boots, trousers, long hair, and leather garments. It was too late to stem the tide of change, however. By the end of the Roman Empire, the traditional sandals and robes of antiquity had been replaced by shoes, fitted pants, and shirts and dresses with sleeves—the forerunners of modern garments. (*See also* **Class Structure, Greek; Class Structure, Roman; Dyes and Dyeing; Economy, Greek; Economy, Roman; Family, Greek; Family, Roman; Gems and Jewelry; Hairstyles; Patricians, Roman; Social Life, Greek; Social Life, Roman; Weapons and Armor; Women, Greek; Women, Roman.**)

CLYTEMNESTRA

MYTHICAL GREEK QUEEN

* **rhetoric** art of using words effectively in speaking or writing

In Greek legend, Clytemnestra was the wife of AGAMEMNON, king of MYCENAE. While Agamemnon was away fighting in the Trojan War, Clytemnestra took a lover, Aegisthus. When Agamemnon returned from the ten-year war accompanied by his mistress Cassandra, Clytemnestra killed him in his bath. For her crime, Clytemnestra was killed by her son, ORESTES. The story of Clytemnestra, her husband, and their children was immortalized by the poet HOMER and by the playwrights AESCHYLUS, SOPHOCLES, and EURIPIDES. Each author presents a different view of Clytemnestra and her motivation.

Clytemnestra was the daughter of Tyndareos and Leda. She and Agamemnon had a son, Orestes, and three daughters. Two of the daughters were IPHIGENIA and ELECTRA. Homer depicted Clytemnestra as a good but weak woman who is misled and manipulated by Aegisthus. In Homer's version of the story, it is Aegisthus who actually murders Agamemnon. The Greek playwrights depicted Clytemnestra as a powerful woman who is driven to murder by years of pent-up grief and rage. In Aeschylus's *Agamemnon* (part of the *Oresteia* trilogy), Clytemnestra mourns the sacrifice of her daughter Iphigenia by Agamemnon and kills him when he returns home. She then seizes power by the force of her public rhetoric*. In Sophocles' *Electra*, Clytemnestra is depicted as an evil woman whose horrendous act is avenged by her children, Orestes and Electra.

As these different portrayals of Clytemnestra show, women in ancient Greek literature were given a wide range of qualities—from wise to foolish, from pure to corrupt, and from strong to weak. In general, early Greek poets, such as Homer, tended to show women acting rationally and intelligently, while later Greek writers focused on women acting against society's rules. The Greek tragedians often used the themes of murder and revenge to illustrate how these rules were broken. (*See also* **Drama, Greek; Women, Greek.**)

| CODEX | See *Books and Manuscripts*. |

COINAGE

* **die** device used for shaping, cutting, or stamping, as in coining money

* **anvil** iron block on which metals are hammered and shaped

* **city-state** independent state consisting of a city and its surrounding territory

* **Hellenistic** referring to the Greek-influenced culture of the Mediterranean world during the centuries after Alexander the Great, who died in 323 B.C.

The Greeks and Romans both used coins for money. They made coins of precious metals—usually bronze, silver, or gold. Like today's currency, their coins came in different sizes and values. Some of these coins are very beautiful and highly prized by modern-day collectors.

Ancient coins were produced by hand in mints. Coins had designs on one or both sides. To make a coin, a mint worker placed a piece of metal of the desired size over a die* that rested on an anvil*. Using a hammer, the worker punched the metal onto the die with a bar. In this way, the metal took on the design on the die. The first coins had a design on only one side. To make a coin with a design on the other side, called the reverse, the worker used a bar that had the desired design engraved on the end that struck the metal.

GREEK COINS. Lydia, a kingdom in Asia Minor, issued the first coins around 650 B.C. They were made of electrum, a mixture of silver and gold. Within a few decades, communities in Greece were issuing coins made of silver. The silver came from mines in northern Greece.

Each Greek city-state* made coins with a characteristic design. Commonly, a god or goddess closely associated with the community was depicted on one side. The other side might have a scene or animal connected with the god or goddess. The first Athenian double-sided coins, for example, showed the goddess ATHENA on one side and, on the other side, the owl and the olive branch, both sacred to Athena. Athenian coins have been found all over the eastern Mediterranean region, indicating their widespread use. Athens minted coins in many denominations, smaller coins being worth less than larger ones.

The most beautiful Greek coins come from the Greek cities in Italy and Sicily. They were minted from 400 to 300 B.C. An especially striking one is from Syracuse on the island of Sicily. On one side, it has the head of a water nymph encircled by dolphins. The reverse side shows a chariot drawn by four horses.

The coins issued by ALEXANDER THE GREAT were standardized and circulated throughout his vast empire. Mints in different parts of the empire produced coins with the same designs. During the Hellenistic* period, rulers for the first time minted coins that were stamped with their portraits.

ROMAN COINS. Coins depicting generals and rulers were typical of the last years of the Roman Republic and of the Roman Empire. The first Roman "coins," however, were quite different. This early money, issued around 280 B.C., consisted of large bronze bars that weighed about five pounds each.

A decade later, Rome issued heavy round bronze coins that weighed one pound. Around the same time, Rome began minting silver coins that

Coins from Athens were among the most popular forms of currency in the ancient world, and they have been found throughout the Mediterranean region. This silver coin from Athens, which dates from about 440 B.C., has the head of the goddess Athena on one side, and an owl and an olive—items associated with Athena—on the other.

depicted the famous scene of Roman history in which a she-wolf nurses ROMULUS AND REMUS, the legendary founders of Rome.

In 211 B.C., Rome issued a silver coin, the denarius, and smaller denominations in bronze. The denarius remained the basic Roman coin for about five centuries. For a time, the officials who were in charge of the mint put their names on the coins together with scenes from their families' history.

During the civil wars of the Roman Republic, powerful generals issued their own coinage, usually in gold. They did this, in part, so they could pay their soldiers. CAESAR began the practice of putting portraits of himself on his coins. BRUTUS, one of the assassins of Caesar, issued coins with his own portrait on one side, and daggers, symbolizing the assassination, on the other.

Under AUGUSTUS, the first Roman emperor, Rome returned to an orderly issuing of coins by the government. Augustus had some of his coins marked SC, for *senatus consultum,* to assure people that the coins had the approval of the Roman Senate. Emperors customarily issued coins with their portrait on one side and scenes depicting their achievements or policies on the other. For example, CLAUDIUS had a coin minted that showed a triumphal arch commemorating his conquest of Britain.

The emperors frequently altered the metal content of new coins. When people realized that the new coins contained less gold or silver than older ones, they tried whenever possible to pay their taxes with the new ones. The counterfeiting of coins became a serious problem, and a new profession developed to detect forgeries. Rome stopped issuing the denarius in A.D. 270 because the coin had declined so much in value. Constantine I had a new coin minted in A.D. 310, the gold solidus, which remained the standard until the end of the Roman Empire. (*See also* **Banking; Money and Moneylending.**)

COLLEGIA

See *Social Clubs and Professional Associations.*

COLONIES, GREEK

The ancient Greeks spread their influence and culture through much of their known world by establishing colonies in other lands. During two great periods of colonization, the Greeks founded settlements in Sicily, Italy, North Africa, and western Asia. Modeled on Greek cities, with Greek-style temples, public buildings, and houses, these colonies brought Greek architecture, art, customs, and language to many regions.

THE FIRST WAVE. The first wave of colonization lasted from the 750s to the 580s B.C. It was not a unified Greek enterprise, however. Instead, a number of city-states* established colonies at different times for various purposes. The first to do so were Eretria, Chalkis, and Kyme, city-states on Euboea, an island off the eastern coast of the Greek mainland. The Euboean cities joined together to found two colonies to exploit the region

* **city-state** independent state consisting of a city and its surrounding territory

west of Greece that was rich in metals such as iron and tin. One colony, Cumae, was established on the western coast of Italy. The other colony, Ischia, was located on a small island north of the Bay of Naples. These colonies served as centers for trade and mining.

Soon the Greeks realized that colonies could be more than just trading outposts or isolated mining settlements. Colonies offered a solution to a serious problem—the shortage of land in Greece. As the Greek population had grown, many farms had been divided and subdivided among sons until the plots that remained were too small to support families. Aristocrats possessed all the best land around the cities, and discontent rose among the landless poor. If people were willing to settle overseas, however, they could obtain land. Driven by this hunger for land, as well as the desire to trade and to exploit new resources, many Greek city-states founded dozens of colonies.

Chalkis was a leading colonizer, establishing settlements in southern Italy and on the island of SICILY. Eretria placed settlers on Corfu, an island off the western coast of Greece. CORINTH founded SYRACUSE, an important harbor city in eastern Sicily. Greeks from the region known as ACHAEA colonized most of the southern coast of Italy with settlements, such as Sybaris, that became great cities by Greek standards. Sparta founded its only colony, Taras (modern Taranto), at a location that offered the best port in southern Italy. Phocaea, a Greek city on the coast of western Asia, protected its western Mediterranean trade routes by setting up colonies as far west as southern France and northern Spain. One of them, Massalia, was the ancestor of the French city of Marseilles.

With colonies established in the west, the Greeks looked to expand in other directions. In the east, MILETUS, which was itself thought to be a colony of Athens, founded many colonies on the coast of ASIA MINOR in what is now Turkey and in the fertile, grain-producing regions around the Black Sea. Greeks from the island of Thera established the colony of Cyrene, in northern Africa, which flourished until about 440 B.C.

Some of the colonies founded colonies of their own, called daughter colonies or daughter foundations. The Achaean colony of Sybaris, for example, founded Poseidonia and other colonies on the west coast of Italy. Over time, the colonies and daughter colonies developed new relationships with their founding cities. Some colonies remained tightly controlled by their founders, while others enjoyed almost complete independence.

THE SECOND WAVE. The second period of colonization began in the 330s B.C. under ALEXANDER THE GREAT. Eager to spread Greek civilization throughout the lands he conquered, Alexander founded numerous settlements. According to the historian PLUTARCH, Alexander established 70 cities, many of them named Alexandria, throughout the Middle East and as far east as modern-day Afghanistan and Pakistan.

Most of the colonies established by Alexander the Great began as military encampments rather than cities, but ALEXANDRIA in Egypt was an exception. Alexander planned the city to be a great capital, and it became one. A leading commercial and trading center, Alexandria was also the most important intellectual center of the Hellenistic* period.

See map in Migrations, Early Greek (vol. 3).

* Hellenistic referring to the Greek-influenced culture of the Mediterranean world during the three centuries after Alexander the Great, who died in 323 B.C.

* **dynasty** succession of rulers from the same family or group

After Alexander's death, the Seleucid dynasty* ruled his conquests in Asia, establishing new cities and creating Greek-style buildings and institutions in older cities. Greek cultural heritage, which in the first wave of colonization had traveled to the western Mediterranean, had now taken root in Egypt and in western Asia. A far-flung web of Greek colonies and influences reached from Spain to India, ensuring that, even after Greece's political power faded, its cultural importance would still be felt across much of the world. (*See also* **Greece, History of; Migrations, Early Greek.**)

See map in Migrations, Late Roman (vol. 3).

The Romans established colonies for a variety of reasons. The primary one was to secure strategic defenses for the Italian peninsula. The secondary reason was to resettle the poor and to find homes for discharged veterans. Colonization reached its peak under CAESAR and AUGUSTUS, and came to an end during the reign of HADRIAN.

As the Romans pushed invading Gauls from the Italian peninsula in the 300s B.C., they established colonies in the region. These colonies were located on the borders of LATIUM, the area surrounding Rome. The people living in these communities included allies as well as Romans. They gave up their existing citizenship and became citizens of the colony. These communities were known as Latin colonies. Other people—those who had fought against Rome—were given only half-citizenship. This latter group had to serve in the army and pay taxes to Rome, but had no vote in the assemblies and could not hold office.

Minor settlements established along the coast of Italy took the place of a navy in helping to defend the peninsula. These strongholds were too small to be self-governing, and inhabitants kept their Roman citizenship. These settlements became known as "colonies of Roman citizens."

After 338 B.C., the Romans founded more colonies in the area south of Rome. The settlers of these colonies were drawn mainly from Rome and had to give up their Roman citizenship in exchange for generous parcels of land in the new colony. Called "Latin colonies" like the older colonies, these settlements contributed to the eventual unification of Italy under Rome. Latin colonies ceased being founded after 181 B.C., however. At that time, Rome found it increasingly difficult to persuade colonists to give up their Roman citizenship. There were other reasons as well. By 177 B.C., the strategic lands in the Po River valley had been secured and most of the suitable land had been distributed.

Gaius GRACCHUS revived the practice of colonization as a means of relieving the poverty among the landless and as a way to provide for the resettlement of soldiers. He attempted to establish the first overseas colony at CARTHAGE in northern Africa, but he was killed before his plans for large-scale colonization could be put into effect. Emigration of Roman citizens to colonies was revived by Caesar, who settled more than 80,000 citizens, including the poor and veterans, in more than 30 colonies. Caesar's policy was greatly expanded by Augustus, who founded approximately 75 colonies in faraway regions of the empire such as Africa, Sicily, Macedonia, Spain, and Asia Minor.

Eastern colonization continued under the emperors CLAUDIUS and VESPASIAN, but it came to an end under the emperor HADRIAN. The title of *colonia* became a mark of status for an existing city. (*See also* **Cities, Roman; Citizenship; Economy, Roman.**)

COLOSSEUM

* **gladiator** in ancient Rome, slave or captive who participated in combats that were staged for public entertainment

* **tier** one of a series of rows arranged one above the other, as in a stadium

The Colosseum was the greatest Roman AMPHITHEATER of ancient times. Located in the city of ROME, it became a symbol of Roman power and grandeur—and also of violence. For hundreds of years, the Colosseum presented gladiator* fights, wild animal spectacles, and other types of entertainment. Much of the entertainment was violent and bloody, with thousands of gladiators, slaves, prisoners, and animals killed each year.

Construction of the Colosseum began about A.D. 75 during the reign of the emperor VESPASIAN. The dedication ceremonies for the amphitheater took place five years later, and it was named the Flavian Amphitheater in honor of the Flavian family of emperors who had supervised its construction. However, it later became known as the Colosseum after a colossal statue of the emperor NERO that stood nearby.

The Colosseum was a marvel of engineering. The oval-shaped building had a massive stone and concrete facade with numerous arches and columns. Its outer walls stood 157 feet high. The central arena, which measured 290 feet by 180 feet, was surrounded by tiers* of seats and standing areas capable of holding from 45,000 to 50,000 people. Arched corridors, ramps, and staircases within the outer walls provided access to the seating areas of the building.

Spectators in the Colosseum were seated according to rank. The lower tiers of seats belonged to public officials and members of the upper classes of society. Above this area were the seats reserved for the middle classes. The lower classes had to climb even higher to reach their seats near the top of the amphitheater. A complex ticketing system controlled

Although many Roman cities and towns had amphitheaters, the Colosseum was the greatest of them all. Originally built between A.D. 75 and 80, the Colosseum was used for gladiatorial games for the entertainment of Romans, holding approximately 45,000 to 50,000 people at a time.

the admittance of spectators to the arena and determined the location of their seats. Tickets, which were free, indicated a specific entrance, row, and seat. A canvas awning stretched over the seating areas, providing shade for the spectators on bright sunny days.

The floor of the arena was made of wood and covered with sand. Two levels of rooms and corridors ran beneath the arena floor. Cages in this underground area housed wild animals. An elaborate system of narrow passageways, pulley-drawn elevators, and trap-doors facilitated the safe movement of the animals to the arena. A net was hung around the arena to protect spectators in the front rows. Skilled archers stood by in case they were needed to provide further protection.

Among the most popular entertainments in the Colosseum were gladiator fights and wild animal hunts. Gladiators generally fought to the death. If a fight ended with injury instead of death, the life of the loser could be spared by a signal from the emperor. Gladiators also participated in animal hunts, sometimes in the midst of elaborate settings and scenery. Wild animals fought each other or attacked slaves and criminals, who were thrown into the arena unarmed. For some unusual events, the floor of the arena was flooded using underground pipes, and spectators rooted for staged sea battles or amphibious animal fights.

After the adoption of Christianity in the Roman Empire, violent and bloody amusements declined in popularity. As a result, the importance of the Colosseum declined and the building fell into disrepair. The ruins of the Colosseum still stand—an impressive reminder of the past glory of ancient Rome. (*See also* **Games, Greek; Games, Roman.**)

COLUMNS

See color plate 9, vol. 2.

Columns, which are among the most familiar symbols of ancient Greek and Roman architecture, are often seen in what remains of ancient structures. Columns served as vertical supports for buildings, and they all had two standard parts: a tall, cylindrical shaft and a capital, the section at the top of the shaft that connected the column to the rest of the building. Some columns also stood on a base. Because stone columns were large and extremely heavy, builders usually made columns in sections and assembled them at the construction site.

Early Greek columns share certain similarities with the human form. Female (and, more rarely, male) figures were sometimes used as columnar supports, as in the caryatids of the ERECHTHEUM in ATHENS. Also, the proportions of the column appear human. The relationship of width to height is the same as that of the human body—roughly one to seven. Furthermore, the ancient Greek names for the various components of the column reflect human body parts. For example, the capital is called the head in Greek, and the base is referred to as the foot, which has led some scholars to see the column as an abstract representation of the human figure.

Greek architects developed three styles of columns: Doric, Ionic, and Corinthian. These styles of columns defined the three main architectural styles, known as orders, of ancient Greece. The Romans adopted the Greek orders and based much of their own architecture on them.

COLUMNS

Columns provided vertical support for buildings. Although the most familiar columns are simply tall cylinders, sometimes caryatids—figures in the shape of women—were used. These caryatids, on the Erechtheum in Athens, are among the most famous. On rarer occasions, buildings were supported with figures in the shape of men, called atlantes.

The Doric was the oldest order and also the simplest. Doric columns had shallow grooves, called fluting, down the length of the shaft. The capital was a round block of stone with a curved edge above the shaft, topped by a plain square block. Doric columns had no base.

The Ionic order appeared soon after the Doric order in the 500s B.C. Ionic columns were more ornate than Doric ones. The Ionic column stood on a carved base atop a square block. Its fluting was deeper than that of the Doric column. Its capital was ornamented with carved decorations that resembled two scrolls curving down toward the shaft.

The Corinthian order was still more elaborate. The base and shaft of the Corinthian column were similar to those of the Ionic column, but the Corinthian capital was shaped like an upside-down bell decorated with carved leaves. Sometimes this capital was topped with a scroll. The Corinthian column became popular in Rome, where builders continued to use the Greek orders for some time. (*See also* **Architecture, Greek; Architecture, Roman.**)

COMEDY

See *Drama, Greek; Drama, Roman.*

COMMERCE

See *Economy, Greek; Economy, Roman; Trade, Greek; Trade, Roman.*

CONFESSIONS

See *Augustine, St.*

CONSTANTINE

A.D. 272–337
FIRST CHRISTIAN
ROMAN EMPEROR

Although Constantine I, the Roman emperor from A.D. 306 to 337, was an able and efficient leader of the empire, he is best known for his support of the Christian church. Constantine worked throughout his reign to promote Christianity, and he was baptized a Christian on his deathbed.

Constantine I ruled the Roman Empire from A.D. 306 to 337. During that time, he made several important changes in the ways in which the empire was administered. He was also the first Roman emperor to encourage Roman citizens to become Christians. In addition, Constantine gained fame as the builder of the city of CONSTANTINOPLE, which became the capital of the Eastern Roman Empire and the center of Byzantine* civilization for more than 1,000 years.

Constantine was born in Naïssus, a city in present-day Serbia. He was the son of Constantius Chlorus, one of four contenders for the imperial* throne of Rome. His mother was Helena, a Christian who was believed to have discovered the cross on which Christ died. When Constantine's father died in York in BRITAIN in A.D. 306, Constantine was declared *augustus,* or emperor, by his father's soldiers. However, not until A.D. 324 did Constantine defeat his rivals for the throne and become the sole ruler of the empire. Meanwhile, he ruled his father's territories in Spain, Gaul, and Britain and married Fausta, daughter of the former emperor Maximian.

In A.D. 312, Constantine invaded Italy. The night before the battle against Maxentius, Constantine supposedly had one of a series of visions and dreams, some of which involved Christian themes. (Two years earlier he had seen a vision of Apollo accompanied by Nike, and the numeral XXX—meant to symbolize the years of his reign. In another vision, he saw a cross above the sun with the words *in hoc signo vinces,* which means "In this sign shall you conquer.") As a result of the dream he had at Saxa Rubra, on the night before the battle against Maxentius, Constantine ordered his soldiers to paint crosses on their shields before going into the battle. Although heavily outnumbered, Constantine defeated his rival. He attributed this victory to the Christian God, and from that time forward, he felt the need to maintain the Christian God's support for himself and the empire. To that end, he built a great triumphal arch in Rome to commemorate the victory.

A year later, Constantine and the new eastern emperor, Licinius, issued a series of decrees, commonly called the Edict of Milan, by which they extended religious toleration in the empire to all religions, including Christianity. Constantine personally rejected paganism* and worked hard to convert the Roman Empire to Christianity. He intervened in church controversies in order to maintain religious harmony (and to

* **Byzantine** referring to the Eastern Christian Empire that was based in Constantinople

* **imperial** pertaining to an emperor or empire

* **paganism** belief in more than one god; non-Christian

* **bureaucracy** large departmental organization that performs the activities of government

* **succession** transmission of authority on the death of one ruler to the next

solidify his power) and allocated money to build new churches. He founded the Church of St. Peter in Rome and, in his boldest move, established a new, Christian city on the site of the ancient BYZANTIUM. The city was dedicated as "Constantinople" in A.D. 330, and it became the capital of the Eastern Roman Empire in A.D. 453.

As an administrator and military leader, Constantine did much to maintain and strengthen the empire. He created a larger and more mobile field army, with new commanders directly accountable to him. He also strengthened and reorganized the frontier armies. He allowed non-Romans to advance through the army ranks. He enlarged the government bureaucracy* and gave senators civilian posts that enabled them to recover some of their lost political influence. However, not all of Constantine's reforms were popular. New taxes on all forms of trade and commerce were bitterly criticized. The establishment of the *solidus,* a new gold coin, led to the depreciation of other currencies. Constantine was an able, practical, but often ruthless leader. He had his wife and oldest son executed on suspicion of treason and is suspected of eliminating his relatives in order to secure the succession* of his sons Constantine II, Constantius II, and Constans. Ironically, none of his sons lived long enough or were able enough to have a major influence on the empire. (*See also* **Christianity; Rome, History of.**)

* **strait** narrow channel that connects two bodies of water

See map in Visigoths (vol. 4).

* **acropolis** a high, fortified site in a Greek city

onstantinople was the capital city of the Eastern Roman Empire (later known as the Byzantine Empire). Located on a triangular-shaped peninsula on the western side of the Bosporus, one of the narrow straits* that separates Europe from ASIA MINOR, the city had great strategic importance. It controlled the sea route between the Black Sea and the MEDITERRANEAN SEA, and its location at the crossroads of Europe and Asia made it an important trade center. After the decline of the Western Roman Empire, Constantinople replaced Rome as the most important city in Europe. Today, the city is known as Istanbul, and it is the largest city in Turkey.

EARLY HISTORY. The city of Constantinople was founded in A.D. 324 by the Roman emperor CONSTANTINE I on the site of the ancient Greek city of BYZANTIUM. Constantine had wanted to build a great city near the important industrial centers of Asia Minor and SYRIA and the agricultural areas of EGYPT. He chose the site of Byzantium because of its strategic and protected location and its excellent harbor, which was known as the Golden Horn.

Constantine quickly rebuilt and enlarged Byzantium and constructed protective walls around the city. According to legend, the emperor himself traced the new city boundaries before construction began. It took builders six years to expand and fortify the city, which was formally dedicated in A.D. 330. Originally called Nova Roma, or New Rome, the city soon became known as Constantinople in honor of the emperor.

Like Rome, Constantinople had seven hills. One of these was the old acropolis* of Byzantium. Constantine built impressive public buildings and monuments on these hills. He brought statues and art works from

* **forum** in ancient Rome, the public square or marketplace, often used for public assemblies and judicial proceedings

* **granary** storage place for grain

* **aqueduct** channel, often including bridges and tunnels, that brings water from a distant source to where it is needed

* **basilica** in Roman times, a large rectangular building used as a court of law or public meeting place

* **Holy Land** Palestine, the site of religious shrines for Christians, Jews, and Muslims

* **doctrine** principle, theory, or belief presented for acceptance

around the Roman Empire to adorn the city. The main imperial buildings of Constantinople, modeled after Roman buildings, included a forum*, a senate house, and a royal palace. Constantine also enlarged the hippodrome, a race course and sports arena modeled after Rome's CIRCUS MAXIMUS. Later emperors added theaters, baths, granaries*, and aqueducts*.

A convert to CHRISTIANITY, Constantine wanted Constantinople to be a great Christian city. To help achieve this goal, he built many churches and basilicas* and brought religious relics from the Holy Land* to place in these churches and around the city. The greatest religious building in the city was the church of Hagia Sophia (Holy Wisdom in Greek), completed around A.D. 360. In 381, the office of bishop of Constantinople became the second highest office in the Christian church after the bishop of Rome. In later years, Constantinople played a major role in the evolution of Christian doctrine* and belief.

RISE TO GREATNESS. Constantinople rapidly outgrew its original boundaries. By A.D. 413, new city walls had to be constructed to accommodate the city's expansion. These new walls, a marvel of engineering, protected the city from attack for over 1,000 years.

Constantinople reached the height of its growth and splendor in the A.D. 500s. After fire destroyed much of the city in A.D. 532, the emperor JUSTINIAN I rebuilt it on an even grander scale than before. One of his greatest achievements was the rebuilding of Hagia Sophia, which became the largest and most beautiful church in the world. During Justinian's reign, Constantinople's population reached about 500,000, and the city became the most important political, commercial, religious, and cultural center in all of Europe. It remained Europe's greatest city for the next several hundred years until its decline in the late Middle Ages. (*See also* **Aqueducts; Architecture, Roman; Cities, Roman; Forum; Government, Roman; Rome, History of: Christian Era.**)

CONSTITUTION

See *Rome, History of.*

CONSTRUCTION MATERIALS AND TECHNIQUES

The Greeks and the Romans were ambitious and skillful builders. Their elegant and massive TEMPLES, PALACES, and public buildings are some of the most familiar images of ancient Greek and Roman culture. Even though most ancient buildings that survive today are in ruins, the structures are still impressive. The Greeks and the Romans also built humble, everyday structures, such as HOUSES and apartment buildings. By studying ruins and ancient writings, scholars have learned much about how the people of Greece and Rome constructed their buildings.

EARLY GREEK BUILDING TECHNIQUES. The Mycenaeans and the Minoans, the very early peoples who lived in Greece and on the nearby island of CRETE, mastered sophisticated building techniques and constructed large

See color plate 1, vol. 2.

palaces. By about 1100 B.C., however, these civilizations had disappeared, and many of their construction techniques were lost. From then until 700 B.C., Greek construction was more modest, consisting mostly of houses and a few temples and city walls.

Greek builders used materials found locally. In many areas, the standard material for walls was mud-brick, made by mixing clay with water and straw, pressing the mixture into rectangular wooden forms, and letting it dry. When constructing a wall, builders started with a few layers of stones to raise the mud-bricks off the ground, then continued with rows of mud-bricks. Sometimes, they used timber beams to strengthen the walls. In some parts of Greece, stone was more common than clay. In these areas, people built with rubble masonry—small blocks of limestone roughly chipped from quarries. Walls consisted of stacks of these stones, with smaller stones and mud filling the space between. Both mud-brick and stone houses had dirt floors that were stamped flat.

Whether made of stone or mud-brick, a house had either a flat, clay roof or a steep, thatched roof. A clay roof began with crossbeams, a frame of timbers resting on the tops of the walls. The builder laid reeds across the crossbeams and covered them with clay. A thatched roof was made of bunches of straw woven together into a tight pattern and supported by a framework of poles inside the house.

For centuries after 700 B.C., the Greeks built houses, sheds, workshops, and other modest structures of mud-brick and rubble masonry. They also used these materials for a few public buildings. In the mid-400s B.C., for example, the Athenians built a mud-brick council chamber. By that time, however, they had largely turned to a new kind of construction, called monumental construction. The new construction methods produced buildings that were bigger, more impressive, and longer-lasting than earlier ones—buildings that were monuments.

GREEK MONUMENTAL CONSTRUCTION. Monumental construction included all the elements we now regard as characteristic of Greek architecture, such as COLUMNS, stone platforms for large buildings, shallow peaked roofs, and decorations of statues or carved panels. The Greeks introduced this style in the 600s B.C., having invented new building techniques and designs, as well as borrowing others from the Egyptians. The Greeks first applied this style to temples, but by the 400s B.C. they also used it for other public structures, including treasuries, council halls, and walls of cities.

Stone, especially marble, was the main material of monumental architecture, and the Greeks became experts at building with finely cut stone. Stonecutters carved blocks of different sizes and shapes from quarries: rectangular blocks for paving, square ones for building walls, and thick cylinders that formed columns when stacked on top of one another. From the Egyptians, who had been building large stone monuments for centuries, the Greeks learned how to move large, heavy blocks of stone using rollers and ramps. Each block was delivered to the building site a little larger than necessary, in case the stone was chipped during transport. Masons at the site trimmed the blocks to exact size.

Remember: *Words in small capital letters have separate entries, and the index at the end of Volume 4 will guide you to more information on many topics.*

Greek builders developed techniques for fastening blocks of stone together. Dowels (thin rods of wood or metal) secured sections of columns. Builders also used wooden pegs or metal clamps to lock each block of stone in a wall to the blocks around it. The clamps, sunk into the centers of the blocks, were invisible when the wall was finished.

The roofs on monumental structures were made from tiles of terracotta, baked clay that was usually reddish-brown in color. These tiles, which may have been a Greek invention, are still used throughout the Mediterranean and elsewhere. Laid in overlapping patterns, with channels to carry off rainwater, they create a sturdy, waterproof roof.

Although Greek architects and builders knew how to construct ARCHES, they made little use of them, preferring their traditional architecture of columns topped by flat crosspieces. While the Romans developed a style of monumental construction based on arches, the Greeks continued to build in their own style during the Roman Empire.

ROMAN CONSTRUCTION. Early Romans constructed buildings using the wattle-and-daub method, in which walls made of interlocking sticks (wattle) were coated (daubed) with mud. While easy to make, especially in the country, wattle-and-daub structures presented a fire hazard in a

---

Features of Monumental Masonry
Early Greek structures consisted of either mud-brick or small, roughly-cut limestone blocks, stacked and held together with mud. By the age of monumental construction, building techniques had greatly improved. The Greeks learned to carefully shape and smooth, or "dress," blocks for a secure fit. They reinforced the joints with clamps that held the blocks in place.

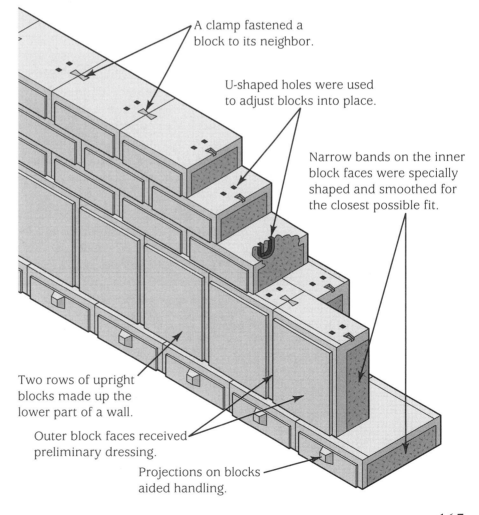

A clamp fastened a block to its neighbor.

U-shaped holes were used to adjust blocks into place.

Narrow bands on the inner block faces were specially shaped and smoothed for the closest possible fit.

Two rows of upright blocks made up the lower part of a wall.

Outer block faces received preliminary dressing.

Projections on blocks aided handling.

CONSTRUCTION MATERIALS AND TECHNIQUES

* **imperial** pertaining to an emperor or empire

* **terra-cotta** hard-baked clay, either glazed or unglazed

* **forum** in ancient Rome, the public square or marketplace, often used for public assemblies and judicial proceedings

crowded city. As the Roman architect VITRUVIUS POLLIO wrote, they were "like torches ready for kindling."

Buildings made with mud-brick walls proved more durable, and the Romans built their first temples with this material. The Romans soon turned to stone slabs instead of mud-bricks for temples, city walls, and public buildings. They probably learned how to quarry, transport, and build with stone from the ETRUSCANS, a neighboring Italian people whom the Romans later conquered. The Etruscans may have learned their stoneworking techniques from the Greeks.

The first stone the Romans used for building was tufa, a stone found in and around the city. For centuries, tufa served Rome's builders well. By 100 B.C., however, the Romans wanted to copy the precise edges and hard, smooth surfaces they saw on Greek marble buildings. Rome was becoming the capital of an empire, and the Romans felt that only marble was grand enough for their public buildings. They imported marble from all over the known world—white marble from Greece and northern Italy, purple and golden marble from North Africa, and white marble with purple veins from central Turkey. Roman builders used these expensive marbles for columns and veneers, or thin outer coatings, on walls of coarser stone.

The Romans also built with concrete, which they made by mixing crushed stone or gravel with lime and sand. To protect the concrete from the weather, they covered the walls with rows of small stones or bricks. Brickmaking became such an important industry that in the A.D. 200s the government established imperial* brickyards to manufacture bricks, roof tiles, and terra-cotta* pipes for plumbing.

Wood remained in use as a construction material throughout imperial times. The walls of many apartment houses were wooden frames filled with concrete or stones. Houses of better quality had walls of concrete faced with brick, but their floors, door and window frames, and shutters were wood. Fire was an ever-present danger in Rome. It spread quickly in districts where buildings stood close together.

REBUILDING ROME. Around 30 B.C., Rome's rulers began rebuilding the city on a large scale. For the next three centuries, each emperor tried to make a permanent mark on the city by erecting temples, arenas, forums*, public bathhouses, or other magnificent structures. Caesar Octavianus AUGUSTUS, the first emperor, boasted that he had found Rome a city of brick and left it a city of marble. After a devastating fire destroyed much of Rome in A.D. 64, the emperor NERO rebuilt the city—and took the opportunity to build a luxurious palace for himself in its center.

Later emperors continued to build new monuments, such as the Temple of Peace and the COLOSSEUM, which were built by VESPASIAN. People in the ancient world, however, regarded the Forum of Trajan, built in the early A.D. 100s, as the most remarkable of Rome's monumental buildings. One writer in the A.D. 300s called it "a construction unique under the heavens . . . and admirable even in the unanimous opinion of the gods . . . a gigantic complex beggaring descriptions and never again to be imitated by mortal men." The Forum of Trajan was a series of courtyards and multistoried buildings that included a law court, Greek and Latin libraries, a

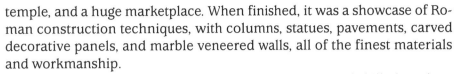

temple, and a huge marketplace. When finished, it was a showcase of Roman construction techniques, with columns, statues, pavements, carved decorative panels, and marble veneered walls, all of the finest materials and workmanship.

The construction of the Forum required experts and skilled workers in dozens of crafts: demolition, stonecutting, marble working, iron-smithing, paving, plastering, painting, and many more. These and other imperial building projects gave rise to a large and diversified construction industry. An imperial department of public works, with a large staff of supervisors and clerks, kept track of the supply of building materials and coordinated the work of architects and construction workers. Rome's apartment houses, mansions, country villas, temples, theaters, and even tombs were the achievements of a vast number of highly skilled craftsmen who were organized into a disciplined and effective workforce. At the command of the emperors, these men transformed Rome. Their buildings survived for centuries. Even in ruins, they continue to inspire architects, painters, and scholars today. (*See also* **Architecture, Greek; Architecture, Roman; Churches and Basilicas; Crafts and Craftsmanship; Mining; Rome, City of; Temples.**)

See
color plate 7,
vol. 2.

CONSULS

* **Roman Republic** Rome during the period from 509 B.C. to 31 B.C., when popular assemblies annually elected their governmental officials

onsuls were the highest officials in the government of the Roman Republic* and in theory, but not in fact, during the empire, since the emperor had supreme authority then. Each year a special assembly elected two consuls, who shared supreme civil and military power. Consuls served for one year. Although the consuls generally worked together, they had the power to veto each other's decisions.

At the founding of the republic in 509 B.C., the consuls assumed the powers that had belonged to the king. Known as PRAETORS until the 300s B.C., consuls were the heads of state. Military command was their most important function, but they also had civil powers. Consuls could arrest and prosecute criminals, issue edicts and decrees, summon assemblies, propose laws, preside at elections, and convene and introduce motions to the Roman Senate. In addition, consuls and former consuls were life-members of the Senate. Consuls had unlimited authority, and some people, such as the historian POLYBIUS, thought that they had far too much power.

Some of the powers of the consuls were limited during the time of the republic. For example, a law granted citizens in Rome the right to appeal to the citizen assembly capital punishment and heavy monetary fines. The right of appeal was to protect a citizen from the severe and arbitrary power of a consul and the misuse of power. The growing power of the TRIBUNES, who represented the lower classes of citizens, also placed limits on the actions of consuls through their right of veto.

Consuls were elected in a popular assembly, which could elect as consul anyone who was willing and qualified to serve. The consuls depended on the support of the Senate. Since they could not take decisive steps—especially those requiring money and heavy expenditures—without the backing of influential senators, consuls generally acted in accordance to the will of the Senate.

The authority of the consuls in the military, however, remained almost unlimited during most of the republic. Consuls commanded Roman forces in the field until the time of Lucius Cornelius SULLA in the first century B.C. After Sulla, consuls remained in ITALY, while former consuls, or proconsuls, commanded the Roman armies.

Although the office of consul remained during the Roman Empire, consuls had less power, since the emperor was then the supreme authority. Usually, the emperor chose the consuls or held the office himself. Although during the republic consuls (called *ordinarii*) served for the entire year and gave their names to the year, consuls during the empire were regularly replaced later in the year by other pairs of consuls (called *suffecti*). Emperors frequently named relatives or friends as consuls. Even children were consuls, and the emperor Honorius was named consul at birth. It was reported that the emperor Caligula intended to appoint his favorite horse to act as consul.

* **imperial** pertaining to an emperor or empire

* **province** overseas area controlled by Rome

Despite this imperial* control, consuls remained important during the empire. Consuls presided at meetings of the Senate and at some elections. They also sponsored games, which increased their popularity with the public. After their term in office, many consuls governed large and important provinces* of the empire. (*See also* **Government, Roman; Senate, Roman.**)

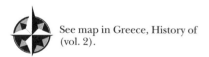

CORINTH

* **Peloponnese** peninsula forming the southern part of the mainland of Greece
* **Neolithic** referring to the latter part of the Stone Age, and characterized by the use of polished stone implements
* **aristocratic** referring to people of the highest social class

See map in Greece, History of (vol. 2).

* **city-state** independent state consisting of a city and its surrounding territory

orinth was one of the most prosperous cities in ancient Greece. Its wealth was the result of the city's advantageous location on the isthmus of Corinth, a thin strip of land that joins central Greece to the Peloponnese*.

Although settled since Neolithic* times, Corinth did not develop into a city until the late the 900s B.C., at which time it rapidly became a center of pottery making. Skilled crafts workers were valued members of Corinth's society and helped develop the Doric order, an architectural style that was used extensively in temples in northwestern Greece.

Corinth was initially ruled by a king. Then, in about 747 B.C., an aristocratic* clan called the Bacchiads gained power. The Bacchiads governed until the 650s B.C., when a series of TYRANTS took control of Corinth. This period marked the high point of Corinth's power and prosperity. Its ships sailed both the Aegean and Adriatic seas. Colonies were established, and silver coins were minted. These coins, with their distinctive stamps of Pegasus, the mythological winged horse, served as the main medium of exchange throughout the Mediterranean world.

The economic power of Corinth began to decline around 550 B.C. as ATHENS grew in economic and political strength. Rivalry and conflict between the two city-states* contributed to the causes of the PELOPONNESIAN WAR in 431 B.C., a conflict in which the Corinthians allied themselves with Sparta. In the 330s B.C., PHILIP II established the League of Corinth in the city. The League consisted of all the Greek states except Sparta, and its purpose was to keep the peace and support Philip's attack on Persia.

Corinth was defeated and destroyed by the Romans in 146 B.C. About a century later, Julius CAESAR founded a colony for former soldiers on the ruins of the city, and Corinth soon regained its role as a major port. In A.D. 50, the Christian missionary St. PAUL addressed Corinthian Christians in a series of letters. Paul's *Letters to the Corinthians* form an important part of the New Testament of the Bible. (*See also* **Architecture, Greek; Christianity; Cities, Greek; Pottery, Greek; Pottery, Roman; Trade, Greek.**)

CRAFTS AND CRAFTSMANSHIP

* **legion** main unit of the Roman army, consisting of about 6,000 soldiers

See color plate 3, vol. 2.

In the ancient world, all manufactured goods—everything from ships to individual nails—were made by hand. This required people skilled in a variety of crafts, such as metalworking, stonemasonry, carpentry, and textile weaving. Although there may have been some craftswomen in ancient Greece and Rome, most skilled workers who earned a living by practicing their crafts were men.

Craftsmen made shoes, dishes, lamps, and hundreds of other things that are used in daily life, as well as more specialized items, such as extravagant gems. For example, potters produced thousands of vases and bowls that were an important part of trade across the ancient world. Some craftsmen made statues, wreaths, and other objects for religious worship, while others manufactured the equipment needed for war. So vital were craftsmen to armies that Roman legions* had their own corps of skilled workers to make everything from military boots to WEAPONS AND ARMOR.

CRAFTS OF THE ANCIENT WORLD. Some crafts, such as leather making and pottery manufacture, were long practiced by ancient peoples. While the Greeks and Romans excelled at these skills, they added few new techniques to those that had already been developed. Other crafts were invented in Greek or Roman times. For example, Greeks in western Asia invented a new kind of metalworking around 625 B.C. when they began minting coins. By striking disks of hot silver or electrum (a mixture of gold and silver) with a bronze stamp on which an image had been carved, they were able to produce many identical coins. Similarly, many early cultures knew how to make glass from melted sand, but because it was costly and hard to transport, it was not widely used. In the first century B.C., Syrians discovered the technique of glassblowing, in which a craftsman blew into a tube and shaped a piece of glassware from the bubble that formed on the other end. Glassblowing enabled craftsmen to produce glassware faster and cheaper than ever before, which in turn enabled glass merchants to reach a wider market in the Roman world.

Crafts often depended on and influenced one another. For example, the availability of inexpensive glass led to a growing popularity of MOSAICS, pictures made of tiny bits of colored stone and glass. By the A.D. 100s, the craft of mosaic making had expanded enormously throughout the empire. In the same way, when the Greeks began constructing large stone temples in the early 500s B.C., stonemasons, who cut and shaped stones, became more important, as did workers who plastered and painted stone walls.

Leather making, or tanning, also supported many other crafts. Tanneries, where animal hides were turned into leather, were usually located outside of town or in the poorest districts because the tanning process

169

produced such terrible odors. Tanners produced sheets of leather, which leather workers then turned into sandals and slippers, leather flasks, workmen's aprons, harnesses, and the writing surface known as vellum or parchment. Glue makers made glue from hides and bones, which was used by woodworkers to hold furniture together. Another very specialized craft related to tanning was the manufacture of rope from tough strands of tendon called sinews. These sinew ropes were a vital part of the siege catapult, a device used to hurl large rocks into enemy fortresses.

Women throughout the ancient world made fabric in their homes for their family's CLOTHING. Home production of textiles continued through the Roman era, but workshops in the Roman empire also produced pieces of cloth and ready-made clothing that people could buy. Linen cloth produced in Egypt was shipped around the Mediterranean Sea for use in clothing and in the sails of ships. One mystery concerning ancient craftsmanship is that almost no information has survived regarding the making of rope and sails. War fleets and cargo vessels used huge quantities of rope and sails, but scholars know little about how the Greeks and Romans crafted these goods.

Because many places lacked metals, merchants had developed a far-reaching trade in ores and finished metal goods, even before the rise of Greek civilization. Perhaps more than any other craft, metalworking led to contacts among peoples of different cultures and geographic regions. Among the most prized trade items of the ancient world, finely crafted metal objects were transported great distances. Jewelry and metal cups from northern Europe, Syria, and Egypt ended up in Greece and influenced the work of Greek craftsmen. In the same way, Roman craftsmen copied designs from Irish and German jewelry and metalwork.

Crafts were a major part of the ancient economy. The prosperity of some regions depended on the number and quality of its craftsmen. Because ATHENS had high-quality marble and clay for masons and potters and abundant silver ore for metalworkers, the city became one of the

Most craftsmen learned their skills from their fathers, while others began as slaves or apprentices in a workshop. They started working for a master craftsman at a very young age, performing menial tasks while learning the trade. This relief shows a metalworker, his assistant, and some of the tools of the blacksmith trade.

LEAVING A NAME

Few ancient craftsmen achieved individual recognition, and even fewer are remembered by historians. Most were obscure in their own time. Still, craftsmen displayed their pride in their work by signing the gold and silver dishes, pottery, statues, coins, gravestones, and even city walls they made. A daring sculptor named Theophilus added his name to the heel of a huge imperial statue. Alxenor, another sculptor, carved "You have only to look and see!" on one of his marble panels. And, in an attack on a rival, a Greek vase painter named Euthymides wrote on one of his pots: "Euphronios never did it like this."

busiest craft centers of the Greek world. Rome built up trade based on crafts, importing raw materials, such as iron and wool, from its provinces and exporting finished goods, such as tools and ready-made clothing, in return.

The Craftsman's Life.   Most craftsmen learned their crafts from their fathers. Several generations of the same family often practiced the same trade. For example, many of the shipwrights who built the warships of Athens were related, and the Athenian sculptor PRAXITELES is thought to have been the son of one sculptor and the uncle of another. Roman records indicate that many architects were related to carpenters or to other architects.

If a craftsman had no sons, he acquired apprentices or bought slaves to help him in his workshop. Many skilled workers were slaves earlier in their lives, having bought their freedom with the money they earned through practicing their crafts. Training started at a young age, with apprentices often spending several years running errands, sweeping floors, and fetching water, before learning the craft. Some teenage boys were considered qualified or even expert craftsmen. Roman grave markers mention 16-year-old sculptors and 11- or 12-year-old jewelry makers.

Most workshops were small. The establishment of a furniture maker, blacksmith, or shoemaker often consisted only of the master and a helper. Some crafts required larger workforces. One Athenian vase painting portrays a pottery workshop with eight people performing different tasks. One man is making a large vase on a pottery wheel that a young boy, an apprentice or slave, is spinning. Another man carries a newly made vase outside to dry, while others prepare to light a fire in the kiln, or pottery furnace. Large operations, such as shipyards, mines, and stone QUARRIES, were often owned by investors who hired craftsmen and bought slaves to work for them.

A master craftsman needed to understand every stage of his craft. A carpenter might cut his own timber, season it, and shape it into finished goods in his workshop. Sculptors often worked on their chosen material from start to finish. They selected their stone in quarries, supervised the stonecutters, carved the blocks of stone into statues, and finally installed the statues in the settings chosen by their purchasers. Some craftsmen had to know how to work with more than one material. A maker of armor, for example, had to use both metal and leather, and a jeweler might work with ivory, gold, and glass. Certain crafts made a wide range of products. For example, some pottery shops produced costly, one-of-a-kind items for wealthy clients, while others mass-produced bowls and jars for everyday use.

In Rome and other large cities, the market for crafts was large enough that some skilled workers could specialize. For example, a shoemaker could make only women's slippers and a metalsmith could make only trumpets. In small towns and villages, though, a skilled man might not be able to make a living as a carpenter but would also have to be the local blacksmith.

The Craftsman in Society.   While today people often regard crafts and arts as two different things, the ancient Greeks and Romans made no distinction between an "artist" and a "craftsman." Painters and sculptors had the same professional and social status as boot makers and blacksmiths.

Different crafts did, however, bring different monetary rewards. In Rome, stonemasons, carpenters, blacksmiths, and boatbuilders earned twice as much as unskilled laborers and shepherds, while shipbuilders, mosaic makers, and marble pavers made even more. Wall and picture painters could earn three to six times as much as unskilled laborers. Famous painters, sculptors, and jewelers commanded much higher fees from wealthy patrons*.

* patron special guardian, protector, or supporter

Craftsmen were united through professional and social ties. In Rome, they formed collegia, associations whose members worked in the same or related crafts. With their collegia, craftsmen celebrated public holidays, such as religious festivals and the emperor's birthday. The collegia also provided proper funerals for their members. Craftsmen might also achieve status by holding offices within the collegium, but the real value of membership was in the companionship and respect that craftsmen found in the company of fellow craftsmen. Members of Quintus Candidus Benignus's collegium displayed this sense of fellowship in the words they inscribed on a memorial marker they put up after his death: "He was a builder of the greatest skill. . . . Great craftsmen would always call him master. . . . No one could excel him. . . . He was sweet-tempered and knew how to entertain his friends—a man of gentle and studious character, and a kindly spirit." (*See also* **Coinage; Art, Greek; Art, Roman; Dyes and Dyeing; Gems and Jewelry; Gold; Marble; Mining; Sculpture, Greek; Sculpture, Roman; Ships and Shipbuilding; Textiles.**)

CRASSUS, MARCUS LICINIUS

112–53 B.C.
ROMAN SOLDIER AND ADMINISTRATOR

* **triumvirate** ruling body of three

* **Roman Republic** Rome during the period from 509 B.C. to 31 B.C., when popular assemblies annually elected their governmental officials

* **consul** one of two chief governmental officials of Rome, chosen annually and serving for a year

Together with Julius CAESAR and Gnaeus POMPEY, Marcus Licinius Crassus formed the First Triumvirate*. By doing so, the three men planned to dominate Roman politics in the late Roman Republic* and reduce the power of the SENATE.

Born into a noble family, Marcus Crassus fled to Spain after his father's death at the hands of a political opponent in 87 B.C. Two years later, he joined the dictator SULLA and acquired a considerable fortune. He rose through the ranks of government to a position of leadership in the 70s B.C. Although he defeated the rebellion led by the slave SPARTACUS in 72–71 B.C., his rival Pompey took credit for the victory. Crassus was deeply offended and refused to support Pompey thereafter. Both men were elected consuls* in 70 B.C. While Pompey waged war against Rome's enemies in the east, Crassus offered his patronage to Caesar, then a young political leader on the rise. Late in 60 B.C., Caesar asked Crassus and Pompey to join him in forming a triumvirate to dominate the government for their mutual advantage. Both agreed, and the First Triumvirate was established. In 56 B.C., Crassus, Caesar, and Pompey renewed their alliance. They agreed that Caesar would retain command of the army for five years, and that Crassus and Pompey would retain their positions as consuls and would be given special, long-term commands in Spain and Syria respectively. Ever ready to compete with Pompey and match his influence, Crassus set out for Syria in 53 B.C. to do battle with the Parthian empire. The Parthians were the only major power threatening Rome's frontiers at that time, and Crassus hoped to achieve military glory and political power by defeating them. However, his army was outmaneuvered at the Battle of Carrhae in

* standard flag or banner of an army

Mesopotamia. Crassus was killed, the Roman army annihilated, and its standards* lost. (Roman dignity would not recover until many years later under the rule of AUGUSTUS.) Crassus's death brought Caesar and Pompey into an even more intense political duel that eventually led to civil war. (*See also* **Rome, History of; Triumvirates, Roman.**)

 rete is the southernmost and largest of the Greek islands. Its important location on sea routes between Greece and the Near East led to early Cretan contacts with ancient civilizations in Egypt and the eastern Mediterranean region. These contacts probably influenced the development of Minoan civilization, which flourished on Crete from about 2000 to 1400 B.C.

See map in Greece, History of (vol. 2).

Crete had been settled for several thousand years before the Minoan period. By the early Bronze Age (ca. 3000 B.C.), the island had well-established farming societies. From 3000 to 2000 B.C., the people of Crete learned to work with bronze and to cultivate OLIVES and grapes—important and versatile food sources that improved their way of life. The Cretans were also excellent seafarers, who engaged in extensive trade with other communities around the Aegean and eastern Mediterranean seas. By this trade, the Cretans exchanged wine, oils, textiles, lumber, and other goods for products such as tin, which they needed to create bronze. Moreover, the Cretans began to build houses and public buildings in large communities, perhaps establishing the earliest towns in the eastern Mediterranean region.

MINOAN CIVILIZATION. The prosperity from Crete's thriving agriculture and sea trade led to the rise of a rich and elegant civilization around 2000 B.C. Historians call it Minoan after Minos, a mythical king of Crete. The heart of Minoan civilization lay in several enormous palaces built around the island. The largest and most famous of these was at Knossos, on the northern coast of Crete. This royal complex covered about six acres and served as the religious, social, and commercial center of the small kingdom. Knossos and the other palaces of Crete were not fortified, which suggests that the Minoans felt little need for the defense of their island home.

About 1700 B.C., an earthquake (or series of earthquakes) destroyed most of the palaces on the island, but the Minoans rebuilt them more magnificently than before. Many elaborate frescoes* decorated the new walls. By about 1600 B.C., the Minoans had reached a new level of wealth, which brought about a golden age of art and culture. Skilled artisans* produced fine cloth as well as metal and gem work, and made pottery that they adorned with flowers, fish, and animals. Life for the Minoans, as depicted in their art, seems to have been peaceful and pleasurable, full of dancing, games, and festivals.

The pleasures of Crete came to an abrupt end, however, sometime between 1400 and 1200 B.C. The circumstances are mysterious, since there are no written records from that time, and Minoan prosperity was apparently still at its peak. Archaeological evidence shows that some

* **fresco** method of painting in which color is applied to moist plaster and becomes chemically bonded to the plaster as it dries; also refers to a painting done in this manner

* **artisan** skilled craftsperson

catastrophe occurred during that time, which damaged or destroyed nearly all the palaces on the island. The cause may have been a natural disaster, such as an earthquake or volcanic eruption, or else a violent uprising or a raid by outsiders. After this time, the Cretans apparently tried to rebuild again, but invaders from the Greek mainland soon overran the island. Minoan civilization disappeared.

GREEK CRETE. Over the next centuries, the culture of Crete became thoroughly Greek. As Greek civilization developed, numerous city-states* arose around the island. This period of Crete's history was dominated by the DORIANS, a group of northern Greeks who spread across the Greek mainland and islands sometime after 1200 B.C.

During the classical* period, Cretan society resembled the powerful military society of SPARTA. In fact, Sparta's constitution may have been modeled after one from Crete. As in Sparta, the city-states of Crete valued order, obedience, and service to the state above all else, and the state directed many family and religious matters. The cultures of both Crete and Sparta were a source of fascination to Greek philosophers from less regimented societies, such as Athens. Both PLATO and ARISTOTLE analyzed Cretan and Spartan customs at length in their writings about law and morality.

These writings, as well as Cretan law codes and a long account by the Greek historian Ephoros, provide a picture of what life was like for the men of Crete. All males had to spend much of their lives in military training and hunting. They ate all their meals together in "men's houses," or mess halls, where they were separated according to age. Boys had to eat sitting on the floor, while the men sat on benches. To toughen the boys, they were made to wear the same shabby clothes winter and summer, and required to wait on the men at meals.

The boys of Crete underwent a complex series of initiations, or rites of passage, to reach manhood. As a boy came of age, he selected an adult man to be his sponsor. This adult taught the boy hunting and military skills and also engaged him in a homosexual relationship. At the end of the initiation period, it was customary for the sponsor to give the young man presents to symbolize his new rank. These included a suit of armor, an ox to sacrifice, and a drinking cup. After a group of young men had passed their initiation, they were all expected to find female brides at once and start households.

ROMAN RULE. Crete remained outside most of the major events of Greek history during the classical era. Crete's city-states periodically fought with each other and with other islands, but Crete managed to avoid the conquests of King Philip II of Macedonia, who by 338 B.C. had brought Greece into his empire. The island kept its independence throughout the Hellenistic* era, during which time it became a haven for pirates.

Meanwhile, Rome arose as the dominant power in the Mediterranean. Even as Rome gained control over Greece and ASIA MINOR, Crete remained an isolated pirate stronghold. Eventually, however, the Romans became fed up with the disruption of trade caused by the pirates, and

* **city-state** independent state consisting of a city and its surrounding territory

* **classical** in Greek history, refers to the period of great political and cultural achievement from about 500 to 323 B.C.

* **Hellenistic** referring to the Greek-influenced culture of the Mediterranean world during the three centuries after Alexander the Great, who died in 323 B.C.

* **province** overseas area controlled by Rome

they were angered by Crete's support of Rome's enemies. In 67 B.C., Rome crushed the Cretans and made the island a Roman province*. Crete remained part of the Roman and Byzantine empires for the next 800 years.

Under Roman rule, both Jews and Christians established communities on the island. In the A.D. 300s, the island was rocked by several major earthquakes that disrupted life and prosperity on the island. In the early A.D. 600s, Crete faced frequent raids by Slavs, and later by Arabs. Arabs captured the island around A.D. 828. (*See also* **Bronze Age, Greek; Greece, History of; Homosexuality; Minos; Philip II; Piracy; Polis; Rome, History of; Social Life, Greek; Trade, Greek; Trade, Roman.**)

CRIME

See *Law, Greek; Law, Roman.*

CROESUS

REIGNED ca. 560–546 B.C.
LAST KING OF LYDIA

* **oracle** priest or priestess through whom a god is believed to speak; also the location (such as a shrine) where such utterances are made

Lydia was a kingdom in the western part of ASIA MINOR, the peninsula east of Greece that is now the nation of Turkey. Beginning in the mid-600s B.C., Lydia became involved in wars and alliances with other ancient peoples, including the Egyptians, the Persians, and the Greeks. This involvement came to a climax during the reign of Lydia's last king, Croesus.

After defeating his half-brother in a struggle for the throne, Croesus conquered EPHESUS and other Greek cities on the coast of Asia Minor. Despite these conquests, Croesus admired Greek culture and wanted to remain on good terms with the people of Greece. His hospitality to Greek visitors was famous as were his lavish gifts to Greek temples. His golden gifts to the temples at DELPHI helped spread the story that he was enormously rich.

Alarmed by the rising power of the PERSIAN EMPIRE under its leader, Cyrus the Great, Croesus urged Babylon, Egypt, and the Greek city-state of Sparta to form an alliance with him against the Persians. Before the alliance formed, however, Croesus and Cyrus found themselves at war. According to legend, the oracle* at Delphi told Croesus that if he made war on Persia, a mighty kingdom would fall. The oracle did not tell him that the fallen kingdom would be his own. Cyrus's forces soundly defeated the Lydians.

Several versions of Croesus's fate appear in ancient Greek documents. According to one story, Cyrus ordered Croesus burned alive but changed his mind when a rainstorm put out the fire. Later, the legend arose that Croesus was saved from the fire by the god Apollo. Other accounts say that Cyrus pardoned Croesus, who was his great-uncle through marriage, and made him an adviser, or perhaps even a governor, in Persia.

Even more widespread and enduring was the legend of Croesus's great wealth. Lydia's capital, Sardis, was located near rich mineral deposits of gold and silver. The first coins in history are believed to have been cast there in the 600s B.C. People still use the phrase "as rich as Croesus" to describe someone with great wealth.

175

See
color plate 6,
vol. 4.

* **sacrifice** sacred offering made to a god or goddess, usually of an animal such as a sheep or goat

The religious life of ancient Greeks and Romans was organized around their many cults. The word *cult* refers to a group of people and the religious activities and rituals they performed to honor a god or goddess. Gods and goddesses were believed to look after human needs, and people would pray, perform sacrifices*, and hold festivals to show their respect and to ask for help. Cults were central to events in both private and public life.

CULT PRACTICE IN ANCIENT GREECE. Cult rituals were held in a place sacred to a god. This place was called *hieron,* meaning "filled with divine power." Every Greek was expected to recognize a sacred place and to know how to behave in or near it. A sacred place could be in the middle of a city, at the top of a mountain, in a cave, or in a grove of trees. Every home had several altars dedicated to the gods. Before entering some sacred areas, a person had to be *katharos,* or in a state of purity suited to religious observance. People bathed themselves before entering to symbolize their readiness to participate in the sacred events and as a sign of respect for the gods. Temples were often built in sacred areas and contained a statue of the cult god. Since the god was believed to live in the temple, rituals occurred at an altar just outside.

Prayer was an important cult ritual. The Greeks would pray to attract a god's attention and ask for help. They prayed for everything—the success of a new venture, triumph in love and war, abundant crops, children, wealth, and good fortune. Prayers were public as well as private, and often were offered at the beginning of political meetings or athletic contests. Hymns—prayers set to music—were sung to the gods. Prayers were performed in a specific order. First, the person called the god or goddess by name. Next, the person stated the reason why the god should respond. Finally, the person made his or her request.

Offerings of gifts or sacrifices to the gods often accompanied prayers. If a prayer seemed to be answered, the god received a gift. A farmer might give a portion of his crop to the god in return for a bountiful harvest, or a warrior might donate a piece of his armor to the god who helped him in battle. The area around a temple contained buildings where worshipers could leave offerings or dedications to the god.

CULTS OF THE FAMILY. Since the family was very important to the ancient Greeks, they honored several gods whom they believed protected the household. Every family kept statues of ZEUS in the house, as well as altars to other gods such as Hygieia, the goddess of health, Tyche, the goddess of fortune, and Agathos Daimon, the god who brought good luck. Statues called *hermae* were placed both inside and outside the house to protect the family. Many families owned sacred objects that were passed down from generation to generation.

Rituals celebrated the important events in family life. The family announced the birth of a child by hanging an ornament on the door—an olive wreath for a boy and a ribbon of wool for a girl. During a ceremony called the Amphidromia, an adult carried the newborn baby around the hearth* to welcome the child into the family. Each stage of childhood was accompanied by certain rituals. A three-year-old boy was accepted as a

* **hearth** fireplace in the center of a house

member of the community with his first sip of wine given to him by his father. At age 18, boys began two years of military training, at the end of which a ceremony welcomed them as adults. Various rituals prepared girls for marriage and motherhood. Athenian girls wove a robe for the goddess ATHENA in the same way they would later weave clothing for their own family. Greek weddings were overseen by Zeus and Hera. The bride bathed in water from a special spring and dressed in special clothing. Friends of the couple sang hymns to the god of marriage as the bride accompanied her husband to her new household.

PUBLIC CULTS. Each city had a patron god who protected the city from harm. For example, Athena was the patron goddess of Athens. The city honored her at a sacred place in the center of the city—the PARTHENON. Each city had such a shrine dedicated to its patron god or goddess, and held many festivals during the year to honor that deity. In Athens, seven days of each month were devoted to festivals of deities who were important to the city, such as Hera, Apollo, and Aphrodite. Major festivals, such as the Panathenaia in honor of Athena, were held only once a year. Some festivals, such as the ELEUSINIAN MYSTERIES, which offered special benefits after death to those who participated, occurred in secret. The participants swore never to reveal the rituals that took place.

CULTS IN ANCIENT ROME. Like the Greeks, the Romans ensured that all aspects of life, both public and private, were watched over by a god or goddess and were accompanied by some form of worship. Romans believed that, just as relations between citizens were ruled by civil law, relations between gods and humans were ruled by divine law. Rituals had to be strictly observed. If a Roman did not recite a prayer exactly right, he or she had to begin again. Roman prayers were quite repetitive, using phrases such as "my farm, lands, and fields," which then might be uttered three times.

The Romans had three main forms of cult worship. Sacrifice was the most common. While they prayed, the Romans offered animals, wine, cakes, or other foods to the gods. A second ceremony was lustration, or purification. A shepherd might sprinkle water on his sheep to cleanse the flock of evil. Vows were the third form of cult worship. A worshiper made a promise to a god that, if his or her request was granted, special offerings would be made. Rome as a whole could make a public vow. For example, in 217 B.C., the Romans promised to sacrifice to Jupiter all animals born in the spring five years hence if the city was spared from HANNIBAL'S invading armies.

Priests and other religious officials presided over the major state cults of ancient Rome. The College of Priests controlled the religious calendar. VESTAL VIRGINS, the only female priests in Rome, tended the sacred hearth of Vesta and kept its fire perpetually lit. Flamines were special priests who each served a single god. An AUGUR observed signs to determine whether the gods approved of a course of action. In times of public emergency, the Senate could order a consultation of the Sibylline Books, which contained the revelations of ancient female prophets called Sibyls. Special priests would then interpret the books to determine the best way to remedy the bad situation or omen.

A GREEK PRAYER

We know about Greek prayers from literature and from inscriptions on pottery and other objects. A famous prayer comes from the *Iliad* by Homer. Chryses, who has lost his daughter to Agamemnon, prays to the god Apollo for the destruction of the Greeks (here called the Danaans):

Hear me, god of the silver bow, you who protect Chryse and sacred Killa and rule Tenedos with your power; if ever I built up a temple pleasing to you, if ever I burned for you fat thighs of bulls or goats, fulfill this wish for me: may the Danaans pay for my tears with your arrows.

177

The Romans held numerous festivals during the year in honor of their gods. The most popular and joyful festival, Saturnalia, spanned several days in the middle of December. A huge banquet was held which anyone could attend. Masters waited on their servants, and people exchanged gifts of wax candles and pottery dolls.

HOME GODS. The cults of private life in Rome centered on the home and household activities. Romans worshiped several "home gods" who preserved the health and well-being of the members of the household. They honored Vesta, the goddess of the hearth, by placing food on a clean plate and tossing it into the fire. The Penates, the spirits of the pantry, received offerings of sacred wine at mealtime. A member of the household leaving on a journey would pray to the Lares, who were spirits of the farmland and the ancestors buried in it. The Lares and Penates were represented by small statues, often placed in a niche inside the house, and were honored at all family festivals. (*See also* **Afterlife; Divinities; Festivals and Feasts, Greek; Festivals and Feasts, Roman; Religion, Greek; Religion, Roman.**)

CUPID AND PSYCHE

Cupid and Psyche are characters in a myth told by the Roman writer APULEIUS. Psyche was the youngest and most beautiful of a king's three daughters. She was so beautiful that humans ceased worshiping Venus (the goddess of beauty, whom the Greeks called APHRODITE). This angered Venus, who told her son Cupid, the god of love, to make Psyche fall in love with the ugliest creature in the world. But Cupid fell in love with Psyche himself and asked the god APOLLO to help him win her.

Apollo ordered Psyche's father to take her to a mountain where a winged serpent would take her for his wife. From the mountain, Psyche was taken instead on a gentle breeze to a fabulous palace. There a voice told her the palace belonged to her and that her every desire would be fulfilled. That night, Cupid came to her in the dark and told her that as long as she did not try to see him or find out who he was, she would be happy forever.

Psyche soon became lonely, however, and asked if her sisters might be allowed to visit her. When her sisters saw the palace, they became jealous and plotted to destroy her happiness. They discovered that Psyche had never seen her husband and convinced her that he was a serpent who would kill her. That night, Psyche took a lamp and a dagger to her bedroom, planning to kill her husband while he was asleep. As she lit the lamp, she saw that he was no serpent but was the handsome Cupid. Cupid awoke and, realizing that Psyche had discovered his identity, fled from her.

Psyche searched for Cupid but was unable to find him. She asked the gods for help, but none of them wanted to anger Venus by helping Psyche. Finally, she offered herself as a servant to Venus, hoping to soften the goddess's anger. Venus, however, was still angry at Psyche and ordered her to perform several seemingly impossible tasks. Psyche managed to complete the tasks, aided each time by friendly spirits. Her final task was to bring Venus a box from Proserpina, queen of HADES (the kingdom of the dead). Psyche, curious about the contents of the box, opened it and was overcome by a deadly sleep. Cupid found the sleeping Psyche and woke her. He then convinced JUPITER, king of the gods, to make Psyche immortal*.

Now that Psyche was a goddess, Venus consented to her marriage to Cupid. This story has often been interpreted as an allegory* that tells how love (Cupid) and the soul (Psyche) overcome all obstacles to find each other. (*See also* **Divinities; Myths, Roman.**)

* **immortal** living forever

* **allegory** literary device in which characters represent an idea or a religious or moral principle

CYBELE

MOTHER-GODDESS

Cybele was the great mother-goddess of Anatolia, or ASIA MINOR. Her main sanctuary was located in Phrygia (now central Turkey), and she is generally shown wearing a crown of towers or carrying a bowl and drum, and accompanied by two lions. She was worshiped primarily as the goddess of fertility, but was also associated with curing diseases and protecting her people.

By the 400s B.C., the cult of Cybele had spread to Greece. She was believed to be the parent not only of the gods, but also the great parent of human beings and animals. In Greece, she was known as *Meter Oreia* (Mother of the Mountains), and special emphasis on her connection to wild nature was symbolized by her attendant lions. As a fertility goddess she was associated with the worship of DEMETER, the Greek goddess of grain and fertility.

During the 200s B.C., the worship of Cybele came to Rome. Romans included her in their spring festival called the Megalesia, which began on March 15 with a procession and sacrifice to ensure the health and abundance of the spring crops. A week of fasting and purification was followed by several days of festivities. On the day of Cybele's festival, a pine tree was cut and carried to the temple. The tree was the symbol of Cybele's youthful lover Attis, who had castrated himself under such a tree and bled to death. At the temple, the tree was honored as the god and covered with violets, which were believed to have sprung from Attis's blood.

From Rome, the rites of Cybele spread to Gaul and Africa. The worship of Cybele was very popular among farmers and women. Scholars think that followers of the cult of Cybele may have believed that in the AFTERLIFE they would be reunited with the mother-goddess. (*See also* **Divinities; Religion, Greek; Sacrifice.**)

CYCLADES

The Cyclades comprise a chain of mountainous islands in the southern AEGEAN SEA. They range in size from a few square miles to over 155 square miles. To the ancients, the Cyclades offered a favorable route across the Aegean because land was always in sight. Naxos and Paros are the two largest islands of the Cyclades.

Most of the Cyclades are volcanic and therefore unsuitable for farming. However, mineral resources such as iron ore, copper, silver, lead, and gold were plentiful during ancient times. Marble was another valuable resource in the region.

Permanent settlements sprang up on the Cyclades during the BRONZE AGE. Later, the IONIANS and DORIANS colonized the various islands. From around the 700s to the 400s B.C., the Cyclades enjoyed independence under the rule of wealthy clans*. During the PERSIAN WARS, many of the islands sided with the Persians and contributed ships to the Persian fleet. The westernmost Cyclades, however, remained loyal to the Greeks. After the war, the Ionian Cyclades joined the Delian League, an alliance of Greek city-states* against the Persians. The Dorian Cyclades kept their independence until the PELOPONNESIAN WAR. After 314 B.C., the Cyclades were caught between the Hellenistic* kingdoms that were competing for control of the Aegean. As a result, control of the islands changed hands several times over the years. The Macedonians, the Ptolemies of Egypt, the Attalids of Pergamum, and the island of Rhodes all ruled the islands at some time. After 133 B.C., the Cyclades fell to the Romans, who administered them as part of the province of Asia. Under the Julian-Claudian emperors, the Cyclades were often used as a place of exile for their political opponents.

The island of Naxos is the most famous of the Cyclades. Its inhabitants developed a style of smooth, white sculpture that came to be known as "Cycladic" statuary, characterized by its elongated, stylized figures. According to Greek myth, Naxos was the birthplace of DIONYSUS and the place where Ariadne was found after her abandonment by Theseus. The coins of Naxos displayed a wine goblet and grapes in honor of the island's patron god, Dionysus.

Paros is the second largest island of the Cyclades. According to Greek myth, the island was settled by the Cretan king MINOS and his sons. During the Persian Wars, Paros allied itself with Darius I against the Greeks and contributed a ship to his fleet at MARATHON. Following the Persian Wars, the islanders of Paros joined the Delian League under Athens's leadership. As a member of the league, Paros contributed valuable marble for construction and higher tribute* than any other island. During the Hellenistic period, the economy of Paros flourished. Eventually, the island came under the domination of the Ptolemies of Egypt, the Macedonians, and the Romans. (*See also* **Greece.**)

* **clan** group of people descended from a common ancestor or united by a common interest

* **city-state** independent state consisting of a city and its surrounding territory

* **Hellenistic** referring to the Greek-influenced culture of the Mediterranean world during the three centuries after Alexander the Great, who died in 323 B.C.

See color plate 14, vol. 2.

* **tribute** payment made to a dominant power or local government

CYCLOPS

Cyclops (plural Cyclopes) is any of several one-eyed giants in Greek and Roman mythology. The word *cyclops* means "round-eye." Traditions relating to the Cyclopes vary from source to source. In Homer's *Odyssey,* the Cyclops Polyphemus, son of the sea-god POSEIDON, captures ODYSSEUS and his crew when they wander into his cave. The giant devours some of the crew and promises to do Odysseus a great "favor" by eating him last. However, the hero cleverly tricks the Cyclops into drinking an excessive amount of wine. The giant becomes drunk and Odysseus drives a hot stake into his only eye. While the blinded Polyphemus rages, Odysseus and his remaining men escape by clinging to the bellies of the giant's woolly sheep.

The poet HESIOD relates that Uranus and Gaia (the gods of Heaven and Earth) gave birth to three Cyclopes: Arges (Bright), Brontes (Thunderer), and Steropes (Lightning Maker). Uranus and his son Cronos confined the Cyclopes in Tartarus, the lowest part of the underworld*. However, ZEUS released the trio, and they became the makers of his thunderbolts. In other accounts, APOLLO slays the Cyclopes in revenge after his son ASCLEPIUS is killed by a thunderbolt they had crafted. The Roman poet VERGIL places the Cyclopes in the workshop of Vulcan, the god of fire (whom the Greeks called HEPHAESTUS). There they forge the spectacular armor of the hero Aeneas.

* underworld kingdom of the dead; also called Hades

The Cyclopes are said to have built the citadel, or fortress, of MYCENAE and the mighty walls around Tiryns, birthplace of HERACLES. In fact, the word *Cyclopean* still refers to such walls made of massive stones with no mortar—and so colossal that supposedly only giants could have constructed them. (*See also Aeneid;* Homer; Myths, Greek; Myths, Roman; *Odyssey.*)

CYNICS

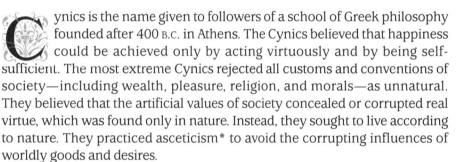

ynics is the name given to followers of a school of Greek philosophy founded after 400 B.C. in Athens. The Cynics believed that happiness could be achieved only by acting virtuously and by being self-sufficient. The most extreme Cynics rejected all customs and conventions of society—including wealth, pleasure, religion, and morals—as unnatural. They believed that the artificial values of society concealed or corrupted real virtue, which was found only in nature. Instead, they sought to live according to nature. They practiced asceticism* to avoid the corrupting influences of worldly goods and desires.

* asceticism way of life in which a person rejects worldly pleasure and follows a life of poverty

The most famous of the Cynics was Diogenes of Sinope (ca.400–ca.325 B.C.). Diogenes lived in a barrel, ate cast-off scraps for his food, and was outspoken and shameless. He is said to have defaced coins to show his contempt for the standards of society. Because of his wild behavior, the Athenians called Diogenes "Cynic," which comes from the Greek word for dog. The name stuck to him and his followers.

The underlying principles of Cynicism were influenced by the teachings of the philosopher SOCRATES. According to some traditions, the school was founded by a student of Socrates, Antisthenes. In turn, the principles of Cynicism influenced the development of STOICISM. Cynicism declined in popularity after about 200 B.C. but experienced a revival during the early Roman Empire. (*See also* Philosophy, Greek and Hellenistic; Philosophy, Roman.)

CYPRUS

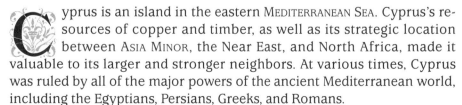

yprus is an island in the eastern MEDITERRANEAN SEA. Cyprus's resources of copper and timber, as well as its strategic location between ASIA MINOR, the Near East, and North Africa, made it valuable to its larger and stronger neighbors. At various times, Cyprus was ruled by all of the major powers of the ancient Mediterranean world, including the Egyptians, Persians, Greeks, and Romans.

Around 1400 B.C., the people of MYCENAE, the forerunners of the Greek civilization, established colonies on Cyprus. The Mycenaeans were followed by two civilizations from the Near East—the Syrians and the Phoenicians. During the 600s B.C., Cyprus was controlled by Egypt and then by Persia. Nevertheless, the Greek influence was the strongest. Greeks founded several city-states*, including Salamis and Paphos, on the island. In addition, many Cypriots—as people living on the island are called—spoke a version of the Greek language. The Cypriots prospered by mining and exporting copper and by harvesting timber for use in shipbuilding.

In the 400s B.C., during the PERSIAN WARS between Greece and Persia, Phoenician communities on Cyprus sided with Persia, and Persia gained control of the island. However, in 333 B.C. all the Cypriot city-states supported ALEXANDER THE GREAT and Greece against the Persians. Alexander defeated the Persians and placed Cyprus under Greek rule. However, in 58 B.C., a stronger power—Rome—took control of the island. At first, Cyprus was part of the Roman province* of Cilicia, but it later became a separate province. The Roman governor ruled from a capital at Paphos.

Around A.D. 115, the Jewish population of Cyprus rebelled against Rome, destroying the city of Salamis. Rome quashed the rebellion and instituted harsh laws banning Jews from the island. Turmoil struck again early in the A.D. 300s, when Cyprus was rocked by a severe and destructive earthquake. Aside from these tumultuous events, however, Cyprus was a quiet minor province of the Roman Empire.

See map in Visigoths (vol. 4).

Dacia was a mountainous region in eastern Europe, north of the Danube River, in the region of modern Romania known as Transylvania. Famous for its rich gold, silver, and iron mines, Dacia was a province* of the Roman Empire for almost 200 years.

The people of Dacia were farmers, miners, and traders. The many tribes of the area united under King Burebistas in the 50s B.C. In the A.D. 80s, under the leadership of a king named Decebalus, Dacia became a military power that threatened the northern borders of Roman territory. The Roman emperor DOMITIAN attempted to bring Dacia under control. In three years of fighting, however, he was unable to conquer Dacia, and he settled for a peace treaty in A.D. 89. The emperor TRAJAN had greater success. In two military campaigns between A.D. 101 and 106, he conquered Dacia, destroying the capital city, Sarmizegetusa, and forcing Decebalus to kill himself. Trajan's Column, a monument in Rome under which the emperor's ashes were later buried, is decorated with carvings that celebrate the conquest.

Trajan made Dacia a province of the Roman Empire and colonized it with thousands of settlers from Italy and the other provinces. Many of these settlers were miners sent to work in Dacia's mines. Several generations later, the Goths, a German tribe, began invading Dacia. Rome found the province too difficult to defend and abandoned it around A.D. 270. The influence of the Romans proved lasting, however. The Romanian language, derived from Latin, survived, even though the Romans held the area for only about 200 years.

DAEDALUS

LEGENDARY INVENTOR

aedalus was a legendary Greek craftsman, artist, and inventor. According to the Roman poet OVID in his work *Metamorphoses,* Daedalus was invited to the island of CRETE by King MINOS, who asked him to build a labyrinth, or maze, to house the Minotaur—a beast that was half-human, half-bull. When Daedalus gave away the secret of how to escape from the labyrinth to the king's daughter, King Minos became enraged and threw the inventor and Icarus, Daedalus's young son, into prison. Since Minos controlled all the ships leaving the island, escape by sea was impossible. Their only hope was to flee by air. Using all of his talent, Daedalus made wings for himself and his son. Fashioned from feathers and wax, the wings were large enough and strong enough to enable them to fly. Before beginning their journey, Daedalus warned Icarus not to risk melting the wax on his wings by flying too close to the sun. Escaping from their prison, the two men soared over the countryside, much to the astonishment of observers on the ground. Icarus was delighted with his newfound abilities and flew up to where the sun warmed the skies. To his horror, the wax on his wings began to melt and the feathers fell apart. Icarus cried out to his father for help, but Daedalus could only watch helplessly as the young man fell into the sea.

The grief-stricken Daedalus flew on to Cumae on the Bay of Naples in Italy. From there, he flew to the island of Sicily where he invented many amazing structures, including a steam bath and a golden honeycomb to adorn the temple of Aphrodite. To form the honeycomb, Daedalus used a special technique with wax.

Daedalus was known for his uncommon skill and ingenuity. He was also a tragic figure because he tried to imitate the gods and was punished by being made to suffer the terrible loss of his son. The story of Daedalus has captured the imagination of artists and writers from Roman times until the present. (*See also* **Theseus and the Minotaur.**)

DAILY LIFE

See *Clothing; Food and Drink; Family, Greek; Family, Roman; Household Furnishings; Houses.*

DANCE

ance was an important part of Greek life. It played a role in Greek religious ceremonies, drama, education of the young, and even military training. The Romans used dance less frequently, though they did enjoy watching dancers called *pantomimi,* or pantomime performers.

The Greeks considered dance a gift from the gods. Dancing usually accompanied ceremonies and special occasions such as weddings, funerals, harvest celebrations, processions, and feasts. The Greeks also enjoyed watching the performances of trained dancers, usually slaves, and held many artistic competitions in dance, drama, and music. Types of artistic dance included the dithyramb, a choral dance to poetry and music, and the dance movements of the chorus in Greek dramas.

DANCE

Dance was often an important part of Greek religious festivals. This vase painting shows women dancing at the Athenian festival of the Lenaea, celebrated in late January or early February in honor of the god Dionysus.

* **classical** in Greek history, refers to the period of great political and cultural achievement from about 500 B.C. to 323 B.C.

Among the most famous dance forms were those associated with the worship of DIONYSUS, the god of wine. In early times, participants in frenzied worship rituals performed wild rhythmic dances. In ancient art, Dionysian revelers are often pictured drinking wine and dancing at night with bulging throats, tousled hair, and startled eyes. During the classical* period, the spontaneous dances of the revelers gave way to well-rehearsed performances. Another famous nighttime dance was a winding, snakelike dance called *geranos,* which was performed at celebrations. The author PLUTARCH described such a dance performed by young men and women with Theseus to celebrate their escape from the labyrinth of Minos.

Greeks also incorporated dancing into education and military training. Athenian youths were expected to take dance classes as a regular part of their education. Men and boys dressed in armor and performed a dance called the *pyrrhic* at the Panathenaia, a large Athenian festival, and also in the military society of Sparta. The philosopher SOCRATES is said to have declared that those who danced best were also best at war. In the *Iliad,* the poet HOMER attributes the warrior Meriones' agility in battle to his expert dancing.

Greek dancing tended to be performed by groups of only men or only women, since the sexes were usually separated in their respective festivals and religious rituals. In Greek drama, the performers who danced as part of the chorus were always male, even those who were playing female roles. Mixed dancing by members of both sexes was mentioned by Homer and other early poets and may have been more common in early times.

Dance was less prominent in Roman culture than it was in Greek culture. Conservative Romans, such as the statesman and orator CICERO, openly expressed disdain for dancers. A few ancient Roman dances were part of certain religious ceremonies, but most types of dancing in Rome were imported, particularly from Greece. Slave dancers usually provided the entertainment at Roman BANQUETS.

During the later years of the Republic, pantomime theater became very popular in Rome. Greek *pantomimi* of both sexes performed solo dancing accompanied by wind and percussion instruments. Elaborately dressed and masked, the mimes excelled at presenting stories from mythology, either serious or comic, with wordless dance and gestures. During the reigns of emperors Nero and Domitian, two pantomime dancers named Paris enthralled Roman audiences and gained the kind of attention from their fans that rock stars have today. (*See also* **Art, Greek; Art Roman; Drama, Greek; Drama, Roman; Music and Musical Instruments; Religion, Greek; Religion, Roman; Slavery; Theseus and the Minotaur.**)

DAPHNE AND APOLLO

* **metamorphosis** change in form, structure, or substance by supernatural means

Daphne, whose name means laurel, was a character from classical mythology who experienced an extraordinary metamorphosis* after an encounter with the god APOLLO. The most famous version of the story of Daphne and Apollo is in the great poem *Metamorphoses* by OVID.

In Ovid's account, Apollo provoked Cupid, the Roman god of love, by insulting his skill as an archer. Angered, Cupid retaliated by shooting Apollo with a golden arrow that made him fall in love. The love god also struck Daphne, the beautiful daughter of the river god Peneus, with a lead arrow that made her despise the thought of love. Although her father wished her to marry and have children, Daphne rejected all of her suitors and decided to live as a huntress in the forest, like the goddess Diana.

When Apollo spied Daphne in the forest, she became the object of his desire. The love-struck god chased her through the woods, pleading with her to stop. Hearing the voice of Apollo, one of the most powerful of deities, Daphne realized she could not escape. In desperation, she prayed to her father for help. (In other versions of the story, she prayed to ZEUS.) At the moment she felt Apollo's breath on her neck, Daphne became transformed into a laurel tree, and Apollo embraced only limbs of wood. Because of his unfulfilled love, Apollo adopted the laurel tree, or bay tree, as his sacred symbol. He vowed always to adorn himself with a wreath of laurel leaves. (*See also* **Artemis; Myths, Greek; Myths, Roman.**)

DEATH AND BURIAL

The Greeks and Romans mourned and disposed of their dead in a variety of ways. Proper and respectful burial rituals, they believed, helped the soul of a dead person enter the next world and protected the living from bad luck and misfortune. The early Greeks and Romans buried some people—rulers, nobles, or the wealthy—in tombs that contained clothing, weapons, and jewelry and other precious objects. This custom of burying the honored dead with grave goods, as these items are called, dates back to prehistory and was practiced in many parts of the world.

GREEK FUNERAL CUSTOMS. The early Greeks believed that an image of a dead person might appear to a sleeping mourner in a dream, usually to announce that it would never come back again. If the image did return, however, this indicated that there had been some sort of religious failure in the burial. An improper or incomplete burial failed to release the soul from the living community, and therefore, it could not join the community of the dead as it should.

The Greeks developed elaborate rites to ensure proper burial procedures. In one Greek custom, mourners showed their respect for the dead person by washing his or her body, anointing it with olive oil, and wrapping it from head to foot in a clean cloth. They cleaned the house and draped it with wreaths of fragrant leaves, such as celery, marjoram, or laurel. The dead person's family sang a mourning song that expressed their love and grief. At night, a funeral procession accompanied the body to the cemetery. After burial, a marker—either a large vase or an engraved stone pillar—was placed on the grave.

Graves excavated around the city of Athens reveal that the Greeks used many different burial methods over the centuries. In the 1000s B.C., people usually buried their dead in small stone-lined graves. Between

Large decorated vases, called kraters, sometimes served as grave monuments in public cemeteries in ancient Greece. This krater, from the late 700s B.C., is decorated with a funeral scene. The mourners, carrying the deceased, follow a chariot to the burial place.

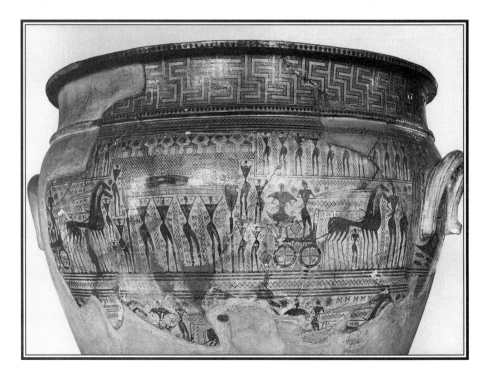

1000 and 750 B.C., most bodies were burned, or cremated, and the ashes were placed in pottery jars, which were then buried. Later Greeks buried bodies in earth-lined pits or cremated them inside the graves. After about 550 B.C., Athenians buried their dead in pits, tile-covered graves, or sarcophagi*.

* **sarcophagi** ornamental coffins, usually made of stone

See color plate 3, vol. 1.

ROMAN FUNERAL CUSTOMS. Roman funeral customs were also varied. Evidence from grave sites in Rome indicates that as early as 900 B.C., some dead bodies were buried, while others were cremated before being buried. Either way, for the Romans, it was important that the body be placed to rest underground.

The grave goods of the early Romans included everyday objects, such as cooking pots and lamps, as well as weapons and armor. The early Romans believed that the dead would need these possessions in the afterlife. Early Roman historical evidence suggests that the government tried to outlaw elaborate and expensive grave goods, which were not only considered wasteful, but also thought to attract grave robbers. In another ancient custom, which survived into the Christian era, mourners held a meal for the living at the burial site. Sometimes, they offered to share the meal with the dead person in the tomb. Some tombs were built with pipes or holes through which food and drink could be passed to the deceased.

The funeral customs during the Roman Republic, from 510 B.C. to 31 B.C., were simple. Most of the dead were cremated. Wealthy families owned private burial plots outside the city walls. A monument on the plot honored the family's dead, whose ashes were buried in urns beneath it. A very wealthy person might build a lavish marble mausoleum, or funeral monument, in preparation for his own death. The dead person's ashes were generally buried in a cavity under the mausoleum floor.

For less prosperous people, trade associations or other clubs paid for funerals. In fact, many associations were formed solely to provide decent, inexpensive funerals for their members. The associations usually arranged for an urn containing the dead person's ashes to be placed in an underground tomb called a *columbarium*. Most *columbaria* had places for a hundred or so urns, although a few held thousands. People who were too poor to afford even a humble funeral were probably buried in mass graves outside the city walls.

In the early years of the Roman Empire, people in the western part of the empire continued to cremate their dead, while those in the eastern part adopted the Greek custom of burying them. Beginning in the A.D. 100s, however, burial became more common than cremation throughout the empire. This may have been connected to the spread of CHRISTIANITY, which opposed cremation. By about A.D. 300, some people in the city of Rome began burying their dead in CATACOMBS—a series of underground chambers or tunnels beneath buildings. Christians held funeral services in the catacombs and used them as hiding places during times of persecution by the Romans. (*See also* **Afterlife; Festivals and Feasts, Greek; Festivals and Feasts, Roman; Religion, Greek; Religion, Roman.**)

DELOS

* **Hellenistic** referring to the Greek-influenced culture of the Mediterranean world during the three centuries after Alexander the Great, who died in 323 B.C.

* **city-state** independent state consisting of a city and its surrounding territory

* **confederacy** group of states joined together for a purpose

* **sack** to rob a captured city

Delos is a small island in the Aegean Sea that became an important Greek religious and commercial center. The ancient Greeks considered Delos the birthplace of the god APOLLO and goddess ARTEMIS, and a famous sanctuary for the worship of Apollo was located there. During Hellenistic* and Roman times, Delos became a thriving port and drew merchants and bankers from all over the Mediterranean region.

Delos lies in the middle of the CYCLADES, a group of islands in the south Aegean Sea. Ionian Greeks colonized the island around 950 B.C., and it came under the control of Athens in the 500s B.C. For a time, Delos served as the meeting place and treasury of the Delian League, an alliance of city-states* formed by Athens after the PERSIAN WARS to protect Greece from further Persian attacks. From ancient times, Delos was important to many Greek CULTS that worshiped particular gods. Especially renowned was the sanctuary of Apollo, which was the site of a large annual festival celebrated with games, singing, and dancing.

Delos gained its independence from Athens in 314 B.C. and formed a confederacy* with other island city-states. After this time, Delos grew prosperous as a center for foreign trade, and it became the most important marketplace for the Mediterranean slave trade. The geographer STRABO reported that the Delos market bought and sold as many as 10,000 slaves a day.

The island's independence ended in 166 B.C., when Rome conquered Greece and returned Delos to the control of Athens. However, the port and slave market continued to flourish. Delos declined in importance after it was sacked* in 88 B.C. by the forces of Mithradates VI, one of Rome's most dangerous enemies in Asia Minor. It was again looted—by pirates—in 69 B.C. (*See also* **Greece, History of; Ionians; Piracy; Religion, Greek; Slavery.**)

DELPHI

See color plate 1, vol. 2.

Delphi, the most important religious center of ancient Greece, is located on the southern slopes of Mt. Parnassus, 2,000 feet above the Gulf of Corinth. Delphi was the site of a shrine to the god APOLLO. Associated with the shrine was an ORACLE, or place of prophecy, which provided inspired advice from the god. Delphi was also the site of the Pythian Games, an athletic festival held every four years which was second only to the Olympics.

According to legend, Apollo himself built the shrine near a spring where he had killed a serpent called Python. He brought a ship's crew from the island of Crete to serve as his priests. By the 700s B.C., Delphi was the most famous oracle in Greece. The ancient Greeks had great respect for the oracle and its predictions. Most Greek city-states belonged to an organization that maintained the temple housing the oracle. This organization could fine or even wage war on any member that showed disrespect to Apollo or his oracle. At the height of its popularity, people came from all over to ask the oracle at Delphi questions regarding personal, religious, or political matters. Greek city-states erected statues at Delphi to celebrate their military victories.

The precise details of the ceremonies at the oracle are not known, although the writer PLUTARCH, who was a priest at Delphi in the A.D. 100s, has given us some clues. Only men could enter the shrine of

The oracle at Delphi played an important role in many Greek myths. In this painting, Aegeus, the king of Athens, is consulting the oracle regarding his lack of children even though he had been married twice. As in many myths, the oracle's response is unclear. Nevertheless, Aegeus later became the father of Theseus, the great Athenian hero.

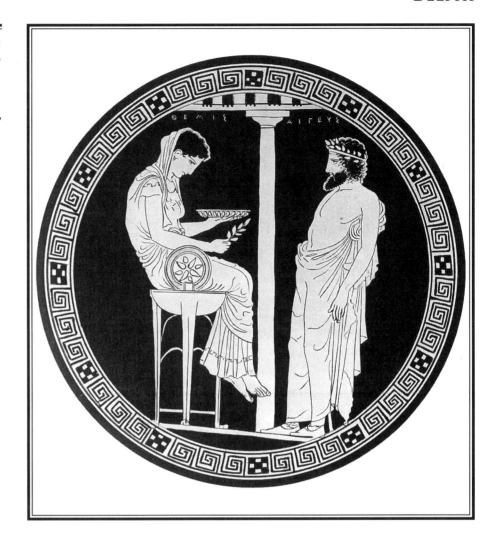

* **omen** sign, good or bad, of future events

Apollo. Before entering the temple, the person seeking advice sacrificed a goat. If the omens* seemed right, the person then paid a fee—often an expensive cake—and was admitted to the adytum, or inner chamber of the temple, which was believed to be the center of the world. Inside the adytum, on a sacred three-legged stool, sat the Pythia, the female prophet who spoke for the god Apollo. The questioner, who could not see the Pythia, submitted his inquiry either orally or in writing. The Pythia then entered a trance, perhaps induced by eating bay leaves, and replied to the question. This divine response, which was also known as an oracle, was interpreted and recorded in verse by the Pythia's attendants. Although the oracle was often ambiguous, it was rarely challenged.

The oracle handled a wide range of issues. Ordinary people came with personal or religious questions. Statesmen, such as the Athenian SOLON, consulted the oracle before making decisions of peace and war. Emigrants visited the oracle before they set out to establish colonies abroad. According to legend, King Croesus of Lydia asked the Delphic oracle whether he should wage war on Persia. The oracle replied that, if he did, he would destroy a great empire. Encouraged by this response, Croesus declared war against Persia, and lost. The

189

* **paganism** belief in more than one god; non-Christian

empire he destroyed was his own. When Croesus complained that he had been misled, the Pythia replied that she was not to blame, since the king should have inquired which kingdom she meant.

After 300 B.C., the influence of the oracle in political matters slowly declined, although individuals still asked it for personal advice. When the Roman emperor JULIAN THE APOSTATE tried to revive paganism* in the A.D. 300s, he sent a representative to ask the advice of the oracle at Delphi. The response indicates that the oracle of Apollo (here he is referred to as Phoebus) had fallen on hard times: "Tell the king, the monumental hall has fallen to the ground. Phoebus no more has a hut, has no prophetic bay, no speaking stream. Even the voice of the water is quenched." The Roman emperor THEODOSIUS closed the oracle in A.D. 390. The ruins at Delphi, however, remain a spectacular tourist destination even today. (*See also* **Cults; Divinities; Religion, Greek.**)